W9-CPF-829

THE Harrods
BOOK OF
ENTERTAINING

THE
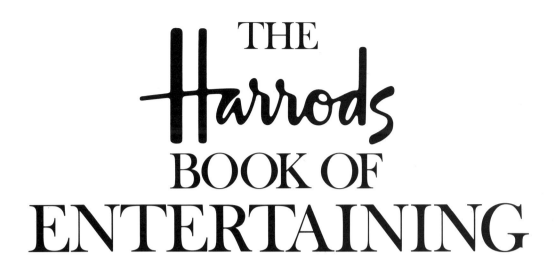
Harrods
BOOK OF
ENTERTAINING

LADY MACDONALD OF MACDONALD

**ARBOR
HOUSE**

NEW YORK

Published in the United States of America by Arbor House Publishing Company
and in Canada by Fitzhenry and Whiteside Limited
by arrangement with Ebury Press, London

Library of Congress Cataloging-in-Publication Data

Macdonald, Claire, Lady.
    Harrods book of entertaining.

    1. Entertaining.   2. Cookery.   3. Harrods Ltd.
I. Harrods Ltd.   II. Title.
TX731.M24   1986   642'.4   86-7968
ISBN 0-87795-824-6

Additional contributions by:
Pat Alburey, Mary Cadogan and Hilary Walden

Edited by Veronica Sperling, Norma MacMillan and Susan Friedland
Art Director Frank Phillips
Design by Bill Mason
Illustrations by Kate Simunek
Photography by Jan Baldwin
Styling by Cathy Sinker
Cookery by Susanna Tee, Maxine Clark and Janet Smith

Filmset by Advanced Filmsetters (Glasgow) Ltd
Printed and bound in Italy by New Interlitho, S.p.a., Milan

CONTENTS

FOREWORD

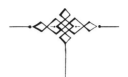

Godfrey, my husband, and I run a small hotel here on the Isle of Skye, and so one could say that entertaining is our way of life. The hotel is also our home, so we live, work, and entertain in the same house. Because it is also our livelihood, it means that we do things properly—good napkins at breakfast and dinner, gleaming silver and sparkling glasses, and more beeswax polish rubbed into the dining-room tables than ever meets the furniture in our private sitting-room.

Entertaining at home tends toward informality these days and I love it. It is always fun to dress up and decorate the table splendidly with lovely flowers everywhere, but equally I enjoy relaxed suppers when a few friends are staying (because living where we do means that most of our friends come to stay rather than just for dinner). We have a candle-lit supper around our kitchen table, eating pasta, hot brown rolls dripping with garlic butter, thick vegetable soups—all those dishes which belong to informality.

My regular trips from Skye to London more often than not include a visit to Harrods. In Harrods I know I can find the quality and excellence that I am always looking for, not only in the freshness of the food in the magnificent food halls, but also in their range of tableware, which is a positive treasure trove of matching glasses, mats, napkins, flatware and candles in a choice of styles to enhance any type of party from the simplest supper to a more formal dinner. And when I can't get down to London, I've always found Harrods an invaluable place to shop by telephone. For example, when I heard that I was selected as a finalist in a champagne picnic competition, I decided I must get a really pretty picnic cloth on which to lay out my picnic, so I immediately phoned Harrods' linen department. Nothing could be simpler.

I love cooking, eating, talking about food and writing about food, too. If I become panic-stricken before we have a party or friends to stay, it is only because I worry that I haven't done everything I possibly can before their arrival, so that I can enjoy being with them as much as possible. I try to plan my menus accordingly, with dishes that can either be cooked in advance ready just to heat up, or frozen. The great thing about entertaining is being with the people you have invited. It is a bit discomfiting for your guests if you are slaving over the stove, and emerge, hot and rather martyred, just in time to sit down at the table with your guests!

Parties are fun and they should be for the host and hostess, too. If you enjoy your party, your guests will surely enjoy it too. The most pleasurable memories of all are those of parties you have enjoyed, being with old friends and meeting new ones. Even despite the odd disaster, I can't think of anything more satisfying than entertaining.

Claire Macdonald

Claire Macdonald, Skye, 1986

THE PLEASURES OF ENTERTAINING

◆•●•◆

Entertaining is having anyone apart from your immediate family to share food and drink with you and the pleasure lies in the anticipation of sharing, and of actually having your friends around you. There is so much pleasure in being with people, be they friends or acquaintances, who are enjoying themselves. I find I get great pleasure in the anticipation of entertaining right from the beginning— planning who to invite, and what food and wines to give them, then with the actual making and presentation of the food comes more pleasure. The great thing about entertaining is that it must be fun and enjoyable for you, the host and hostess, as well as for your guests.

Entertaining means sharing, on whatever scale, from the simplest to the grandest, most formal affair. When this involves a landmark in life, such as a special birthday, a christening, wedding or anniversary, then it is also connected with nostalgia.

I love entertaining, I love having my friends around me and I get the greatest possible pleasure in planning for their visits. This is probably the most important thing about entertaining—how much you and your guests enjoy it is directly connected to the amount of effort you put into the planning and preparing for the event, and I hope the following pages in which I share my experience of entertaining will be helpful to you for whatever occasion you are planning.

WHAT SORT OF PARTY?

◆•●•◆

The principal aim in entertaining is to give pleasure to your guests, and for you to be able to spend time with them. For centuries the traditional way to express friendship and to celebrate a special event has been by sharing food and wine. There are many different reasons for entertaining, ranging from parties decidedly for pleasure such as dinner parties, cocktail parties, evening parties and Sunday parties to parties to celebrate special events such as Christmas, birthdays, and anniversaries.

Although the trend in entertaining has moved from the formal to the informal, there are still some occasions for the really formal party, such as a twenty-first or eighteenth birthday party, a wedding or a christening. Other reasons for parties include introducing new neighbors to your area and, in the business sphere, entertaining colleagues and clients. The value of this sort of entertaining cannot be overestimated and, although you may regard it at first as a nuisance, it often turns out to be fun: discovering what the client or colleague is like away from work can prove interesting!

Formal parties should not be dreaded, they just need more thinking about than other types of parties. They are usually on a larger scale than less formal gatherings, so you will need more of everything: more food, drink, flatware, plates, glasses and, in particular, advance preparation. The great advantage of large parties is that you can usually prepare very much more in advance with only the sauces, salads and garnishes to be organized on the day itself. It's important for your guests that you are not exhausted by the day of the party.

If you have children, you will find many reasons for parties for years to come! The most important are birthdays but there are other sorts of parties for children, too—Halloween presents a wonderful reason for a party. Children's Christmas parties are fun, too, with the Christmas decorations setting the scene beautifully. All you need is a willing father to dress up as Father Christmas to add authenticity to the proceedings.

Religious celebrations such as christening parties, confirmation parties, bar mitzvahs and weddings are joyous occasions for parties—I recently went to a wonderful lunch party following the ordination of my aunt as a Deaconess. On a larger scale, great carnivals are held in many countries to celebrate religious events—the mardi gras in New Orleans, for example, which is held just before the beginning of Lent. Mardi gras is the final celebration before the solemnity of Lent descends, and similar types of festivals are held in many places.

The greatest Christian celebration of the year is Christmas: if anyone ever needs a reason for giving a party, this is the time! The Twelve Days of Christmas have always been synonymous with festivities and party-giving. Christmas dinner itself is a party, whether there are just four of you, or whether like us you have friends and relations staying. The whole Christmas season is one huge party, which the hostess can enjoy as much as the guests, provided she has made sufficient preparation. Preparation means thinking about:

- the reason for the party
- where you will hold it
- how many guests you wish to invite
- sending out the invitations
- planning the menus with the numbers involved taken into account and thought given to balance, aesthetics and presentation
- wines and other drinks
- creating a party atmosphere—
  table settings: *linen, mats, decorations, flatware, glasses, the seating plan*
  flowers
  music
  candles and lighting
- organization on the day of the party: receiving your guests; whether you will have servants to help

Whatever the reasons for a party, just as important as any reason for giving it must be that the giver of the party, be it host or hostess or both, must be able to enjoy the party too. We used to give wonderful parties when I was growing up, and I remember my mother worked hard for several days before a party. She maintained that the more work you put into a party the more your guests—and you—enjoyed it. She was so right! No matter how simple an occasion or how elaborate, the success (or otherwise) all depends on the work you put into it beforehand—in one word, planning!

The only way to plan successfully is by making a list of what needs to be done: the first item on your list will be sending out the invitations. You need to make a guest list, keeping track of the acceptances or refusals as they come in. Make a shopping list of the food you will need, and the drink, and lastly all the other items. Keep a main list of each of the things you are going to do, in the order you intend to do them—for example, checking the fresh soap and hand towels in the bathrooms, arranging where coats and wraps are to go and that there are adequate car parking facilities.

Making your guests feel welcome and relaxed is the most important thing because it sets the atmosphere for the whole evening.

Where to Hold the Party

Where to hold your party depends entirely on what sort of space you have available. Whatever sort of party you hold and wherever you hold it—whether it's in your kitchen or dining room, or outdoors —the priority is to create an impression of welcome and tranquillity. If you know that everything is ready and that the flowers are arranged, the table set, the coffee tray is complete and that the candles just need to be lit, then you can achieve a tranquil atmosphere.

The sort of room you intend to eat in helps to set the scene. Many families nowadays have large kitchen/dining rooms, with no separate dining room. A kitchen/dining area sets an informal note and if you have a fireplace in your room, a blazing fire creates a perfect, welcoming atmosphere in the winter months.

If your home consists of one living room, and your kitchen is a tiny, functional area, when planning for a party you need to be scrupulous in your organization. Ideally and obviously, having two or four friends to dinner or lunch will suit your environment, but there will inevitably come the occasion for entertaining on a

A well-prepared room offers welcome and tranquillity

larger scale, and it is perfectly possible, providing that your home is geared entirely for the event!

The main importance is tidyness—there will be no space available for any clutter when your room is full of your guests, their glasses, plates, knives and forks! If your kitchen is too small to get a flow of people in—and out—of, don't attempt to serve the food from there. To avoid creating a bottleneck, arrange the drink, food (plates, flatware and napkins) on a table at one end of the room for your guests to stand or sit and enjoy their dinner.

When planning your menu, keep it restricted to items which can be served from a minimum of dishes. Get everything prepared beforehand, and all the washing-up done, dried and put away.

The kitchen is the room you will use to eat in for Halloween parties, and it is especially important that it is warm as your guests will have been outside before eating. To come inside to a warm, welcoming room—bright with the glow of lots of candles, some of them in pumpkins which have been scooped out and had faces of gap-toothed witches carved in them—helps set the scene! Decorations, such as pumpkins, flowers and table napkins in combinations of orange, yellow and black help to create a Halloween type of atmosphere!

If you are lucky enough to have an enclosed porch or patio which catches the evening sun, nothing could be better for a dinner party setting. If your porch furniture is white wrought iron table and chairs, you can incline towards a more formal setting; if, on the other hand, you have a wooden table and chairs, aim for an informal supper. Whichever you have, a porch or patio makes a lovely setting for a party. Surrounded by plants and flowers, I would be inclined to have a simple flower centerpiece for dinner.

A formal dinner party in a dining room, with a polished table, gleaming silver, sparkling glasses, and with beautiful flowers in the middle of the table, cannot fail to create the impression that you have given every thought to your guests' comfort and entertainment. If you intend to have a buffet party, serve food from a table set in the middle of the room.

For a large, formal party, a dance or a wedding, with a large number of guests which cannot be accommodated in your house, think about the possible alternatives. If you have a garden, you could rent a tent to provide the extra space. If you live in an area where more than one firm rents tents, get estimates from all of them, not only for the rental of the tent with its decorative lining, but also for the type of flooring you would like inside it and, if in winter, for the heaters, and restroom facilities. Tent rental firms are booked well in advance, so reserve the tent as soon as the date is decided.

An alternative location for a large, formal party is a room or rooms in a hotel. Ask around among your friends and acquaintances who have had experience either as guests at a party given in a hotel in your area, or who have themselves given a party at a hotel. Bear in mind that not only must the hotel be attractive, but it will also be responsible for the catering at your party, so make sure that it has a consistently good reputation for its food and try out *all* food before a reception or wedding lunch. When it comes to important details such as flower arrangements, discuss with the hotel before you make a firm booking whether they will arrange the flowers to your specifications, or whether you need to organize this yourself with a florist. For weddings, a toastmaster should be booked and for a dance there should be someone to reject any gatecrashers.

Another alternative is to use the house of nearby relations or friends. However good the friends are, having a large, formal party in their house will naturally involve them in a certain amount of disruption, and it is up to you to minimize this as much as possible. Discuss with your friends the arrangements you make with the caterers, or, if you are preparing the food yourself, when you will be arriving, and keep your friends fully informed about the times other people, such as the florist, are expected. Make sure that any valuable ornaments are tucked safely away. Make sure that you provide lots of ashtrays and fire buckets with sand in corridors and other areas where there is nowhere to put ashtrays.

Any party given outside your own home will mean more work for you to create the right atmosphere, but with careful planning and preparation it can be done (see *Planning the Menu*). An alternative to arranging the party yourself is to hire a firm of professional party organizers. They will take care of all the arrangements for you, starting with writing, addressing and sending the invitations and finishing with serving the last coffee and dishwashing.

Parties Outside the House

Outside parties include barbecues, picnics, garden parties and country lunches.

If you are giving a country lunch, it will most probably be in a barn, set with trestle tables, or a similar farm building—the lunches we go to on the Black Isle north of Inverness take place in the drying room of a large farm! You can't do a great deal about the surroundings for such a lunch—the warmth of your welcome lies in the food and drink and the conviviality of the fellow guests. I often think that country lunches are among the best sorts of parties. The food should be hot and filling—good stews and potatoes, fruit cake or gingerbread and Stilton cheese, red wine and sloe gin or cherry brandy to drink afterwards.

Barbecue parties create their own atmosphere of relaxed informality. The role of cook is often reversed, with the husband presiding over the glowing charcoals, the wife having done the preparation! Organize the drinks on an outside table, with glasses and ice. Plates, paper napkins, knives and forks, and salads and sauces will need another table. Organizing a barbecue or picnic is rather different from organizing other sorts of parties

Barbecues have a unique atmosphere of informality and there is usually room for one or two uninvited guests

since the menus and type of food to be served often have special requirements. Organizing these parties is described in a separate section (see *Parties Outside* on page 40).

The Invitations

The main points to make when issuing an invitation are:

- date   • time   • place
- purpose (if birthday, for example)   • dress

It is also essential to use the correct forms of address to those of your guests who have titles or ranks: see *Forms of Address* on page 44 for general guidelines.

Formal invitations eliminate any confusion over time and location

If you are giving a formal party, a dance or a wedding, and want to have invitations specially printed for you, go to a good stationery store, which will have books of examples of different styles of invitation. Having decided on the style you like best to suit the occasion, ascertain from the stationers how long they will take to be printed. Bear in mind that engraving takes much longer than printing. Avoid silver edging or lettering for wedding invitations. For all invitations choose a good quality thick card with clear plain lettering and give care to the layout.

Invitations are often issued by telephone, but for safety's sake follow up a telephone invitation with a reminder card or postcard. This is a wise precaution, because not only can the guest forget about the invitation, or confuse the date, but so can the host or hostess. A written reminder to a verbal invitation helps to clarify any confusion as to just what the invitation was for—it is very embarrassing to arrive at a house for a drink, perhaps before going on to dinner somewhere else, only to discover that what you thought was an invitation for drinks was in fact for dinner.

If you are having a formal dinner party, ask your guests two or three weeks in advance to make sure that they can accept, or, if they are unable to accept, to give you time to invite other friends, without it seeming like a last-minute invitation. A formal invitation card should be sent, with Black Tie added at the bottom if you would like your male guests to wear dinner jackets. This will be the indication to the women what to wear, too. Printed "At Home" cards will do for all invitations except the most special occasions, such as a dance or a golden wedding anniversary party. Wedding invitations should be sent not less than six weeks before the wedding.

If you are having a Halloween party, make the invitations yourself: using yellow or orange cardboard, cut into a pumpkin shape, with a face drawn on the pumpkin and the necessary information on the back. Write inside the date, the time, the place and, most important for a children's party, the time you expect the party to end—or you will have all the parents telephoning to enquire what time they should collect the guests.

When I was about nineteen, we gave a wonderful Regency dance and the invitations were exactly as they would have been in Regency days. So, if you are having a theme party, specially styled invitations give a taste of what is to come.

PLANNING THE MENU

The aim of entertaining is to give pleasure to your guests, but it is equally important that you, the host or hostess, should enjoy the occasion, too.

The first priority is planning the menu, taking into account several considerations.

- keeping it simple—how much time do you have?
- the season. The time of year will suggest not only the kind of menu that is suitable but will also dictate to some extent what ingredients are readily available. For example, a good, rich oxtail stew will be greeted with cries of delight in the middle of winter, when your guests may have had some exercise outside, and have come inside for lunch, hungry and cold. In the summer, however, how much more appealing it is to offer something light and refreshing—a chilled pea, mint and cucumber soup, or cold poached salmon served with a crisp salad and an herb mayonnaise.
- the numbers involved. Hot soufflés are lovely for two or three but not practical for six or eight. Cost must be a consideration when you are thinking about numbers. Avoid very expensive ingredients like caviar, smoked salmon and dishes that contain almost nothing but heavy cream when you are planning for very large numbers.
- balancing the menu so that you do not produce too rich a dinner, or a menu which features cheese in the first course and the main course.
- health: no one these days will welcome three courses, all of which are rich and creamy (see *Special Diets*, page 16)
- aesthetics: how to make food attractive (see *Textures* and *Garnishes*, page 17)

The second priority is planning when you are going to prepare each course, according to your capabilities and time. Don't schedule seven hours non-stop cooking or you will be exhausted! Everything depends on planning, and once you have planned what you are going to cook and when you are going to cook it, you will feel much more relaxed.

Keeping it Simple

Don't be tempted to create an elaborate menu, or an elaborate dish for your menu, if it means you have to resort to packaged or convenience foods. It is far better to serve something simple as long as it is fresh and of the best quality rather than a dish which calls for, perhaps, a can of soup. It would be far better to serve, for example, fresh pineapple, sliced, with some kirsch poured over it. Although you can buy hollandaise sauce mix, don't be tempted to dress up your vegetables with it! If you want to serve hollandaise sauce with your broccoli and you don't feel confident enough to make your own, instead melt some butter and finely grate some lemon rind into it, and pour the lemony butter over the broccoli spears just before serving.

There is a desire, naturally, to offer special food to your guests, but it is much better to make dishes that you know will work, rather than attempt for the first time a slightly tricky recipe. You will find it a worry and it will stop you from feeling relaxed. Experiment with recipes with which you are unfamiliar before you give a party.

The Time Factor

When planning your menu, think about how much time you are going to have to prepare the food just before the dinner—ideally, you should have everything more or less ready to serve before your guests arrive, but if you are going to be busy and occupied with other things before dinner—like putting children to bed, for example—plan to serve at least one course cold, preferably two. Balancing a menu means a balance between hot and cold, too, so don't be tempted to give your guests three courses, all cold, just for the sake of convenience! Have a cold first course, a hot main course and a cold dessert. If it is winter, don't be afraid to give your guests an ice cream, because you can make a hot sauce to go with it, which can be keeping warm in the oven or on top of the stove. A ginger ice cream served with a hot chocolate sauce makes a delicious dessert in the winter. If you decide to give your guests just such a dessert, it is a good idea to offer them a choice of desserts, with a fruity alternative to something rich, such as a dish of stewed fruits—raspberries, strawberries and black currants in the summer—or baked dried fruits in the winter—apricots, peaches, figs, prunes and fresh bananas in rum. You can add chopped preserved ginger to a dried fruit concoction as I have described, provided you don't include ginger elsewhere in the menu. For an informal supper party, serve warm fudge brownies with vanilla ice cream.

Balancing the Menu

As you plan your menu, aim for a balance of richness and lightness between the dishes. Don't be tempted to have a menu where each course has something with cream or cheese in it as it will be heavy and indigestible. The best party food is that which you have taken time to plan, have bought the best ingredients for, and which you have clearly gone to some trouble to make. If you want to give your guests a fairly rich main course, with a creamy dessert to follow, serve a simple, smooth soup as a first course—a carrot soup flavored with orange and coriander, for example. If the soup is made with good chicken stock, is puréed and sieved to ensure that it is velvety smooth, and if it is garnished with small croûtons and finely chopped parsley (no cream) it will be a perfect introduction to a rich main course. (Incidentally, such a soup is delicious served chilled in the summer; if it is to be served cold, leave out the croûtons and garnish it with finely chopped parsley and chives, and a spoonful of yogurt.)

If you plan to serve a plain main course, dress it up with the vegetables. If you give your guests roast lamb, or lamb chops, you could give them two vegetable dishes to accompany the meat and a good salad to follow. Mixed vegetable dishes are delicious and are good enough to serve as the main course for a lunch party. I am thinking of such dishes as ratatouille, and mixtures of red, yellow and green peppers, with garlic—both of these dishes need to be stewed in the best olive oil. Thinly sliced potatoes and onions, layered in a buttered dish with a few anchovies in the middle, and the whole dish baked in milk flavored with grated nutmeg makes an interesting and delicious accompaniment to any main course. Equally convenient is broccoli with a good tomato sauce poured over it, or a dish of cooked leeks, with a parsley sauce poured over them. There are numerous vegetable dishes like these which dress up a simple main course, and which can conveniently be made ahead.

The easiest dish to offer your guests is a casserole of meat, fish or vegetables. Nearly all casserole dishes, with the exception of fish, benefit from being made in advance and reheated. Their flavor improves enormously by being made a day or two in advance, and then thoroughly reheated before serving.

Formal Dinner Parties

Dinner parties, whether formal or informal, need to be planned and prepared in advance if you are to enjoy them. Formal dinner parties need rather more in the way of advance preparation. Start by making a list of the food you intend to give your guests at each course, bearing in mind how busy you will be around the day of the dinner party, and choosing dishes therefore that will fit into your schedule. Start your menu with one or two items to offer your friends with drinks before dinner—a dish of pecans, which have been toasted and sprinkled with salt and a little cayenne, or a dish of crudités served on a large platter with a bowl of tomato and cream cheese dip in the middle of the platter.

If you wish, offer more elaborate hors d'oeuvres with the pre-dinner drinks and dispense with a first course at the table. Small savory profiteroles, triangles of whole-wheat toast spread liberally with smoked fish pâté, smoked salmon rolled in wholewheat rolls with walnut butter, little deep fried balls of cheese served with a tomato dip—are among numerous delicious things to be eaten with the fingers with drinks before dinner.

If you do not have much time available on the day, plan at least one cold course, if not two—ideally, the first

course and the dessert. If you can set the first course out shortly before your friends begin to arrive, and if you have the desserts ready made and finished, then you need to think only about the main course. First courses that can be put out ready at each place include an avocado terrine, a fish pâté, a savory mousse or shellfish served with an interesting sauce, such as a fresh herb and lime mayonnaise.

THE FIRST COURSE

If you plan to serve a hot first course, choose something that can be cooked and kept warm for an hour or preferably two. You may decide on a good soup, with a garnish of tiny crispy croûtons, ready to ladle into the soup plates, or deep fried cheese choux balls, which can be fried two hours ahead and kept warm without spoiling. Don't plan a soufflé, as it has to be eaten the moment it is cooked. As with all parties, the seasons dictate to a certain extent your menu. For example, during the winter months, you may choose game as your main course. Only in really hot weather is it advisable to serve all courses cold, and even then I would suggest one hot item—new potatoes, for example, with cold poached sea trout or salmon.

THE MAIN COURSE

A casserole makes the perfect main course for a dinner party. Dishes such as chicken baked in curry cream with brandy, or pheasant baked with apples and Calvados (or cider), pork tenderloin baked in sherry with a creamy tomato and mustard sauce are all delicious and impressive. The term casserole does *not* mean a simple beefy stew; it can also be an elegant and delicious dish, which is, at the same time, convenient because it can be made a day or two in advance.

When planning your vegetables, don't feel compelled to include potatoes. Potatoes are delicious, cooked in a variety of ways, but we tend to believe that they are a permanent fixture on any menu. During the winter months you could have potatoes puréed with another root vegetable—potatoes puréed with Jerusalem arti-chokes, or puréed with parsnips, for example. It is wise to serve a garnish that makes a good contrast in texture to the purée—sautéed cashew nuts, or crisp bacon pieces. As an alternative to potatoes, you could serve noodles, tossed in a cream and garlic sauce, or plain boiled brown rice if it is to accompany a particularly rich main course dish. Plain brown rice looks attractive and tastes good with a couple of tablespoons of finely chopped parsley stirred in just before serving.

If you dispense with potatoes and rice, offer a choice of two vegetable dishes, one of them an interesting salad. There are so many different greens available now that a green salad makes a positive talking point. One such green is arugula, which adds a new dimension to

The perfect setting for a formal dinner party, with gleaming cutlery, china, glasses and an attractive low flower arrangement in the center of the table

salads—it is delicious. Another is nasturtium leaves: most gardens have clumps of nasturtiums growing somewhere, and half a dozen leaves torn up into a salad add a different flavor as well as a slightly different leaf texture. The nasturtium is a slightly thicker leaf than lettuce, spinach or arugula. There are also the numerous chicory leaves and the deep red of radicchio.

THE DESSERT

If you are having a formal dinner party, it is a good idea to have two desserts for you friends to choose from—or to indulge in both! A contrast in desserts is a good idea—perhaps a rich, creamy meringue dessert, and a light, fruit mousse alternative. There are very few desserts which need last minute attention, and these are to be avoided anyway, because the aim of a good dinner party is for the hostess to be present as much as possible, not out in the kitchen cooking right up to the point of serving dinner, and then during the meal popping out to attend to something for the following course. Fruit mousses, like a lime and grape mousse, or a lemon and clementine mousse, a raspberry mousse, or a strawberry and orange mousse, can all be made a day or two in advance, and kept, covered, in the refrigerator until a couple of hours before dinner. Take them out of the refrigerator to let the mousse come to room temperature, otherwise the gelatin in the mousse will be too stiff. As the mousse relaxes at room temperature, it regains its creamy texture. Meringues can be made well in advance, and vanilla meringues just need to be sandwiched together with whipped cream and served with either a hot vanilla fudge, chocolate, or fruit purée sauce—such as puréed and sieved raspberries and mint.

Ice creams make ideal dinner party desserts. If they are very rich, like brandy and chocolate, freeze them ready to serve in ramekins. If you are going to serve them from a bowl, chill the bowl by putting it in the refrigerator for an hour or so, then spoon the ice cream into the bowl and put this into the refrigerator just before you and your friends sit down for dinner. This way the initial icy edge will be taken off the ice cream ready for serving when the time comes for dessert. I love to serve a hot sauce with ice creams—vanilla fudge and chocolate are my favorites. You can have a bowl of crushed praline to serve as a garnish over ice cream—coffee ice cream with hot chocolate sauce and a spoonful of praline sprinkled over it is very good.

A simple but rich cake makes a perfect dessert. My extremely rich chocolate cake is so rich that it needs no filling or icing, just a bowl of whipped cream to serve with it. Alternatively, offer a coffee and praline cake, cinnamon sponge with strawberries (or raspberries) and cream, or a feather light lemon sponge with fresh lemon curd and whipped cream.

CHEESE

If you plan to serve a cheese course, which more and more people do these days, decide whether to serve it before or after the dessert. Personally, if we have served red wine with the main course, I like to serve cheese before the dessert to eat with the rest of the wine. I also find that most of the guests staying here at Kinloch prefer to help themselves to cheese before they have dessert. I know that I am not alone in liking to finish a meal on a sweet note. On the rare occasion when we give guests a savory, I find that they invariably eat chocolates or fudge after dinner with their coffee.

Maintain a balance with the cheeses as in the rest of your menu. A blue cheese such as Stilton is loved by many, but don't have Gorgonzola as well. Offer one creamy cheese, such as a wedge of good Brie, or a semi-creamy cheese like Reblochon, with a hard cheese as an alternative—there is nothing better than a good, sharp Cheddar. If I were to add anything else, it might be to include a goat's cheese.

As with all things, it is the quality of the cheeses rather than the quantity of the choice. Remember to take your cheeses out of their wrappings (which should be wax paper rather than plastic wrap or bags, which make cheese sweat) and out of the refrigerator a couple of hours before dinner. This lets the cheese come to room temperature at which its flavor is at its peak.

COFFEE AFTER DINNER

It is wise to plan to offer good, strong coffee as well as decaffeinated coffee. If you have any herbal teas, you may find some appreciative guests gratefully accepting a cup of one of these delicious and fragrant teas as an alternative to coffee. The herbal teas which I keep in stock are peppermint and rosehip, both of which are very good after dinner. You can set the coffee tray ready in the morning, pour the cream into the jug and keep it covered in the refrigerator until coffee time, and fill the coffee pot ready to make the coffee just as you serve the dessert. This all saves time and worry at the end of a dinner party.

To complete a formal dinner, offer chocolate truffles or fudge with coffee. You can make them several days in advance and store in an airtight tin.

Special Diets

If one of your guests is allergic to any sort of food, he or she will be quite sure to tell you. Food allergies can produce such dramatic reactions that their sufferers will always warn a first-time hostess. Food causing allergies include shellfish, gluten (basically wheat) and eggs, while common special diets are vegetarian and fat-free. Some guests may be prohibited from eating certain foods by their religion. If you are not absolutely sure about what your guests are allowed to eat, ask them whether they are permitted to eat meat, for instance, or fish. Moslems and certain other religious sects (Mormons, for example) do not drink any alcohol, so beware when planning your menu of including any dishes which contain it.

16

Textures

When planning your menu consider the different textures of each dish you wish to serve and aim for contrasts. If you are serving a smooth soup, provide a contrast in texture with crisp croûtons served as a garnish. (If you need a contrast in texture it can often be provided with the garnish.) I serve a purée of root vegetables as one of the vegetables, but alone it is too smooth and no matter how well seasoned it is it can be boring. So we garnish our purées with toasted cashew nuts, or with small crisp bacon pieces. A smooth ice cream benefits from the addition of a contrasting texture such as ginger ice cream with small pieces of preserved ginger in it. A tart, with a creamy filling, either savory or sweet, contrasts well with the crisp pastry case. A stuffing for a bird—be it turkey, pheasant or goose—should have a contrast in texture, otherwise it is too bland in texture. This contrast is usually provided by nuts—cashew nuts, walnuts, chestnuts or almonds. (Crisp bacon becomes flabby in a stuffing, as it cooks inside the bird, so it doesn't do as a contrast in texture in this case.)

Garnishes

Many herbs make beautiful garnishes. Feathery fronds of dill, for example, on a salmon cream tart, the same dill laid along a cold salmon, or chervil instead of the dill, all add the finishing touch. The best thing about garnishing with herbs is that their purpose is twofold: they both look good and also impart their delicate flavor to the dish. I use thin slices of lemon to garnish a spinach and turmeric soup as the lemon gives just the right amount of lemon flavor to the soup.

A useful garnish for fish pâtés or mousses is lemon (or lime) wedges dipped in finely chopped parsley—the parsley sticks to the cut sides of the lemon and looks very effective, with the green contrasting with the lemon skin. If you are serving a fish dish containing shellfish, a simple and most effective garnish is to use four or five unshelled shrimp.

With texture in mind, I always decorate a good trifle with toasted sliced almonds sprinkled around the sides of the dish over the whipped cream. The contrasting crunch of the almonds and their delicious taste combine beautifully with the rest of the trifle, the cream, the vanilla egg custard, the sherry soaked sponge cake, the strawberry jam and the fruit.

Too much decoration makes a dish look fussy and false as if the food itself hardly matters. It can be useful, however, to resurrect a mold that has not unmolded successfully or to conceal any other infelicities of presentation.

The only time when you can afford to decorate as lavishly and as brightly as you wish is for food intended for a children's party. It is fun to put faces on cookies with pieces of chocolate or nuts, to make a cake look like a clock, or a hedgehog, or make a maypole cake with sticks of candy and satin ribbons. You can buy all sorts of cutters and shapes for cakes and cookies and molds in the shape of rabbits and fish and so on for mousses and gelatins. Use gelatin of different colors for extra effect—a red rabbit on green grass, for example.

Having Friends to Stay

Your food planning and advance preparation will be on an altogether larger scale if you have friends to stay. The same principles apply, however, to planning food for friends visiting as friends coming for just one dinner: the aim is to give your friends special food, while at the same time planning menus which can, for the most part, be prepared before your friends arrive so that you can enjoy their company.

Plan dishes that can be frozen—those which are complete dishes, such as a seafood lasagne, can be taken from the freezer in the morning for dinner that evening. You only have to make the salad to accompany it. If we have a lot of friends staying for a number of days, I invariably give them roast smoked ham as the main course the evening of their arrival. This way I have cold ham to serve with scrambled eggs, which seems to be a favorite breakfast, as well as cold ham for lunch one of the days of the visit, served with baked stuffed potatoes (which can be baked, stuffed and frozen, thawed for a couple of hours and popped back into the oven for twenty minutes to heat up before serving) and leeks in a cheese sauce (if this is a winter visit) which can also be prepared and frozen, and later reheated.

Having guests to stay means that you have to plan for four meals each day. If there are children you need to fill the tea-time tins with cookies, cakes and gingerbread, which you will find the grown-ups eating just as much as the children.

To make this sort of entertaining appear effortless, which it must so as to make your guests feel relaxed, remember to:

- order more milk (if there are to be children visiting you will need to double your usual order)
- have a good supply of breakfast cereals
- keep a stock of good breakfast rolls, croissants or brioches in the freezer for breakfasts—just pop a tray of them into the oven instead of making endless rounds of toast
- have plenty of butter, both unsalted and salted—keep some extra in your freezer
- have a stock of orange juice
- keep coffee beans in the freezer in reserve, and grind as you need them. Grind enough coffee to last the visit, keeping it in a large screw-top jar
- stock up on household items

BREAKFAST SUGGESTIONS

- **Eggs baked in buttered ramekins**
- **Scrambled eggs with cold ham**
- **Sausages, bacon and broiled tomatoes keep warm well for those guests who may not get up too promptly for breakfast!**
- **Kedgeree (a mixture of smoked fish and rice)**
- **Croissants**

LUNCH

When you have friends to stay, lunch falls into two categories. If there are children staying, it is the main meal of the day, so you want to provide them with something good and sustaining, whereas if your friends are grown up and have had a good breakfast and are going to have a good dinner they will probably want just a light lunch. Aim to make dishes that will keep well in

Breakfast in bed gives guests a relaxing start to the day

the refrigerator or that freeze well.

First course dishes which keep for two or three days in the refrigerator:

- soups (don't forget to make the croûtons—they store and reheat very well)
- fish pâtés
- egg mousse (I like to chop the eggs rather than purée them)
- fish mousses
- fresh crab or shrimp (you can make the accompanying mayonnaise and refrigerate it, covered)

Quick and easy first courses:

- avocado
- smoked salmon—make sure you have plenty of lemons to serve in wedges

Main courses:

- a good casserole made several weeks ahead and frozen, or made the day before your friends arrive, and reheated for dinner on the second night
- good lamb chops are simple
- fish, such as turbot or halibut which needs poaching

These main courses rely on the vegetables served with them to add some color and interest to the course. Prepare all the potatoes before your friends arrive and keep them in a huge bowl, covered with water, which you change each day. They keep well like this for three days. Pick over Brussels sprouts in advance, putting a small nick in the base of each sprout. Preparing sprouts is a fiddly and time-consuming business, and much better done before your friends arrive. Leeks can be trimmed, washed, and cut to whatever length you require. Prepared carrots become slimy if kept in water, and parsnips do the same as well as turning brown, so only prepare a few hours ahead.

Wash any salad stuff and keep it in a large plastic bag in the refrigerator, with a tissue with it to prevent it turning brown at the edges. Make up French dressing and keep it in a screw-top jar in the refrigerator.

Desserts

- ice creams, with fudge or chocolate sauces ready made and stored in the pantry or refrigerator ready to heat up
- fruit mousses can be made and kept in the refrigerator for two or three days. Take them out of the refrigerator two or three hours before you serve them, particularly if they contain gelatin
- meringues can be made well ahead, and stored in airtight tins. Offer vanilla meringues, filled with cream, with hot fudge sauce. They will be extremely popular! So are brown sugar meringues, served with lemon curd
- fresh strawberries
- have a good supply of fresh fruit, and yogurts, too, both for children and adults

Decorations add so much to Christmas festivities

Christmas

Planning food for a visit of family and friends over Christmas needs extra thought to leave you free to be with your guests. Plan menus for each day and plan dishes that can be frozen either in their entirety or in part. There is so much food given as presents around Christmas time, in the form of chocolates and crystallized fruits, and traditional Christmas food, such as mince pies, plum pudding and cake, is so filling that you should plan menus consisting of fairly light, simple dishes. Instead of heavy desserts, offer sherbets such as fresh pineapple, or raspberry or lemon. Steer clear of chicken dishes, as it is similar to turkey, and think of meat casseroles or fish dishes. Have baked ham for dinner on the first evening: I like country ham, which will need soaking to get rid of excessive saltiness. If you are going to have a lot of people and you buy a very large ham, remember you will need a large enough container in which to soak the ham. The ham can be eaten for breakfasts and can accompany cold turkey for lunch during the holidays.

Make three or four batches of good soup to store in your freezer and buy lots of wholewheat rolls; butter them generously with garlic butter, then wrap them and freeze them. Don't do this more than two weeks before Christmas. When you want to serve them, pop them, wrapped in foil, in an oven to heat until the butter has completely soaked into the roll.

Another useful standby for Christmas are frozen stuffed baked potatoes. You will only have to thaw them for an hour or so and bake in a moderate oven for about

20–25 minutes before serving with cold roast turkey and salad. To make: scrub the potatoes, bake them until they are soft, then cut them in half lengthwise. When they are cool enough to handle, scoop out the potato into a bowl, and mash until smooth, then beat in plenty of grated cheese, butter, salt and freshly ground black pepper, finely chopped parsley and egg yolk. Divide the cheese-flavored mashed potato among the potato skins, and put them on a baking sheet in the freezer. When they are hard, just tip them into a large freezer bag and put them back in the freezer. You can take out as many as you need at any one time.

Order a fresh turkey from your butcher—there is a world of difference between a fresh and a frozen turkey. Collect it from your butcher a few days before Christmas and store it in a cool place, covered with wax paper, not with plastic wrap.

You can make and freeze the stuffings for the turkey (or goose, if you prefer), the bread sauce and the cranberry sauce.

Brandy butter can be made weeks ahead and stored in a sealed container in the refrigerator. Mince pies can be stored in tins in the refrigerator. You can make the plum puddings and Christmas fruit cake three months before Christmas, and get them well out of the way. (See also *Afternoon Tea by the Fire* on page 23.)

If you plan to give a party around Christmas time, plan something that is as different as possible from roast turkey. Individual smoked salmon mousses, followed by a mixed game casserole, rich with port and red currant jelly, and served with forcemeat balls, can all be frozen. I would serve two vegetables with this, but no potatoes or rice—the forcemeat balls are filling.

An easy and delicious dessert to follow this would be a chocolate roulade filled with whipped cream flavored with Tia Maria, the coffee liqueur, which lifts a chocolate roulade into the realms of the sublime. This can be frozen filled and completely ready to serve, except for a last minute dusting of sugar. As an alternative dessert to the rather rich chocolate roulade, I would offer a fresh lime mousse, containing shreds of lime peel to contrast its texture with that of the smoked salmon mousses of the first course. This meal only needs to be thawed, and the casserole and forcemeat balls reheated, to serve to your guests.

If you plan your menus for the busy days around Christmas Day involving lots of frozen foods, do make a list of the items to remove for thawing for use the following day and place it in a prominent position.

Buffet food should be simple but attractively garnished and easy to eat with a fork (see menu on page 126)

Buffet Lunch or Supper Parties

The food you plan to serve your guests must be able to be eaten with just a fork. It is no use having slices of meat or turkey, chicken or ham that need to be cut with a knife, because if you are sitting down balancing a plate on your knee—or, worse still, standing balancing a plate (and possibly a glass, too) in one hand—you can't

possibly cut anything on your plate. So most food must be cut into bite-sized pieces; only soft vegetables, fish and fruits can be left in large slices—such as avocado, melon, peaches and nectarines—because these, like fish, can be cut with a fork. Large lettuce leaves should be shredded. Mousses of all sorts, both entrée and sweet, are ideal buffet food.

As the food will all be laid out together, color co-ordination is important. The food must be attractive to look at and tempting but this does not mean hours spent on garnishing. As with all garnishes, the simpler the better. The plates you use can provide all the decoration necessary: for instance, a plain white or glass cake stand just asks for individual items, like meringues, to be piled in a pyramid on them. Huge, beautiful cut glass bowls ask for cut up fruits in them—the different colors of the fruit are set off spectacularly by the facets of the cut glass. Another simple idea for serving food attractively, yet

simply, at a buffet is to line a dish with edible leaves which bear some relation to the content of the food: for example, a molded dessert of soft summer fruits turned out on top of a wide, shallow dish or platter lined with raspberry leaves.

If you have enough space to leave the table in the middle of the room, so much the better, because your guests will be able to walk around the table as they help themselves to the food. If your guests are rather elderly, it is a good idea to have several small tables so that they can sit down and rest their plates and glasses on a firm surface. They will also find it less tiring if they are able to sit while chatting and eating, rather than having to stand for an afternoon or evening.

Brunch

Planning food for a brunch party, combining breakfast and lunch, means getting everything as ready as possible the previous evening as people may arrive as early as 10:30 a.m., probably having had only a cup of coffee since they got up. However, you can set the time— 11:30 a.m. is perfectly acceptable. Lots of freshly squeezed orange juice ready in jugs, with champagne to mix Mimosas, makes the most perfect start to brunch whether it is winter or summer. To start the meal, serve fresh fruit attractively sliced and arranged on serving plates, with lime or lemon wedges to squeeze over the fruit. Plan to serve a choice of three main dishes:

A weekend brunch is a relaxing way to entertain (see menu on page 50)

Guests of all ages enjoy a warming afternoon tea (see menu on page 70)

- scrambled eggs with smoked salmon stirred into them. The evening before you can cut up the smoked salmon, and beat the eggs in a bowl, ready to pour into a saucepan of melted butter to scramble over a low heat the following morning
- thinly sliced bacon, placed on the broiler rack or in a frying pan, ready to be cooked in the morning
- salmon cakes—delicious served with crisply broiled or fried bacon. The fish cakes need only shallow-frying in the morning
- chanterelles or mushrooms (preferably the large, flat field mushrooms), wiped and ready to fry gently in butter
- a choice of two or three types of rolls—wholewheat rolls, croissants, or muffins—to warm through and offer your guests with honey and marmalade
- stewed and fresh fruit
- lots of hot, strong coffee with milk or cream

Afternoon Tea by the Fire

Nearly everyone I have ever met has a weakness for tea as a meal rather than just as a drink. A proper afternoon tea might include:

- drop scones (similar to pancakes)
- warm cheese scones
- buttered tea bread—such as apricot and walnut
- crumpets dripping with butter
- homemade jam—raspberry, or strawberry and elderflower
- homemade lemon curd
- homemade cookies
- a good chocolate cake, an essential
- a light vanilla sponge cake
- small éclairs, some coffee and some chocolate
- a choice of tea: Indian, Earl Grey and Lapsang Souchong, with a plate of lemon slices for those who like their tea without milk. Have a thermos of hot water ready to fill the teapot, as you refill the teacups

DRINKS

W hat you give your guests to drink is just as important as the food. The time of day and the season, to some extent, will give you guidelines. Pimms and other long, cool drinks, chilled white wine and fruit wine cups are welcome for summer parties while in the winter, a warm glass of mulled wine or punch makes an attractive welcoming drink. (See recipes for delicious hot wine drinks and for cold wine cups.)

With the growing concern about health and drunk-driving more people are choosing wine instead of spirits, which makes party giving much easier. A light, fruity red and a medium-dry white with perhaps champagne for a more special occasion are good, generally acceptable choices for most parties, but you may also like to offer a choice of spirits, such as gin, whiskey and vodka, with their usual accompaniments of tonics, sodas and ginger ale, dry or medium sherry and white and red vermouths. When you put out the glasses remember to put out Worcestershire sauce, a stirrer, a saucer with slices of lemon or lime, cocktail sticks and an ice bucket full of ice with tongs or a spoon. If giving a party single-handed ask one or two people to lend a hand serving the drinks.

Do remember to have a good choice of nonalcoholic drinks; bitter lemon, tonic water, tomato juice, mineral water, orange, apple and grapefruit juices.

Depending on the length of the party, allow about $\frac{1}{2}-\frac{3}{4}$ bottle of wine per person; for a dinner party, 1–2 glasses of an aperitif, 1–2 glasses of wine with the first course, 2 with the main course and another with the cheese and/or dessert. One bottle of table wine should give 6 glasses. If the wine is a good one, don't fill the glass more than about two-thirds full.

Choosing Wine

One good way to learn more about wines is to seek out a wine merchant whom you trust, and who will appreciate that you are serious in wanting to learn more on the subject. It is worth keeping notes of wines, the ones which you particularly like, with what foods they were served and how well the two went together. The most expensive wines are not necessarily the best and there are some very good buys from the classic (i.e. Burgundy and Bordeaux) areas of France and the rest of the wine-producing world. America and Australia, for instance, now produce some of the best wines around. The more important the occasion, the more thought you will probably put into choosing the wine. For special dinners a knowledge of vintages, or an up-to-date vintage chart can help you make the most suitable choices for the whole meal.

Pre-Dinner Drinks

For meals where expensive wines are being served the choice of aperitifs is just as important as the choice of wines to accompany the food. An aperitif should stimulate the palate and the appetite. Therefore it is best to avoid sweet drinks, such as cream sherry and many cocktails, and those that have a high alcohol content, such as spirits and, again, cocktails, as these will deaden both the appetite and the taste buds. Good choices are fino (dry) sherry, sercial (dry) Madeira, dry vermouths and dry white wines still or sparkling. This could be the same as that being served with the first course or one that is slightly lighter in body.

Matching Food and Wine

To gain the maximum enjoyment from both the food and the wine, as well as the occasion and to avoid wasting money or suffering a disappointment it pays to serve an appropriate wine.

- **match the quality and style of the wine to the quality and style of the food, i.e. serve a light wine with light food, a full-bodied one with full-flavored dishes**
- **serve white wines before red, dry before sweet, light bodied before more full-bodied, young before old, less expensive before expensive ones**
- **wines of a country are the best accompaniments for the foods from that country**
- **if a wine has been used in the making of a dish it will be the most suitable one to serve with it**
- **select wines that are appropriate for the occasion, i.e. lesser quality wines for informal affairs reserving the finer wines for special occasions where the guests will appreciate the qualities of the wine**

FIRST COURSES

Consommés, meat and game soups—*fino sherry, sercial Madeira.*

Light fish soups—*good quality light dry white wines.*

Vegetable purées—*more full-bodied white such as a Graves, Pinot Grigio or mature white Rioja.*

Mixed hors d'oeuvres and antipasto—*fairly assertive white such as those made from the sauvignon grape or semillion if the wine is dry, or perhaps a fruity light red such as Bardolino, Valpolicella, Bandol or a young Zinfandel.*

Cold meats, smoked meats and sausages such as salami—*strong rosé such as Tavel or a medium weight white such as Sauvignon Blanc.*

Game and meat pâtés—*a medium-bodied red.*

A wide variety of drinks are suitable for serving before dinner

FISH AND SHELLFISH

Served as a first course or plainly cooked and simply presented—*a light white wine such as Soave, a Loire Chenin Blanc or Pouilly Fuissé.*

Lighter fish such as sole with a creamy, not too rich, sauce—*Mosel.*

Firm fish such as turbot—*Bulgarian, Australian or California Chardonnay, white Burgundy, white Rhône, Rioja, Orvieto.*

Oily fish—with sardines *vinho verde*, with trout *Alsatian Sylvaner or Riesling*, with salmon *good white Graves or Burgundy, California or Australian Chardonnay.*

Mussels are good partnered by a *dry white wine such as a good quality Muscadet or Gros Plant*, scallops *with Savennières or Alsatian or other good dry Riesling.*

Shellfish need *a completely dry but medium-bodied wine such as good white Burgundy and other Chardonnays or good white Rhône.*

Smoked salmon—*Sancerre or a Fumé Blanc or a fairly full-flavored champagne.*

POULTRY

Chicken plainly cooked or cold—a *fairly light, dry white* in any price bracket. With a creamy or full-flavored or textured sauce or stuffing a more full-bodied white with some acidity such as an *Alsatian Riesling.*

Turkey simply cooked and served—*fairly full-bodied white such as white Burgundy or other Chardonnay, white Rioja, white Rhône.* Cooked in a richer or more flavored way, *try a light red such as a lesser growth Bordeaux or other light Cabernet Sauvignon, Italian or Bulgarian Merlot, Chianti Classico.*

Duck *medium-quality Bordeaux or other Cabernet Sauvignon* unless an acidic or fruity sauce accompanies the duck then *drink a fairly assertive, not too serious wine such as an Australian Shiraz or a Zinfandel.*

Goose *serve a full-bodied assertive red wine or a full-bodied sweet white wine with some acidity such as an Alsatian Reserve Exceptionelle or a German Rheinpfalz spatlese.*

MEAT

Lamb plain roast lamb—*a good Bordeaux or other Cabernet Sauvignon.* With chops *Bulgarian or Chilean Cabernet Sauvignon.* With barbecued lamb and Mediterranean-style lamb dishes *a full-bodied rosé such as Tavel, Provençal or Rioja.*

Beef plain roast or fairly simply cooked steaks—*red Burgundy.* Richly flavored beef dishes—*red Rhône, Dão, Barolo, Australian Syrah/Shiraz.*

Pork and veal plainly roasted—*medium quality, medium weight red or white such as Beaune, Graves, Bordeaux or other Cabernet Sauvignon.* With broiled or fried pork chops—*a dry white with some acidity such as Alsatian Pinot Gris, Valpolicella or Penedes.* Creamy sauced or casseroled dishes—*Maçon blanc, a strong rosé or Sauvignon Blanc.*

Kidneys *Pomerol, St. Emilion or a Barbaresco.*

Sweetbreads and brains *a good, medium-full-bodied white wine such as a Hermitage blanc.*

GAME

Young feathered game plainly cooked or with a light sauce—*a good Bordeaux or a medium-bodied Cabernet Sauvignon* from California or Australia.

Venison and hare *a good Burgundy or other Pinot Noir.*

Richly-flavored game casseroles *a good Graves, full-bodied Cabernet Sauvignon, Barbaresco* or, with a really "meaty" dish, *Portuguese Dão, a Barolo or Rioja.*

CHEESE

Soft, creamy fresh cheeses, including soft goats' cheese, *a light-medium white wine with just a touch of acidity such as Sancerre or a Sauvignon or Pouilly Fumé.*

Not too strong blue cheeses such as Bleu de Bresse—*sweet white wines such as Monbazillac, Barsac and Sauternes.*

Very strong blue cheeses *Marsala, Madeira or Malaga.*

Stilton—*port.*

Full-flavored hard cheeses such as sharp Cheddar—*a mature full-bodied red wine such as a good Burgundy or Rhône.*

Milder flavored, slightly softer cheeses *slightly lighter red wines e.g. Bordeaux wines, Beaujolais, Bergerac, California Gamay.*

DESSERTS

Cake-type, non-citrus and not too creamy desserts *a sweet white wine such as Sauternes, Monbazillac, sweet Loire e.g. Vouvray, German Auslese or BeerenAuslese and late-harvest Rieslings from California and Australia.*

Rich-cream desserts and pastries *port, Madeira or cream sherry.*

DIFFICULT FOODS

Some foods do not actually blend well with any wines and can do more harm than good. Acidity in foods makes wine taste sharp so avoid using too much dressing on a salad and use lemon juice instead of vinegar to make the dressing; avoid too much lemon with fish, citrus fruits such as oranges, lemons and grapefruit, gherkins, chutneys etc. and tomatoes. Watercress and eggs and egg-based dishes including mayonnaise, can also cause problems and chocolate spells death to any wine as it completely coats the mouth. Very rich and creamy desserts also spoil wines. Really strong cheeses can overpower all but the most robust of wines, such as Barolo or a good Rhône or an Australian Shiraz, or fortified wines. Red wines do not go with desserts, with the exception of pears, peaches and strawberries, and avoid serving full tannic red wines with fish as they can make the fish taste metallic, but light, fruity red wines, such as red Loire can partner richer fish such as salmon. It can be difficult to find wines that go well with Chinese and Indian foods either because their heat and spiciness makes it impossible to taste anything else or because they contain contrary flavor combinations of sweet and sour.

Serving Temperatures

Wines are always more enjoyable if they are served at the temperature that shows off their particular characteristics to their best advantage. Coolness enhances the crisp acidity of white wines, whether sweet or dry, while a certain degree of warmth is needed to bring out the aroma and flavor of red ones. Within each category, different wines will benefit from being served at slightly

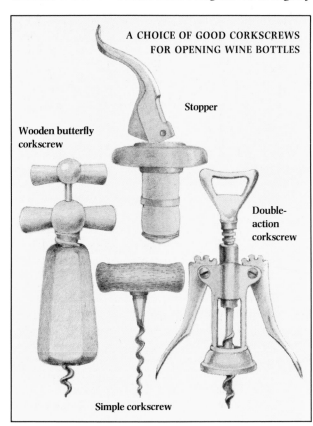

A CHOICE OF GOOD CORKSCREWS FOR OPENING WINE BOTTLES

Stopper

Wooden butterfly corkscrew

Double-action corkscrew

Simple corkscrew

A bottle of chilled champagne offers a sparkling start to a more formal meal

different temperatures according to their quality and weight or "body." Generally, the cheaper or sweeter the wine the cooler the temperature should be with a minimum of about 45°. About an hour in the refrigerator is long enough for cooling good white wines, about 1½ hours for medium quality with about 2 hours for the cheaper ones although, obviously, the initial temperature of the wine and the temperature of the refrigerator will influence the time taken to reach the right temperature. Fruity light red wines such as Beaujolais, red Loire and Valpolicella can be served cool, everyday red wines at about 60° while more full-bodied red wines are most enjoyable if served at about 63–65°. When serving white wines make sure the glasses are cool.

Keeping Wine Cool

The best way to cool more bottles than there is room for in the refrigerator is to place the bottles up to their necks in a mixture of ice cubes and water. In winter the bottles can be left out of doors if you like, once they have been chilled. Wine coolers are very good for keeping wines cool after they have been chilled.

Opening the Wine

There are many different corkscrews available and experts each have their own preferences, many favoring the double-action corkscrew, so see which suits you best.

Cut the foil just below the top of the cork, remove the top of the foil so that it cannot come into contact with the wine, and push the point of the corkscrew into the middle of the cork. Screw until the point of the corkscrew has reached the bottom of the cork and then pull out the cork. If the cork breaks, try and rescrew and pull it out. If this does not work, push the cork into the bottle and decant the wine, pouring it through cheesecloth, a paper coffee filter or a strainer if the cork has broken.

Decanting Wine

There are some far more important reasons for decanting wines other than merely showing off handsome cut-glass decanters. Indeed, it is not even necessary to use a decanter—any clean bottle will do. Wines are decanted to remove from them any deposit that may have settled at the bottom of the bottle as would be the case with, for example, a fine old Bordeaux or vintage port, which would make the wine cloudy as it was poured. Decanting will also aerate the wine and speed up the maturing process, making it softer and easier to drink. If you find that a wine is too "hard" when you first taste it, simply pouring it into another bottle can make it more enjoyable. There is some controversy about the length of time ahead of drinking that wines should be decanted but it is generally accepted that 1–2 hours is about right for medium-priced, medium quality wines, about 2 hours for better quality medium-bodied wines, slightly longer for younger ones and earlier for older ones. Good quality full-bodied red-wines, such as Rhône or old-style Rioja need about 4 hours to "breathe" properly, lesser ones about 2 hours. To decant a wine, if it has a sediment, move it carefully from where it has been stored a day, or longer if possible, before it is required and stand it upright, at room temperature, so the sediment settles at the bottom. Remove the top of the

DECANTING WINE

When decanting, keep the bottle as level and steady as possible to ensure that no sediment is transferred

foil then remove the cork as gently as possible, wipe around the neck then, holding the neck of the bottle over a flame or naked light, carefully and steadily pour the wine into the decanter or second bottle until you can see the sediment approaching the neck.

Opening Champagne

To avoid an exploding cork and wasting wine that foams out as the bottle is open make sure the chilled bottle is not shaken or moved violently. Remove the foil that surrounds the wire cage that holds the cork in place. Untwist the wires, keeping your free hand over the cork just in case the cork begins to shoot out. Hold the bottle at a 45° angle to your body. Hold the cork firmly in your right hand, or left if left-handed, and twist the bottle around with the other hand, gently easing it away from the cork.

Keeping Wine

The points to remember are:

- lay the bottles on their sides
- wine must be kept in a cool, dry atmosphere with a *constant* temperature of 45–55°
- wine must be kept out of a strong light and away from drafts
- it must not be shaken, nor constantly moved around

Any wine that is left over after a party will keep for a short while but for how long depends on the wine, and the amount left over. If you have a bottle which has only a small amount left in it, it is best to decant it into a small screw-top glass bottle, so that the wine is not exposed to too much air. If you have nearly a full bottle left over, recork it (corks from sherry bottles are useful for this), or cover the top with a layer of plastic wrap. You can buy stoppers for sealing opened bottles of wine, and stoppers for sealing opened bottles of champagne. Keep the bottle upright in a cool place (for reds), the refrigerator for whites. Depending on the wine, it should be drinkable for two to three days.

After-Dinner Drinks

Many people like to have a drink to round off a good meal. Port, which is passed around the table clockwise, is the traditional gentleman's choice but it can be a little too heavy after a long or rich meal. Cognac, Armagnac, Calvados, malt whisky, eau-de-vie such as Poire William make very good *digestifs*. If you would like to offer liqueurs as well (from the vast number that are available) select an orange-based one, such as Cointreau, one that is reputedly supposed to help with the digestion such as Kümmel or Crème de Menthe.

CREATING ATMOSPHERE

Creating a relaxed atmosphere comes firstly from preparing for your guests as much as possible in advance so that you are not worrying about the cooking as you greet them. Atmosphere, however, can be created in a number of other ways too, all of which need a little thought beforehand. This means attention to the decorative, visual aspects of a party, whether it is a brunch or a formal dinner party. Music is one of the most potent elements in creating atmosphere at a party and should not be overlooked. Music of an inappropriate sort, or music played irritatingly low in the background or stridently too loud are all equally as annoying for your guests.

So, make a checklist for yourself of the elements that help to create an elegant and lively atmosphere:

- table linen: cloths, mats, napkins
- table settings: plates, flatware, glasses, condiments
- seating plan—it is important to have the guest of honor, if there is one, in the correct place and vital to separate couples if you want to encourage inspired conversation throughout the meal!
- flowers: in the hall, in the drawing or sitting room and as table decorations
- candlelight and other lighting effects for parties
- music

The Table

TABLE CLOTHS

These are a matter of preference and convenience. Plain white cloths look good on a breakfast table while old lace cloths suit a tea table, set off with silver cake stands. For lunch and dinner you may prefer to show off the gleam of your wood or glass table, but for brunches, barbecues and informal lunch parties you may think it more convenient to have a white, cream or pastel cloth as there will inevitably be spills. For children's parties, a cloth is essential, either in a strong, rich primary color or in a vivid design on heavy duty plastic of the sort specially made for children's parties. The plainer versions of this sort of cloth are useful for barbecues as well.

Whatever you choose, bear in mind the color of the plates you will be using, the table mats and the flowers with which you will decorate the table.

TABLE MATS

Linen, cork, rush or the really heat-resistant type with pictures on the top side and felt beneath to prevent slipping—the choice is up to you, but remember you will need something quite solid if you are serving hot food on warmed dishes. If you choose a color, try and make sure it goes with the cloth and the color of the flowers you decide upon.

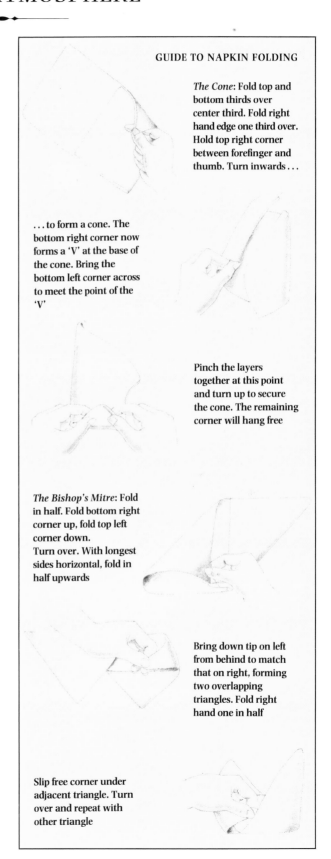

GUIDE TO NAPKIN FOLDING

The Cone: Fold top and bottom thirds over center third. Fold right hand edge one third over. Hold top right corner between forefinger and thumb. Turn inwards . . .

. . . to form a cone. The bottom right corner now forms a 'V' at the base of the cone. Bring the bottom left corner across to meet the point of the 'V'

Pinch the layers together at this point and turn up to secure the cone. The remaining corner will hang free

The Bishop's Mitre: Fold in half. Fold bottom right corner up, fold top left corner down.
Turn over. With longest sides horizontal, fold in half upwards

Bring down tip on left from behind to match that on right, forming two overlapping triangles. Fold right hand one in half

Slip free corner under adjacent triangle. Turn over and repeat with other triangle

TABLE NAPKINS

De rigueur at all times and never more so than for barbecues, informal lunches, tea parties and children's parties. I would recommend paper napkins for children's parties, Halloween parties and barbecues but linen or another fabric for all other entertaining. Nothing looks smarter than white, but if you are using a pastel tablecloth, then napkins in a darker shade look effective. Arrange them in piles or fans for informal parties, and for linen either lay them folded into a triangle on the side or, if you wish, go for something more elaborate such as you would see in a restaurant (see illustrations on page 29). For tea, napkins in fine linen or organdy are particularly suitable and look attractive if you have a lace tablecloth as well.

Table Settings

PLATES

Be sure to go through all your china before a party to make sure you have what you need. The choice of menu is sometimes dictated by what you have to serve it upon.

The only occasions on which it is acceptable to use paper plates are children's parties and for Halloween if necessary. Use china at all other times: if you don't have enough, ask friends to lend theirs. If you are having a large party, it may be impossible to have plates all of the same design, but that at least is the aim. Don't waste precious plates from your dinner service in turning out pies or cheesecakes: use other decorative dishes for these.

Food looks much better on plain dishes. Advocates of nouvelle cuisine regard a plate as the frame for a picture: the food is usually so perfect in its design and appearance that the visual element is clearly as important as taste. Very richly patterned dishes are unappealing to eat food from, so reserve these for something completely plain like a lime tart or a cheesecake, both of which can use some dressing up.

- you will need for the first course: ramekins for individual pâtés or mousses; soup plates or tureens; or small side plates
- for the main course: full size dinner plates, and bowls or side plates if you wish to serve a salad
- for the cheese: small side plates
- for the dessert: bowls for desserts such as trifle or fresh fruit salad; side plates for tarts and pies; individual ramekins for mousses; long-stemmed glasses for syllabub
- for serving: oval platters for cold cuts of meat, smoked fish; dishes for salads, vegetables, sauces; baskets or dishes for bread or rolls (or a linen napkin inside a serving dish)

Certain food looks better on special plates: for instance, a bowl of thick minestrone soup looks more appropriate served in an earthenware soup bowl than in a fine bone

Simple but perfect garnishing for a noble salmon

china soup plate. Small round or oval dishes with ears are perfect for first courses of all types, from pâtés to seafood concoctions, mushrooms in garlic to savory mousses. All salads look attractive served in wooden bowls, in earthenware dishes, or in plain white dishes, such as those with leaf shapes in their design.

It is important that the food nearly fills its serving dish. A dish that is too large for its contents looks stingy, regardless of whether there is enough food for the number of guests. On the other hand, you don't want to

fill a dish so full that your guests when helping themselves can't help but spill it over the edges. This is especially important for a buffet lunch or dinner when you want the table to look attractive, despite the large number of guests. A professional cook told me recently that she had bought a mirror on which to serve cold salmon for buffet parties.

FLATWARE
Make sure that the flatware was dried right after it was last washed or there will be water marks. For silver check that it is freshly cleaned and gleaming—don't

inadvertently use a silver fork when you are preparing eggs or it will turn black. You will need:

- large spoons, knives, silver slicers for serving
- soup spoons can either be large like a serving spoon or bowl-shaped
- knives and forks for main course
- teaspoons for mousses, syllabub and ice creams
- forks for tarts, cheesecake
- knives and forks for cheese if you intend to serve it in the French style before dessert, or just a knife
- small teaspoons for coffee and teaspoon for sugar

The perfect table setting for a five course formal dinner

a balloon bowl and a narrow top. The cup fits snugly into the hand which allows the brandy to warm in the glass, and the imbiber to savor the aroma of the brandy.

When setting the table you only need a maximum of three different glasses. Set a glass for each wine to be served and place the glass for the first wine to be served nearest the place setting. Add one final glass, furthest away from the setting, for water.

Seating Plan

The golden rules for a seating plan are that the most important male guest sits on the hostess's right with the second most important man on her left. The most important female guest sits on the host's right with the second most important woman on his left. Men and women should be seated alternately—never two men or two women together. At private functions husbands are always separated from wives but they may find themselves side by side at public banquets or very large parties. A kindly hostess will, however, place engaged couples or boyfriend and girlfriend next to each other.

It is usual to have the host at one end of the table and the hostess at the other. With certain numbers of guests (six couples, for example), it is impossible to arrange this and comply with the paramount principle of alternating the sexes. In these cases, alternation is the principle that wins and the business is best managed by having the host at one end with the chief male guest at the other and the hostess on the latter's left. The whole business is not at all difficult as long as you can decide who is more important than whom.

If you have a party of people who take much the same precedence, the best thing to do is to place your oldest friends in the middle of the table and have the more recently met guests in the positions of importance. This gives you a chance to give them the best of your attention and make sure that they are enjoying themselves.

There is no point in worrying about the finest points of who takes precedence over whom unless you move in

Be sure to set the table some hours before your guests arrive. When setting the table, remember that your guests will use the flatware set on the outside of the place setting, and work their way inward. Flatware for the first course, therefore, is laid furthest from the plate. Most people put the knives, forks and spoons at each side of the plate. The alternative method is to put the dessert spoon or fork at the top of the plate, with the other flatware at each side of the plate. Some people consider this a European table setting, but if you are short of space at the dining table, this is the better way.

GLASSES

Come in many different shapes and sizes, each design intended for a different drink. Within each type, there are also design variations and the informed hostess will know which glass denotes what sort of drink. As a guide, the smallest glass is for liqueurs, the next largest for port and the next for sherry. After these, come the wine, champagne and spirit glasses: next in size after the sherry glass is for white wine, the next for red, which will be a slightly wider glass in order to let the wine breathe, and the largest for water.

Champagne is usually drunk from tall, fluted glasses. There are also wide, shallow champagne glasses. The fizz of the champagne tends to evaporate in the wider glasses. Plain tumblers are used for whiskey, gin and vodka and other mixer drinks.

There are also brandy glasses, or goblets, which have

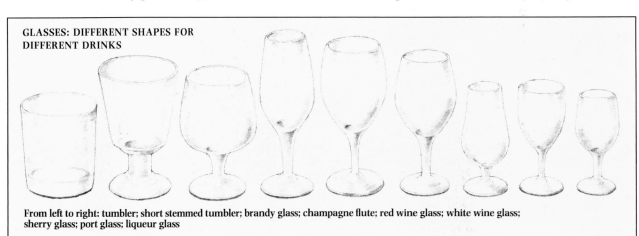

GLASSES: DIFFERENT SHAPES FOR DIFFERENT DRINKS

From left to right: tumbler; short stemmed tumbler; brandy glass; champagne flute; red wine glass; white wine glass; sherry glass; port glass; liqueur glass

royal or diplomatic circles where people may be quite jealous of these things. The business of seniority is usually fairly obvious or else does not matter.

Flowers

Once you have thought about the food and the table setting, you should look at the apartment or house as a whole and consider ways of creating a total party atmosphere. The single, most effective way of doing this is to have large and positive arrangements of flowers, branches of blossom and any unusual greenery that you can obtain. Avoid the temptation to have a lot dotted around in small vases: they will not be noticed. It will prove far more effective to have one or more stunning displays: as a centerpiece on a buffet table and on a small table in the drawing room. Have an arrangement in the hall as a greeting, if you wish.

Choose flowers that smell beautiful, like freesias, for the drawing room or the hall: lots of them look very

Fresh flower arrangements throughout the house create a welcoming atmosphere

pretty displayed simply in a tall glass. Carnations keep well so they would be a good choice if you are having friends to stay. In this case, change the water every day or at least replenish it.

Before you arrange any flowers, immerse them up to their necks in water in a cool place overnight or at least for a few hours. If you are using woody stemmed flowers, be sure to crush the ends of the stems lightly so that they can take in water. The flowers for a party can be arranged one or two days in advance, providing they have been given a good drink before arranging and their containers are kept well topped up with water after they have been arranged.

The greatest boon to flower arranging are oases, blocks of green foam which need to be soaked thoroughly so that they are completely saturated with water before you put them into your vase or bowl. Before you put in the oasis, fix a small pronged plastic disk to the bottom of your vase and then impale your soaked oasis onto the prongs. (Keep surplus oasis in a sealed plastic bag to prevent it from drying out.)

If you are arranging dried flowers and leaves, you can buy a different sort of oasis which is a brownish color and much stiffer. As an arrangement begins to die, you can unpick all the flowers and foliage, cutting off any flowers that are dead, cutting the stalks of the remaining flowers and greenery down and giving them another good drink, up to their necks, for a couple of hours, then rearranging them.

The flowers for a dining table must look pretty from all sides, and this is easy to achieve with the aid of oasis. Take a low dish—a deep saucer will do—and put a piece of well-soaked oasis on the dish, and start by inserting your greenery around the edges, turning the container all the time to put in another piece. Gradually work your way up the oasis, using shorter bits of greenery, and continuing to revolve the container. Then add the flowers in the same way, starting at the bottom, turning the dish, and working your way up. You will end up with an arrangement that is attractive from all angles (see the illustration on the opposite page). Although I love flowers that smell, I do not have scented flowers on the dining room table as their scent can clash with the food.

It is lovely to have flowers on the table for a formal dinner party, but here practical considerations must come first: you must have enough space for all the table settings, serving dishes, sauces, accompaniments and glasses for each guest; and your guests should be able to see each other easily. For these two reasons, then, tall arrangements are out. A collection of small containers, china or glass, look pretty with small bunches of flowers down the center of a dining table. Alternatively, use a wide, shallow glass container, and float a few heads of roses, small lilies, carnations or clematis in the water.

For a buffet lunch or supper party, the flower arrangement on the table should be higher than the level of the food, the opposite to a dinner party, and quite flamboyant.

Dried flower arrangements are ideal for a seasonal touch

If you are having an informal supper, you would not have an elaborate flower arrangement in the middle of the table. It would be more appropriate to have a simple bowl or small jug of flowers, or, in the autumn, a jug of leaves and berries—rosehips are very decorative.

House plants and dried flowers are some of the alternatives to consider when you are unable to get fresh flowers or when the choice is not very exciting. For Christmas, azaleas, cyclamen and poinsettias look warm and beautiful, but remember that they need to be kept in quite cool rooms to thrive. There are some very beautiful dried flowers on the market now, with which you can make superb arrangements. Remember to shake them out now and again as they do get dusty.

Fruit can be used as a centerpiece for the table instead of flowers. Arranged in a shallow basket or dish, it is lovely to look at, with perhaps a pineapple in the middle, surrounded by a wide variety of seasonal fruit. It is also very stylish to have a huge pile of grapes, both black and green, rather than mixing a lot of different fruits. The type of dish in which you arrange the fruit naturally enhances the arrangement: grapes arranged on a low, glass cake stand, for example, will look beautiful. You can use any shallow dish, but glass or white china set the fruit off to best advantage.

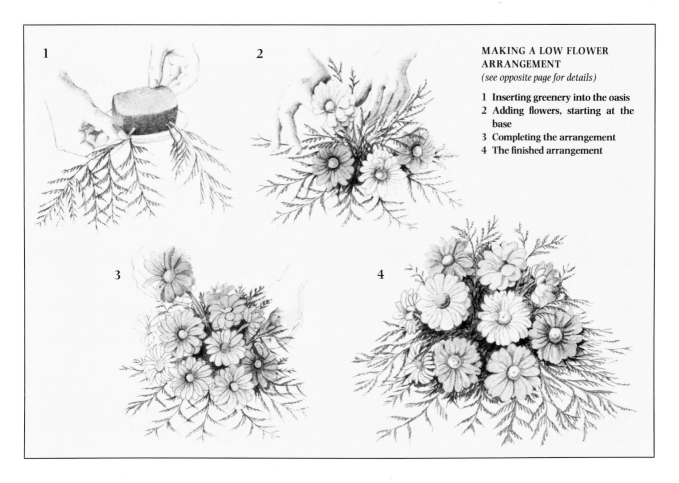

MAKING A LOW FLOWER ARRANGEMENT
(see opposite page for details)

1 Inserting greenery into the oasis
2 Adding flowers, starting at the base
3 Completing the arrangement
4 The finished arrangement

A bowl overflowing with seasonal fruits makes an attractive alternative to a flower centerpiece

SPECIAL TABLE DECORATIONS

Special festivities have their own traditional table decor-ations. If you decide to arrange vegetables, which are particularly suitable for a Thanksgiving table decor-ation, a shallow basket, a wooden board or shallow wooden bowl or tray makes an ideal display. Arrange-ments of preserved corn on the cob, grasses, fruits and vegetables down the center of a dining table at Thanks-giving look most effective. These Thanksgiving decor-ations look good for a Halloween party, too.

At Easter, simple posies of primroses down the center of the table, painted eggs in egg cups at breakfast time and more formal arrangements with daffodils and fresh, bright green foliage are all reminders of spring.

Christmas provides the best opportunity for decor-ating not only the table but the whole house. If you leave the table decoration until Christmas Eve, it will stay fresh over New Year, particularly if you are using foliage like holly and evergreens.

A platter can be used to excellent effect for Christmas decoration: the dish can be covered with glittering Christmas tree balls of different sizes. Use any color combination you like to match the colors of your room, but green, red and gold are especially right for Christmas. In among the Christmas tree balls put ball-shaped or orb candles and around the edges of the dish sprigs of holly. When the candles are lit their glow reflects in the Christmas tree balls, and the whole effect is very pretty.

A Christmas wreath of several varieties of greenery, with a large red bow on the top and streamers hanging from it, hung on the front door spells a welcome to your Christmas guests (see the illustration on page 38).

Christmas trees are beautiful and full of promise for the children and they cannot really be over-decorated. The problem of dropping needles can be overcome to some extent by spraying the tree before you bring it inside with a preserving aerosol spray (from garden centers and some hardware stores). Put the tree in a large bucket with water in it as it needs a lot of moisture. Apart from the Christmas tree lights, the most important tree decoration is luxuriantly thick ropes of gold or silver tinsel. Add the glittering Christmas tree balls, and then all the numerous tree ornaments which families tend to accumulate over the years.

Christmas cards themselves are decorative, and a happy reminder of all your friends. Avoid having them on surfaces because they tend to fall over, and they all need to be collected for dusting and put back: so suspend them on red ribbons over the top of mirrors and so on.

This arrangement of fruit and nuts sets the tone for an autumnal meal

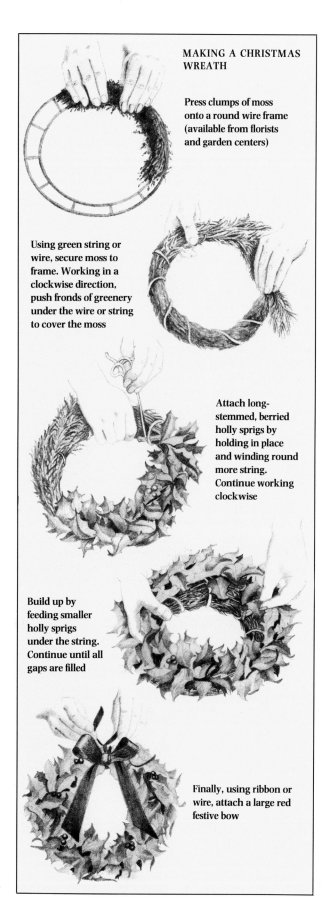

MAKING A CHRISTMAS WREATH

Press clumps of moss onto a round wire frame (available from florists and garden centers)

Using green string or wire, secure moss to frame. Working in a clockwise direction, push fronds of greenery under the wire or string to cover the moss

Attach long-stemmed, berried holly sprigs by holding in place and winding round more string. Continue working clockwise

Build up by feeding smaller holly sprigs under the string. Continue until all gaps are filled

Finally, using ribbon or wire, attach a large red festive bow

Music

Music can set the tone for a party in a way that no other signal can. For a dinner party, something that is melodious playing fairly softly in the background while you have drinks is best, but none while you eat or the general hubbub ceases to be relaxing. Music is not really necessary at "active" parties such as Halloween, brunches, informal lunches and children's parties—except for certain games, of course. Music would be inappropriate for formal occasion parties such as christenings and weddings unless the wedding celebration goes on into a wedding dance—remember that people will be wanting to make speeches and they cannot be expected to

compete with music, no matter how elegant and soft your choice.

The occasions on which you really need music are large evening parties and at Christmas. For large parties it is best to start off with something against which your guests can meet and talk to each other without having to raise their voices: it is rather intimidating to find yourself in a room with several strangers and loud music signaling you to dance! As the evening continues, change the music to something livelier and, at the same time, dim the lights.

For Christmas, put out the music that your family and friends like best and perhaps play some carols, too: it all helps to create a truly Christmassy atmosphere.

Lighting

The golden rule of lighting is not to have the rooms so dark at the beginning that no one can easily be introduced and make new friends. Again, this can be intimidating. Once your guests have had a few drinks you can dim the lights a little in the dining area, either by using only table lamps and spots or candles. Nothing is more flattering and romantic than candlelight and is certain to make your guests feel that the evening is a special one.

Harsh, too-bright light is unflattering and a strain to be in; on the other hand, if you are relying entirely on candles for light, have quite a large number, because too few creates a gloom, with guests peering to identify each other. Avoid candles on a dining table at eye level as your guests will be dazzled and distracted from conversation. Choose either short, fat candles, or very tall, slim ones: they are available in every color you could wish for and all shapes and sizes.

For last Christmas I bought two wooden Christmas tree shapes, which came in two flat halves and slotted together. They contain holders to take short pencil-thick candles and they look very pretty, particularly for an informal or children's arrangement. Always keep a good supply of candles in the house in case of power failures and for impromptu dinners, too!

It is possible to buy small glass disks which sit on the candlestick and catch any wax. (If you do get candlewax on a cloth, just iron it on the wrong side with a piece of brown paper beneath, and peel off the melted wax.)

When you are thinking about lighting, other than candles, you will find that you can create a softer light and warmer atmosphere by using table lamps or spot lights. If the whole room is flooded with center lighting, it tends to look rather business-like. If you are afraid that your room may be too gloomy with just table lamps, fit a dimmer switch to your center light switch so that you can control the amount of light.

Department stores now sell lamps in many different designs: the days of a conventional shade on a lamp alone are past. Lighting is especially important in a kitchen/dining room: when you bring your guests into supper, make sure you turn off the kitchen light in order to emphasize the dining area and create an atmosphere of relaxation and enjoyment.

Simple lights behind large flower arrangements make the most of your decoration and provide the room with a focal point. Pictures can be spot-lit to add a note of elegance to a dining or drawing room.

If you are planning an evening barbecue, you should give some thought to lighting: candles designed for use in the garden are available, and it is also simple to fix a cable from an electrical outlet in the house down the length of the garden on which rainproof holders for light bulbs can be attached.

The soft glow of candlelight enhances Christmas decorations

39

PARTIES OUTSIDE

The principles of buffet parties and brunches can be applied equally to barbecues and picnics as far as presentation of food, forward preparation and the placing of small tables are concerned. People tend to eat more out of doors—somehow the fresh air sharpens appetites, whether it is at a picnic or a barbecue.

Barbecues

Although you may not be doing the cooking, you will be preparing marinaded chicken pieces, kabobs, pieces of fish, barbecue sauces, two or three interesting salads, dips, potatoes for baking, relishes, bread or rolls, and the desserts.

Barbecues have a unique atmosphere of informality, and so they are an ideal way to entertain children, and to entertain guests of mixed ages. For older guests, virtually anything can be barbecued:

- meat in the form of steaks or chops
- meat kabobs—pieces of pork tenderloin threaded on skewers, alternating with pieces of blanched red and yellow pepper, for example
- chicken
- fish such as salmon

The one important thing to bear in mind about barbecues is that the fire needs to be lit early, and the cooking of the food started in good time as it has to be cooked and served in relays. For this reason, limit your guests to twenty, ideally, as otherwise you have to barbecue the first relays of food early and keep it warm in an oven indoors.

The first consideration is what type of barbecue party it is to be. Barbecues are ideal parties for children above the age of about seven. What children like best is often the easiest:

- chicken drumsticks
- frankfurters
- lamb or pork chops
- hamburgers
- a pile of buns, heaped on a tray
- plenty of ketchup
- bowls of salad—two varieties, lettuce and tomatoes, and perhaps an interesting bean salad, made of two or three different varieties of beans and flavored with chopped scallions, or a potato salad
- good vanilla ice cream and piles of brownies, with plenty of marshmallows and skewers to cook them on over the last heat of the barbecue, are the best choices for desserts

Children appreciate jugs of fruit punch, with slices of orange and apple to garnish it. Simple punches can be made from a mixture of sparkling apple juice mixed with orange juice, or, for those who like a slightly sweeter drink, pineapple juice mixed with 7-Up.

For family parties you will want to provide slightly more sophisticated food, perhaps marinated chicken pieces, or kabobs of fish and bacon, or kabobs of pork tenderloin pieces with peppers. Marinate any meat or fish a day or two ahead. You can throw some sprigs of rosemary or thyme on the barbecue before you start to cook, so that they impart their delicate flavor to the food as it cooks. You can provide more interesting salads, too: perhaps a good mixed green salad using greens like spinach, nasturtium, arugula, and a garnish of crisp croûtons of wholewheat bread. Mushrooms in a sour cream and chive dressing make a delicious salad, as do tomatoes with pesto. Make a barbecue sauce to accompany the food: plenty of finely chopped onion sautéed until soft, cooked with canned tomatoes, ketchup, brown sugar, a very little amount of wine vinegar and a dash of Worcestershire sauce. Simmer until it is thick.

Bananas baked in their skins on top of the barbecue make a quick and easy dessert, especially if they are accompanied by rum, raisin and chocolate chip ice cream.

As with all parties, start by making lists of:

- **the guests invited**
- **the food you plan to serve**
- **the items you can prepare in advance**
- **the shopping list**

Dips, for large platters of crudités, can be made two or three days in advance and kept in covered containers in the refrigerator. Two dips such as Stilton and garlic or sardine and mushroom make a good choice, and bowls of dip and plates of crudités can either be placed on each table or on a central table with the drinks, so that guests can help themselves to both.

If you plan to serve a first course, choose a chilled soup, such as gazpacho or almond and garlic that can be set out in advance. Serve hot garlic bread, or bread with garlic and mixed herbs. You can prepare the bread in the morning, by splitting the French loaves lengthwise and spreading both sides liberally with garlic herb butter; wrap the loaves in foil ready to pop into the oven to heat through before you start barbecuing.

Individual pieces of meat such as chicken or meat on kabobs are convenient for barbecuing but if you decide on a really elegant evening barbecue, then try a leg of lamb or loin of pork. Give a 6–7 lb leg of lamb an hour in the oven first and a loin of pork (spread with a mixture of Dijon mustard and parsley breadcrumbs) about 40 minutes in the oven. You will need a firm table outside so that you can carve easily.

If you decide on individual pieces for the barbecue, try,

An inviting setting for a party outside

as a change from the usual chicken pieces, steaks and sausages:

- **steaks of oily fish, such as swordfish, brushed once with sunflower oil**
- **salmon, wrapped in foil. Make several slits in the foil to allow the charcoal flavor to penetrate the fish**
- **chunks of turbot or monkfish, wrapped in bacon and put on skewers**
- **scallops, cooked the same way, or jumbo shrimp**

Serve a good tomato and garlic mayonnaise or an herb and cucumber mayonnaise to accompany barbecued fish.

To accompany the barbecued meat or fish, make small packages of new vegetables wrapped in foil. Tiny new potatoes, with olive oil, garlic and parsley, cooked in a foil package, or foil packages consisting of sliced zucchini, tomatoes and basil, all brushed with olive oil,

are delicious. Large bowls of interesting salads—such as steamed snow sugar peas with a mint vinaigrette dressing, and leeks vinaigrette—make delicious accompaniments to either fish or meat main courses.

For dessert, a large spiced meringue cake covered with strawberries (or raspberries) and whipped cream makes an impressive and delectable finale to a barbecue, as do fruit tarts, made with a rich sweet pastry and served with whipped cream, or meringues, piled into pyramids, and served with platters of fresh fruit such as raspberries, strawberries or cherries (pit the cherries).

For family and children's barbecue parties disposable plates, cups and napkins ensure no breakage and great convenience when it comes to clearing up afterwards. For more elegant barbecue parties, I would still use paper napkins, but not paper plates.

Picnics

A simple impromptu picnic means packing some food for lunch or tea and taking it to the beach or river bank. Such a picnic should, ideally, consist of food to be eaten in the fingers:

- cold sausages
- chicken legs
- meat pies cut in wedges
- wholewheat rolls filled with delicious mixtures of cream cheese, pieces of crisp bacon and garlic; mashed sardines with chopped tomatoes; egg salad and crisply cooked bacon; bacon, tomato and cold cooked chicken. Spread the rolls with mayonnaise instead of butter
- chunks of iceberg lettuce, washed, in plastic bags
- tomatoes, quartered
- cheese
- fruit
- chocolate cookies
- pieces of fruitcake or ginger cake
- brownies
- two vital items: paper towels and an ointment for insect bites and bee stings.

A more formal picnic for a sporting event, such as a football game, may mean you are picnicking in chilly weather, so your picnic must be warm and filling:

- wide-topped thermos full of hot, rich stew
- baked potatoes packed into another wide-topped thermos
- a thick, hot soup, with hot garlic bread, packed in its foil wrapping in a thermos
- hard-boiled eggs
- salad
- a good cheese such as a sharp Cheddar or Stilton
- fruitcake or ginger cake
- apples and chocolate cookies for your friends to eat during the day
- chilled beer and white wine for a hot day
- sherry, Whisky Mac (a mixture of Scotch and ginger wine) and plenty of hot coffee for a cold day
- salt, pepper, sugar, milk, teaspoons and bottle opener

For an elegant picnic you will want to provide food that is deliciously special, yet portable and not too messy. The drink at such occasions is the easiest part, for champagne is perfect—or alternatively, a good white wine. You will need a large insulated bag for transporting the food and wine.

When you plan food for such a picnic, you are looking for the combination of very good ingredients with simplicity. A smoked salmon roulade, for example, for a first course, is easy to transport, easy to slice, and needs no accompanying bread or rolls and therefore makes a perfect first course. The cooled roulade is spread with a sour cream, slices of smoked salmon and diced

cucumber and then rolled up. Other possible first courses are pâtés, of either meat or smoked fish, with good wholewheat bread. Cream puffs with a savory filling make a good first course for this type of picnic, too.

FOR THE MAIN COURSE
- cold, sliced beef tenderloin, cooked very rare, with a creamy horseradish sauce to accompany it
- chicken breasts, which have been dipped in sesame seeds and cooked in a non-stick frying pan brushed with oil, then left to cool before being packed in a plastic container. A slightly curried sauce goes well with this
- a whole poached salmon or sea trout, with lime and parsley mayonnaise
- two salads—one perhaps of three peppers—red,

yellow and green—each of which you have cut into six, and gently cooked in olive oil and crushed garlic until soft. Leave to cool, then seal in a container
- walnut and radicchio salad with their contrasting textures and flavors with a walnut oil dressing is a good choice. Take the dressing for this or any salad in a screw-top jar and dress the salad at the picnic
- rice salad, with brown rice, chopped apricots, and toasted almonds, goes well with fish, chicken or meat

THE DESSERT
A fresh lime or lemon tart is ideal. Alternatively, take brown sugar meringues, with a bowl of ready whipped cream, a jar of lemon curd. Take fresh strawberries to accompany the meringues, which you fill with the curd

An elegant summer picnic is enjoyed in the sunshine

and cream when you assemble the picnic at the site.

Remember to pack a dishtowel, and pack the glasses individually in paper towels. A low, folding table will prove a great help. Try to find a corner to tuck in a small vase or jug, with a posy of roses or flowers to decorate the middle of your picnic cloth. Pack a pretty cloth, with matching napkins, and plates for each course, with knives, forks and spoons. Remember to pop in a couple of shopping bags, in which you can pack the used flatware. Take coffee, cream and sugar, and brandy, with perhaps one liqueur, and the appropriate glasses, and you are all set for a delicious and elegant picnic!

THE DAY OF THE PARTY

The day arrives and with all your preparation you should be perfectly in control of everything with the table laid, the flowers arranged, the seating plan worked out and all the food awaiting only the last minute preparation and garnishing.

Servants and Hired Help

Some people rather enjoy entertaining in a formal way and others are obliged to do it by virtue of their job or rank. Those who do it because they enjoy it will tend to give parties for people who are fairly well known to them and, because this makes for more relaxed circumstances, find it easy enough to produce a controlled and formal atmosphere without the use of servants. For those whose position requires them to offer formal hospitality to a number of distinguished strangers, it is impossible to hold a formal dinner party without help. It does not really work to have the host and hostess offering dishes as well as trying to introduce everyone and keep the drink flowing at the same time.

If you are in the difficult position of arranging formal entertainment without servants you will find caterers who provide reasonably trained temporary staff in most big towns. There are also agencies which will provide freelance butlers and waitresses, while there are professional cooks available for hire—but try them out first.

The Guests Arrive

To take a formal dinner party from its beginning you will station a servant in the hall to let your guests in and take their coats or show them to a bedroom where they can leave their things. The time to invite people for is usually eight for eight-thirty and it means exactly that. They should all have arrived by ten past eight ready to join you in one or two cocktails before being shown into the dining room at eight-thirty.

For many parties it may seem too icy and daunting to adhere rigidly to the rules. A gathering of old friends, for instance, may expect to arrive at eight-thirty and drink cocktails for an hour or so before starting to eat. And that's perfectly acceptable. The important thing is to be aware of the ground rules for the most impersonally formal party so that you do not offend anyone, and you can then ease them to suit the guests you invite on a less formal occasion.

Introductions

You should be reasonably careful to introduce people in the right way. It is simplicity itself to be correct and therefore unforgivable to get it wrong. The rule is to introduce men to women on all occasions: "James, come and meet Henrietta." In the same way, always introduce the junior to the senior—the captain to the colonel—and the younger to the older. If you are a bit confused about whether to introduce 30-year-old Captain Stewart to 30-year-old Doctor Cutting or vice versa, there is no need to worry, for there is little dilemma over formal precedence when the status of two guests being introduced is roughly comparable.

Forms of Address

Using the correct form of address has always been tricky and the informality of the 1980s has only made it more so. People sometimes object to the old forms—not without justification. Feminists, for example, are less than enthusiastic about being totally submerged by their husbands' names or titles. The old form was that when Henrietta Smythe married James Banyard she became Mrs. James Banyard—which left no trace of her former self. No one has come up with a satisfactory alternative to the old form which is generally acceptable (Ms. Henrietta Smythe-Banyard would leave us all with impossibly long surnames within a generation). The disagreement has left us with a great deal more informality generally and a higher tolerance of minor social mistakes.

Despite this, there is no greater security than knowing what is absolutely correct. Henrietta Smythe, for instance, might be addressed in a number of ways throughout her life: she would start as Miss H. (or Henrietta) Smythe (the old custom of addressing the oldest or only daughter as simply Miss Smythe while a younger sister would be Miss Charlotte Smythe has become ignored as too confusing), go on to becoming Mrs. James Banyard and then, if divorced, become Mrs. H. (or Henrietta) Banyard or Mrs. Smythe Banyard; if she remains with her husband, she would become Mrs. J. Banyard on being widowed and simply Mrs. Banyard when she became the senior Mrs. Banyard—her mother-in-law and the wife of James's older brother having died.

Men, too, can go through a number of changes on life's path. As a schoolboy a man might be addressed simply as James Banyard but become James Banyard Esq. (on the envelope) when he leaves school while being addressed as Mr. James Banyard at the top of an invitation. As he goes through life and gains military rank, becomes much decorated and elevated to the peerage, he can go through more changes. The subject of addressing people correctly, sending them invitations or replying to their invitations is varied enough to have had books written about it.

The one thing no book can tell you is whether and when you should proceed from formal to informal personal address. When do you change from calling her Mrs. Banyard and start calling her Henrietta? Luckily, the answer is usually fairly obvious. If you are of much the same age and type you will probably have been introduced by Christian name: "Edward, I want to introduce you to James and Henrietta Banyard," and you never look back. Difficulties arise with people of an older generation and markedly conservative appearance. You may feel that it is as well to stick to Mr. and Mrs. on the first couple of meetings but, if you begin to know them at all well and certainly if you know them well enough to invite to your house, no one is going to object to using Christian names and you may be invited to do so in any case.

Things are not quite the same with people of immensely senior social rank. It is always a useful thing to have a diminutive or nickname so that, when the Duke of Loamshire switches from calling you Edward to calling you Ned, you might feel it fair to switch from calling him Duke to calling him George. However, don't try this with members of the Royal Family: with them you start with Your Royal Highness and progress to Sir or Ma'am (rhyming with clam) and that is as informal as you may ever be in any social circumstance.

Drinks Before Dinner

The basic minimum choice you can offer is gin (with tonic or bitter lemon), whiskey (with soda or Malvern water) and sherry (dry, medium and sweet). Avoid elaborate cocktails: if you wish to offer a further choice then have dry gin Martinis and pink gin. It is also very acceptable and not too expensive to offer two or three glasses of champagne. As far as soft drinks are concerned, orange juice is a strong favorite, backed up by ginger beer or Coca Cola and, most essentially, mineral water. (See also *Drinks*, page 24.)

The moment for going in to the dining room is either announced by a servant—"Dinner is served"—or the host may announce it himself. Your guests will be prepared for this with "There should be time for another one" as you refill glasses ten minutes or so before dinner will be announced.

The hostess leads the way and the women enter the dining room first, closely followed by the men. As everyone reaches the table, it is the hostess who instructs him or her where to sit according to the seating plan (see page 32).

Serving the Dinner

It is usual to start with the most important female guest and go around the table counter-clockwise. Do not bother about serving the women first or leaving the hostess until last. No one starts eating any course until the hostess either does so herself or urges everyone else to begin. At formal parties complete with servants, let the guests wait until everybody has been served. It is no bad idea, however, to let an informal party of old friends begin eating a hot dish as they are served.

Food is served from the left but the butler approaches the wine glasses from the right. You will be serving wine at every level of occasion these days from a shared spaghetti in your kitchen upwards. Choosing and buying it is a subject in its own right (see *Drinks*, page 24).

As far as food is concerned you could, at a formal dinner, provide five courses (soup, fish, main course, cheese and dessert), but three (appetizer, main course and dessert) is quite adequate. Your choice of dishes and the way you serve them are dictated by the knowledge that there are two main aspects of a dinner party that your guests should enjoy: the food and drink, of course, but also the conversation and company. It is something of an art to pace things correctly so that people do not feel rushed or that time hangs heavily between courses.

The first thing to remember is that each course should be completely cleared away before the next one is served. It makes the whole party far too much of a gallop if the next course is plonked down just as the last is whisked away. It is unwise to leave a gap of more than a few minutes between clearing away a light appetizer and bringing on the main course. At the end of the main course it is a good idea to pause for several minutes for people to savor their wine and chat before bringing on the dessert or cheese.

Eating Difficult Foods

There are a number of foods that are difficult to eat with any elegance and you should give it some thought before serving them. On the most utterly formal occasions small birds, such as quail, remain half eaten because your guests are unwilling to pick them up in their fingers. It is best, perhaps, to keep them and corn on the cob (which presents the same problem) for more relaxed occasions. The list of foods that can be properly enjoyed only at the expense of elegance is quite long and obvious—spaghetti is a notorious example. They can all be eaten easily enough on more relaxed occasions.

There are other foods that need just a little technical expertise but which are more managable. Fish such as sole, mackerel, trout and mullet are frequently served unfilleted. The expert will eat one side of his trout, remove the spine and bones, and then tackle the other; with sole he will cut off the fringe of bone around the edge, cut down the center from top to tail and eat both fillets before removing the spine and eating the rest.

Slippery oysters are simply taken from their half-shell, delicately balanced on a fork, and eaten whole. Snails are usually served with special eating implements: tongs and a narrow fork. Hang onto the shell with the tongs and fork the whole snail out—and mop up the delicious sauce with bread if you wish.

Other dishes are rather messy as they have to be

Fine liqueurs, cigars and chocolates are welcomed after dinner

picked up by hand: asparagus and globe artichokes are in this category. Asparagus is picked up by the end and the tip is dipped in the accompanying sauce before it is bitten off all the way down to the part where the green turns white. With artichokes you should begin at the outside and pull out one leaf at a time, dip its white base into the sauce and bite it out. The used leaves are piled on the side of the plate. The leaves near the heart have no tasty white base and are piled up uneaten until the heart is exposed. The heart is then eaten with knife and fork, having first scraped away the hairy choke at the base. Some people give their guests finger bowls to rinse their fingers with when eating these messy foods.

Withdrawing After Dinner

After dinner your guests will be served coffee and a decanter of port will be placed on the table for guests to help themselves and pass it on (always to the left). At this time it is still quite common, particularly among the older generation, for the women to withdraw to another room, leaving the men to their port. Alternatively, the women may also drink a glass of port, then leave the men at the table. Whether you do this yourself depends upon what you feel about the custom. There are quite a number of people today who resent this separation of the sexes just when the party is at its height and you do run some risk of a mutiny from a strong-minded female guest if you attempt to organize a withdrawal. The pro-withdrawal lobby is not very widespread and strong feelings in favor are only likely to occur at the most rigidly formal occasion. You may feel happiest if you keep the custom for use only when you are entertaining the old guard in the most formal manner.

If you do withdraw, the hostess should not let the men talk all night. Twenty minutes or so should be perfectly adequate and then, when you have your party complete again, you may offer everybody a liqueur.

Having House Guests

Some house guests will be close family friends who may be prepared to put up with a certain amount of discomfort and will certainly expect to be treated with informality. On other occasions, your guests may be complete or comparative strangers with fairly set ideas about the sort of courtesies that should be extended to them during their stay.

Whether your house guests are old friends or rather grand acquaintances, you should make sure that their stay is as comfortable as possible.

As coats and so on are shed, you can ask your guests whether they wish to go straight to their room or have a drink first—assuming that it is an appropriate time of day for a drink. Make sure, ideally, that your guests arrive at least an hour before you intend to serve lunch or dinner, or you will have too many different things to organize.

Throughout their stay your guests will expect a certain minimum of eating and entertainment. This runs along the lines of breakfast, pre-lunch drinks, lunch, tea, pre-dinner drinks and dinner. The size and scale of all this depends upon your resources and the sort of guests you have. Even the grandest guest will expect only one formal party a day—but they *will* expect that. The best solution is to make lunch the less formal affair, but have people in for dinner.

Having friends to stay takes a fair amount of planning. There is no need to be afraid of it but you must recognize that it calls for quite a bit of preparation and foresight: the watch-words for entertaining on whatever scale if your guests and you are to enjoy the occasion to the full.

MENUS
FOR
ENTERTAINING

—◆ •●• ◆—

Food for entertaining should be special food. This doesn't necessarily mean it has to be elaborate, but the ingredients should be of the highest quality, presented well. The planning of the menus is best centered around seasonal availability, and also must strike a balance in texture, color and richness.

Whatever the occasion, you will need to plan your food carefully, but more formal occasions need rather more planning, since a greater number of courses will probably be served. The presentation of food for entertaining is important, too. I don't mean overgarnishing, but the food should be simply presented and should look beautiful. The beautiful color photographs in this book illustrate how lovely the food can look.

Preparing the food for your party should be fun, and so that you should be able to enjoy its preparation, try to plan the cooking over several days, rather than cook the entire meal in one day, leaving you feeling exhausted.

There is a great deal of inspiration in this section, with a choice of suitable menus for a wide variety of seasons and occasions whether informal, formal, traditional or fun theme parties. I hope you get much pleasure from reading these ideas and planning for your own parties.

INFORMAL ENTERTAINING

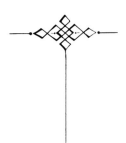

Few people these days have an abundant supply of help available whenever they give a party. This has resulted in more and more informal entertaining, which doesn't mean giving a party with second-rate food, decorations, etc. It means giving a party where the food is simple, the setting and the atmosphere relaxed and informal, and where your guests play their part in creating the atmosphere by dressing informally.

Informal parties can be brunch parties, cozy fireside tea parties, or suppers in the kitchen, bright with candle-light and with attractively colored cloth and napkins. Another type of informal party is an aftertheater supper, when no one would want to sit down to a dinner of several courses. Sunday lunch, a country weekend lunch, a children's Halloween party and a barbecue are all more ways to entertain your friends informally.

After-Theater Supper for 4–6 (see page 64)

SUMMER BRUNCH FOR 6

Inviting friends to brunch gives you the opportunity to entertain them for a long, leisurely meal
eaten toward the end of the morning, with the
afternoon ahead of you to enjoy—talking, or going
for a walk or swim, or playing a game of tennis.
Your guests will arrive at about eleven o'clock,
ready for a delicious breakfast cum lunch—brunch.

Welcome them with a glass of Mimosa.

When your guests go to the dining table to sit
down for brunch, have ready a plate of fruit salad at
each place. This is not a fruit salad in the traditional
sense, that of fruit in a heavy sugar syrup, but
rather an arrangement of sliced fruit on a plate, to
look attractive and to taste good. What fruit you
decide on is up to you, but an assortment of slices of
melon and peach, and clusters of blueberries,
strawberries and raspberries is lovely. If you are
having a buffet brunch party, arrange the fruits on
a large serving platter, and your guests can help
themselves.

SUMMER BRUNCH FOR 6

FRUIT SALAD PLATE

PRUNES IN ORANGE SYRUP

COLD ROAST HAM WITH MINTED PEACHES

FRESH SALMON CAKES

CRISPY BACON WITH FIELD MUSHROOMS OR
CHANTERELLES

PIPÉRADE

SLICED TOMATOES WITH GINGER AND BASIL

OATCAKES

DRIED APRICOT JAM

GRAPEFRUIT AND LEMON MARMALADE

SUGGESTED DRINKS: MIMOSA TO WELCOME YOUR
GUESTS; COFFEE AND TEA

Prunes in Orange Syrup

We always have these prunes on the breakfast menu
here at Kinloch. They are extremely popular, and are
ideal for a brunch party, because they can be made 1 or
2 days in advance. The prunes are cooked slowly in an
orange-flavored syrup, and served cold. You can serve
plain yogurt with them for those who would like it.

1 cup sugar
1 orange, cut into 3 or 4 slices
1 tea bag, Earl Grey preferably (optional)
1 lb prunes

Put the sugar, slices of orange and the tea bag into a
saucepan and add 5 cups of water. Heat, stirring, until
the sugar has dissolved. Add the prunes to the saucepan
and cover the pan with a lid. Simmer very gently for
1½–2 hours, until the prunes are well plumped up. Cool,
then pour the prunes and their syrup into a glass bowl.
Cover and chill until ready to serve.

Cold Roast Ham with Minted Peaches

Cold roast ham is an ideal dish for a brunch. It serves a
dual role, both as an item on the menu, and as the
centerpiece of the brunch buffet table—or dining table
if your guests are sitting down for brunch. A handsome
piece of ham, honey-glazed and studded with cloves,
with a few wafer-thin slices carved off it, looks so
tempting. The peaches poached in a minty syrup make
a very good accompaniment for the ham. Buy a piece of
ham larger than you will need for the brunch alone, as
you can eat it for several days afterward, and a too-
small piece of ham looks so stingy. The ham and
peaches can both be prepared the day before.

5-lb ham
1 onion
1 carrot
3 tablespoons thick honey
2 tablespoons Dijon mustard
about 12 cloves
MINTED PEACHES
2⅔ cups sugar
handful of fresh mint, stalks and all
6 peaches, peeled
juice of 2 lemons
1 tablespoon finely chopped fresh mint, preferably applemint

If the ham is smoked, soak it overnight in cold water, to
get rid of any excessive saltiness. Put the ham in a large

Fruit Salad Plate

saucepan with fresh water to cover it and add the onion and carrot. Bring to a boil and simmer for about 1 hour. Drain.

When cool enough to handle, cut the skin off the ham, leaving as much of the fat on the ham as possible. With a sharp knife, score the fat into diamond shapes. Put the ham in a roasting pan. Mix together the honey and mustard and smear over the ham. Stud with the cloves at even spaces.

Roast the ham in a preheated 350° oven for 1 hour. Allow to cool completely.

To prepare the peaches, put the sugar in a saucepan with 5 cups of water. Heat, stirring, to dissolve the sugar, then bring to a boil. Add the handful of mint to the syrup, and boil for 5–7 minutes.

Add the peaches to the mint syrup with the lemon juice. Simmer for 5 minutes, turning the peaches over in the syrup occasionally. Remove from the heat, and let the peaches cool in the syrup.

Place the ham on a serving platter. Carve off a few very thin slices and arrange around the ham, with the drained peaches and sprinkle the chopped mint over.

Fresh Salmon Cakes

Ideally, leftover cooked salmon should be used for this recipe, but if you don't happen to have any salmon in the refrigerator, it is well worth buying some and cooking it just to make these delicious fishcakes. Alternatively you could use canned salmon. You can make up the fishcakes and leave them in the refrigerator overnight, ready to shallow fry just before brunch.

1 lb cooked salmon, skinned, boned and flaked
2 cups mashed potato
1 tablespoon finely chopped fresh parsley
grated nutmeg
salt and pepper
1 egg, beaten
1–1½ cups fresh wholewheat breadcrumbs, lightly toasted
3 tablespoons sunflower oil
4 tablespoons unsalted butter

Mix together the salmon and mashed potato. Add the parsley, a little nutmeg and seasoning. Divide into 12 equal-sized balls and flatten each into a round cake. Dip in the beaten egg and then in the toasted breadcrumbs. Pat on the crumbs to help them adhere.

Heat the oil and butter in a frying pan. Add the fishcakes, in batches, and fry until golden brown on all sides and piping hot throughout. Drain on paper towels and serve hot.

Sliced Tomatoes with Ginger and Basil

A dish of sliced tomatoes, subtly flavored with ginger and fresh basil leaves, goes so well with all the other items on this brunch menu. This accompanying dish takes very little time to assemble at the last minute.

6 large tomatoes, or 8 if they are smaller, thickly sliced
ground ginger
sugar
salt and pepper
fresh basil leaves

Arrange the tomato slices in a shallow dish and sprinkle a little ginger, sugar and seasoning over each slice. Strew the surface with basil leaves. Serve as soon as possible after assembling.

Crispy Bacon with Field Mushrooms or Chanterelles

Which bacon you choose for this depends entirely on your personal preference—I love sweet Canadian bacon as well as ordinary bacon. If you are lucky enough to live where you can pick your own chanterelles, as we do here in Skye, they can be fried in butter to serve with the broiled bacon. A marvelous combination! Cultivated mushrooms can be used instead, of course. The finished dish can be kept warm, covered, for up to 30 minutes before serving.

1½ lb sliced bacon (about 18 slices)
½ lb field mushrooms or chanterelles
6 tablespoons unsalted butter
salt and pepper

Cook the bacon under a preheated medium broiler until golden brown on both sides.

Meanwhile, quarter or slice the mushrooms if they are large. Melt the butter in a frying pan, add the mushrooms and fry until wilted, stirring occasionally. Continue cooking until the liquid exuded from the mushrooms has evaporated and they are golden brown. Season.

Arrange the bacon and mushrooms in a warmed serving dish and serve hot.

Pipérade

Scrambled eggs are delicious, but pipérade is even better and dresses up plain scrambled eggs for your brunch party. The stewing of the onions and chopped peppers can be done the previous evening, then all you need to do on the morning of the brunch is to stir the beaten eggs into the reheated pepper mixture. I like to garnish this with triangles of bread fried in a mixture of olive oil and butter, with a clove of garlic in the frying pan to flavor the bread. Serve the pipérade in a shallow serving dish and place the triangles of fried bread around the sides.

3 tablespoons olive oil
4 tablespoons unsalted butter
1 onion, finely chopped
1 green pepper, cored, seeded and chopped
1 sweet red pepper, cored, seeded and chopped
1 garlic clove, very finely chopped
12 eggs
¼ cup milk or light cream
dash of Tabasco sauce
salt and pepper
finely chopped fresh parsley, for garnish (optional)

Heat the oil and butter together in a saucepan. Add the onion and cook for 3–5 minutes, then add the chopped peppers and garlic. Cook, stirring occasionally, for 7–10 minutes, until softened.

Lightly beat the eggs with the milk or cream, Tabasco and seasoning. Add to the pepper mixture and cook over a medium heat, stirring, until the eggs scramble. Pile onto a warmed serving dish and sprinkle with parsley, if you like. Serve hot.

Grapefruit and Lemon Marmalade

Grapefruit and lemon marmalade makes a refreshing change from the more usual orange marmalade. And, of course, you can make it at any time of the year.
Makes about 2 lb.

2 lemons
1 grapefruit
3½ cups (1½ lb) sugar

Thinly pare the rind from the lemons and grapefruit, being careful not to take very much of the white pith as well. Cut the rinds into shreds and put them into a bowl. Cut the white pith from the lemons and grapefruit, and put this and the seeds from the fruit into a piece of cheesecloth. Tie the cloth into a parcel. Cut up the fruit. Put the fruit and the cloth parcel into the bowl with the shredded rind. Pour on 2½ cups water, and leave to stand overnight.

Next day, put the contents of the bowl into a saucepan and bring to simmering point. Half cover and simmer gently for 1 hour.

Add the sugar and stir until it has dissolved completely. Bring back to a boil and boil fast for about 15 minutes or until setting point is reached. To test, remove the pan from the heat, drip some of the marmalade onto a saucer and leave it to get quite cold. Push the marmalade with the tip of your finger; if it wrinkles, you have a set. If it doesn't wrinkle, put the pan back on the heat and boil fast for a further 5 minutes, then repeat the setting test.

Remove the cloth bag, pressing it against the side of the pan to squeeze out all the liquid, and discard. Pack the marmalade into warmed jars, cover and process in a boiling-water bath, then complete the seals. Store in a cool place.

Dried Apricot Jam

This delicious jam can be made at any time of the year. It makes a perfect alternative to marmalade at a brunch.
Makes about 6 lb

1 lb dried apricots, finely chopped
3 lb (7½ cups) sugar
½ cup (3 oz) blanched whole almonds (optional)
juice of 1 lemon

Put the apricots into a large saucepan and add 8 cups of water. Leave to soak overnight.

The next day, put the saucepan on the heat and bring to a boil. Warm the sugar, and add it to the pan with the almonds and lemon juice. Stir until the sugar dissolves, then bring to a boil. Boil fast for about 10–12 minutes, until setting point is reached. To test, remove the pan from the heat, drop a trickle of jam onto a saucer and leave for a few minutes to cool. Push the jam on the saucer with the tip of your finger; if it wrinkles, you have a set.

If it doesn't wrinkle, put the pan back on the heat and continue boiling, testing every few minutes until you have a set.

Stir the almonds into the jam, if using. Pack into warmed jars. Cover and process in a boiling-water bath, then complete the seals.

Store in a cool place.

Oatcakes

Oatcakes make the perfect vehicle for butter and marmalade, jam or honey. They can conveniently be made several days before your brunch party and stored in an airtight tin.
Makes 12–15.

1½ cups oatmeal, preferably Scottish
1½ cups wholewheat flour
½ teaspoon salt
8 tablespoons (1 stick) unsalted butter
8 tablespoons lard

Mix together the oatmeal, flour and salt. Rub in the butter and lard until the mixture resembles crumbs. Add a little cold water and knead to a stiff dough.

Roll out on an oatmeal-dusted surface, to a thickness of about ¼ inch. Cut into 2½-inch rounds or triangles and arrange on baking sheets. Bake in a preheated 400° oven for 10–15 minutes or until set and lightly browned. Cool on a wire rack.

BARBECUE PARTY FOR 6

A barbecue lunch or dinner is a wonderful way to entertain your friends informally during the summer months. The only snag about planning a barbecue is the weather—so you'll have to keep your fingers crossed. It will be worth the worry, though, because food eaten outdoors does seem to taste better than food eaten indoors.

Get the fire lit in good time, so that it can burn down to the white hot glow which is the right moment to start cooking. If you are limited in your barbecue cooking space, start cooking early and keep the cooked food warm in the oven. That way all your guests can eat at the same time, instead of half of them eating while the remaining half wait for their food to be cooked.

In this barbecue menu there are many wonderful summer flavors—fruits and vegetables and seasonal herbs. I suggest you offer your guests a fruity wine cup before eating because it is a perfect summer drink, refreshing on a warm day or evening.

BARBECUE PARTY FOR 6

MONKFISH, BASIL AND BACON KABOBS WITH LIME AND PARSLEY MAYONNAISE

ORANGE MARINATED PORK TENDERLOIN WITH COLD ORANGE AND CHIVE SAUCE

PEPPER SALAD

RICE, WALNUT AND APRICOT SALAD

TOMATO, MELON AND MINT SALAD WITH HERB VINAIGRETTE

FRESH RASPBERRIES

STRAWBERRY AND CINNAMON MERINGUE CAKE

SUGGESTED DRINKS: SUMMER WINE CUP BEFOREHAND; A DRY WHITE WINE, SUCH AS A MUSCADET, WITH THE MEAL

Monkfish, Basil and Bacon Kabobs with Lime and Parsley Mayonnaise

Monkfish is one of the best fish, in my opinion, because it is very firm-fleshed with a good flavor, and it has no bones except its backbone. It is easy to cut the flesh off this main bone and into chunks for kabobs. Each chunk is wrapped in bacon and threaded onto a skewer for barbecuing. Fresh basil leaves on the skewers will impart a wonderful flavor. The mayonnaise to accompany the kabobs can be prepared the day before and kept, covered, in the refrigerator.

2 lb monkfish, boned, trimmed of its membrane and cut into 1 inch chunks
1¼ lb bacon (about 30 slices)
fresh basil leaves
sunflower oil, for basting
LIME AND PARSLEY MAYONNAISE
1 whole egg
1 egg yolk
1½ teaspoons dry mustard
½ teaspoon salt
1½ teaspoons sugar
pepper
½ cup sunflower or olive oil
2 tablespoons white wine vinegar
2 tablespoons chopped fresh parsley
grated rind and juice of 2 limes

To make the mayonnaise, put the egg, yolk, mustard, salt, sugar and pepper into a blender or food processor and blend until smooth. With the motor running, add the oil drop by drop to start with. As the mixture begins to thicken, add the oil in a steady trickle until it is all incorporated. Blend in the vinegar. Add the parsley and lime rind and juice. Transfer to a serving dish.

Wrap each chunk of fish in a bacon slice. Thread onto 6 skewers, with a basil leaf between every chunk. If you have plenty of fresh basil and love the taste as much as I do, use more basil.

Brush the kabobs with sunflower oil. Cook on the barbecue for 12–15 minutes, turning the kabobs over occasionally so that they cook evenly. Serve hot with the mayonnaise.

Monkfish, Basil and Bacon Kabobs; Tomato, Melon and Mint Salad; Pepper Salad; Summer Wine Cup

Orange Marinated Pork Tenderloin with Cold Orange and Chive Sauce

— ◆ ◆ —

Prepare the pork tenderloins and put them to marinate 2 days before the party. The sauce can be prepared a day in advance and kept in a cool place.

3 large pork tenderloins ($\frac{3}{4}$ lb each)
MARINADE
grated rind and juice of 2 oranges
$\frac{1}{2}$ cup olive or sunflower oil
10–12 black peppercorns, crushed
1 onion, sliced
2 tablespoons soy sauce
ORANGE AND CHIVE SAUCE
3 large oranges
$\frac{1}{2}$ cup wine vinegar
2 tablespoons sugar
$1\frac{1}{4}$ cups chicken stock (see page 181)
7 teaspoons arrowroot or cornstarch
juice of 1 lemon
2 tablespoons snipped fresh chives

Make a cut in the tenderloins lengthwise, not cutting all the way through. Open out the pork. Place them cut sides down on a working surface. Cover them with wax paper and pound them until thin and flat. Cut in half crosswise.

Mix all the ingredients for the marinade. Add the pork and marinate for 24 hours.

To make the sauce, thinly pare the rind off the oranges with a potato peeler. Cut the rind into fine shreds. Put the shredded rind into a small saucepan and cover with cold water. Bring to a boil and simmer gently for about 10 minutes, then drain. Set aside.

Put the vinegar and sugar into a saucepan and stir to dissolve the sugar. Bring to a boil and boil fast until you have a reduced, caramellike syrup. Add the stock, stirring well, and bring back to a boil. Boil for 10 minutes. Dissolve the arrowroot in the lemon juice. Add some of the hot liquid and stir well, then stir into the remaining liquid in the saucepan. Simmer for 1 minute, stirring until thickened and clear. Remove from the heat and cool.

Cut the oranges into segments, removing all the white pith and membrane. Add the segments to the cold sauce with the orange rind shreds and chives. Pour into a bowl. Cover and chill until ready to serve.

When ready to cook the pork, drain it and pat dry with paper towels. Cook on the barbecue for about 5–7 minutes each side, turning so that they cook evenly. Serve with the cold sauce.

Tomato, Melon and Mint Salad with Herb Vinaigrette

— ◆ ◆ —

This is a most colorful summery salad, full of fresh herbs, the flavors of which are absorbed by the melon and tomato. Don't mix in the dressing until shortly before serving; otherwise it tends to get diluted.

1 ripe cantaloupe or honeydew melon
1 lb tomatoes, peeled
handful of fresh mint, preferably applemint
DRESSING
$1\frac{1}{2}$ teaspoons dry mustard
$\frac{1}{2}$ teaspoon salt
1 teaspoon sugar
pepper
1 tablespoon finely chopped fresh parsley
1 tablespoon finely snipped fresh chives
$\frac{1}{4}$ cup oil, preferably a mixture of olive and sunflower
1–2 tablespoons wine vinegar

Cut the melon in half and scoop out the seeds. Peel the melon and cut it into neat 1-inch chunks.

Cut the tomatoes in half and scoop out their seeds. Cut each half into 4 wedges.

Strip the mint leaves from their stems and chop. Combine with the tomatoes and melon in a bowl.

Put the ingredients for the dressing into a screw-top jar and shake well. Just before serving, pour the dressing over the salad and toss together.

Rice, Walnut and Apricot Salad

— ◆ ◆ —

In this salad I like to use brown rice, but if you prefer white rice it will make no difference to the end result. I like the slight nuttiness of brown rice, and of course it is much better for you than white! This salad has wonderfully contrasting textures and flavors. It can be made the day before the party.

$1\frac{1}{2}$ cups brown rice
2 tablespoons unsalted butter
1 tablespoon oil
$\frac{3}{4}$ cup (3 oz) chopped walnuts
salt
$\frac{1}{2}$ cup finely chopped, ready-to-eat dried apricots
small bunches of fresh parsley, for garnish
DRESSING
2 teaspoons dry mustard
2 teaspoons sugar
2 tablespoons wine vinegar
4 tablespoons oil

Cook the rice in boiling water for 30–35 minutes, until just tender. Drain and rinse with hot water. Put into a mixing bowl and set aside.

Heat the butter and oil in a saucepan, add the walnuts and salt and fry for about 5 minutes, stirring the nuts around so that they cook evenly. Mix the walnuts and apricots into the rice.

Put all the ingredients for the dressing into a screw-top jar and shake well. Pour this into the rice mixture, and mix thoroughly.

Pile the rice salad onto a serving dish or into a bowl. Leave to cool completely before serving, garnished with small bunches of parsley.

Pepper Salad

This is one of my favorite salads, although, strictly speaking, it isn't a salad at all—more a cold, cooked vegetable. The peppers, cut into wide strips, are stewed in olive oil with garlic and then set aside to cool completely before serving. You can, of course, serve them hot as a vegetable dish in the winter. Prepare the dish completely the day before the party.

2 green peppers
2 sweet red peppers
2 yellow peppers
6 tablespoons olive oil
2 garlic cloves, finely chopped
salt and pepper

Cut each pepper in half and remove the core and seeds. Cut each half into 3 strips.

Heat the olive oil in a wide shallow pan, add the peppers and cook over a moderate heat for about 15 minutes, turning the peppers over occasionally so that they cook evenly. Add the garlic and seasoning and continue cooking for a further 15 minutes, until really tender. They will take a surprisingly long time to cook. Turn them into a serving dish and cool.

Fresh Raspberries

Fresh raspberries are such a treat when they come into season. You find them served in so many ways, but to me the most attractive way of serving fresh raspberries is simply to pile them on a large platter lined with raspberry leaves and dust with sugar. This dish makes a most beautiful centerpiece for a buffet barbecue table. If you wish, have a large bowl of whipped cream to serve with the raspberries.

Strawberry and Cinnamon Meringue Cake

The flavor I love with strawberries—and indeed with many other fruits such as raspberries—is cinnamon. This spice enhances the flavor of strawberries so well, and cinnamon in this meringue cake makes a simple dessert almost exotic! The meringue base can be baked on the morning of the party.

4 egg whites
$1\frac{1}{3}$ cups sugar
1 teaspoon vinegar
1 teaspoon vanilla extract
1 teaspoon cornstarch
4 teaspoons ground cinnamon
$1\frac{1}{4}$ cups heavy cream, whipped
$1\frac{1}{2}$ lb strawberries, hulled and halved

Line a baking sheet with baking parchment paper. Draw a 9-inch circle on the paper and set aside.

Put the egg whites into a large bowl and beat until stiff. Gradually add the sugar, beating constantly.

Add the vinegar and vanilla extract, and sift in the cornstarch and cinnamon. Fold them in quickly and thoroughly, using a large metal spoon.

Spoon the meringue into the circle on the paper-lined baking sheet and smooth it evenly. Bake in a preheated 350° oven for 5 minutes, then reduce the heat to 250° and bake for a further hour. Carefully transfer the meringue base, still on the paper, onto a wire rack and leave to cool.

When ready to serve, peel off the paper and place the meringue on a serving plate. Cover with the whipped cream, and then press the strawberries into the cream.

Summer Wine Cup

Offer your guests a refreshing glass of fruity wine cup to begin the party.

Pour 2 bottles of dry white wine into a jug, then pour in 3 cups of 7-Up. Add 1 cored and sliced eating apple, some melon pieces, orange slices and a few strawberries. Add some ice and chill in the refrigerator for 1 hour. Serve very cold, garnished with mint sprigs.

For a predinner drink (if you intend to serve wine to your guests with their food), one large jug of wine cup will be plenty.

SUNDAY LUNCH FOR 6

An invitation to lunch on Sunday is always welcome. The following menu is ideal for lunch, as so much of it can be prepared in advance, leaving the Sunday morning relatively trouble-free. This menu makes excellent use of summer-fresh ingredients, such as elderflowers, if available, fresh peas, mint and dill, and strawberries.

The first course is a light dish of cucumber matchsticks sautéed in butter with fresh dill and lemon juice. Wholewheat bread, or rolls, is a good accompaniment. (See page 68 for a recipe.) Fish features as the main dish—a very simple preparation of baked sea trout or salmon fillets. New potatoes, baked in foil with garlic, and fresh new peas flavored with mint are served with the fish. For dessert, a heavenly combination of brown sugar meringues, sandwiched together with a lemon and elderflower curd, and fresh strawberries.

SUNDAY LUNCH FOR 6

CUCUMBER JULIENNE WITH DILL

MIXED GRAIN BREAD OR ROLLS

BAKED FILLET OF SEA TROUT

NEW POTATOES BAKED WITH OLIVE OIL AND
GARLIC

FRESH PEAS WITH APPLEMINT

BROWN SUGAR MERINGUES WITH LEMON AND
ELDERFLOWER CURD AND
FRESH STRAWBERRIES

SUGGESTED WINE: A FINE CHABLIS

Cucumber Julienne with Dill

This is the lightest of first courses, and also can be a delicious accompaniment to a main course of fish or meat. The flavor of dill is subtle yet fairly intense, and it beautifully complements its classic partner, cucumber. The cucumber can be prepared for cooking the night before.

2 cucumbers, peeled
2 tablespoons oil
2 tablespoons unsalted butter
2 tablespoons chopped fresh dill fronds
salt and pepper
juice of $\frac{1}{2}$ lemon

Cut the cucumbers into 2-inch pieces, and cut each piece into matchsticks. Place in a colander. Sprinkle with salt and leave to drain for 30 minutes. Rinse the cucumber under cold water and pat dry.

Heat the oil and butter in a frying pan and add the cucumber, half of the dill and seasoning. Cook, stirring, for 2 minutes. Squeeze over the lemon juice.

Serve, hot or warm, with the remaining dill laid over the surface of the cucumber.

Baked Fillet of Sea Trout

This method of cooking sea trout or salmon was shown to me by John Tovey, who is a master of inventiveness. It is quite the best way to cook these fish, and is so quick and simple. As an alternative to filleting and skinning the fish yourself, you can ask your fishmonger to do the job for you! If you do it yourself, do it the night before so the cooking of the fish can be accomplished very quickly the next afternoon, just before serving.

3–4 lb sea trout (weakfish) or salmon
12 tablespoons (1$\frac{1}{2}$ sticks) unsalted butter,
cut into 6 equal pieces
fresh mint sprigs, for garnish

Cut the head and tail off the fish. Slit open the belly from the head end to about three quarters of the way toward the tail. Under cold running water, clean the fish thoroughly.

Lay the fish on a board. Using a very sharp filleting knife, cut the fish open. Turn it skin-side down, and fillet it off the bones. Skin the fillets and cut into 6 pieces.

Put the pieces of fish on a baking sheet and top each with a piece of butter. Bake in a preheated 425° oven for 5 minutes. Garnish and serve immediately.

**Baked Fillet of Sea Trout; New Potatoes Baked with
Olive Oil and Garlic**

New Potatoes Baked with Olive Oil and Garlic

———◆●◆———

This is a most delicious way to cook tiny new potatoes. You can add mint to the contents of the foil package too, if you like. Prepare the foil package, ready for cooking, first thing on Sunday morning.

3 tablespoons olive oil
1½ lb tiny new potatoes, scrubbed and patted dry
3 garlic cloves, finely chopped
salt and pepper

Put a large piece of foil in a roasting pan. Pour the olive oil into the foil and add the potatoes, garlic and seasoning. Wrap the foil into a package around the potatoes.

Bake in a preheated 400° oven for 35–40 minutes. Serve hot.

Fresh Peas with Applemint

———◆●◆———

There are very few vegetables which give as much pleasure as a dish of tiny fresh peas. The flavor of mint enhances them perfectly. To save time on Sunday morning, shell the peas the night before.

3 cups shelled fresh peas
1 teaspoon sugar
salt
handful of fresh mint, preferably applemint
unsalted butter, for serving

Put the peas into a saucepan, together with the sugar, salt and mint. Add boiling water to a depth of about ½ inch and cover the saucepan. Allow the water to come back just to a boil, then drain immediately. If you like vegetables cooked a bit more, let them simmer for a couple of minutes before draining.

Serve dotted with butter which will melt into the peas.

Brown Sugar Meringues with Lemon and Elderflower Curd and Fresh Strawberries

———◆●◆———

This is one of my favorite desserts. The flavors go together so well, and the contrast of the crispy meringues with the tender strawberries is wonderful.

The lemon curd benefits greatly from having the delicate flavor of elderflower added to it. The meringues can be made several days in advance, and stored in an airtight tin. The curd can be kept, in sealed pots, in the refrigerator for up to a week.

1¼ cups heavy cream
2 lb strawberries, hulled
sugar
MERINGUES
3 egg whites
½ cup brown sugar
½ cup granulated sugar
ELDERFLOWER AND LEMON CURD
2 large eggs
1 egg yolk
6 tablespoons unsalted butter
½ cup granulated sugar
grated rind and juice of 2 lemons
handful of elderflower heads (optional)

To make the meringues, line a baking sheet with baking parchment paper. Set aside.

Beat the egg whites until stiff. Mix the sugars together and add gradually to the egg whites, beating all the time. Spoon the meringue into a pastry bag fitted with a wide nozzle. Pipe in 12 blobs on the paper-lined baking sheet.

Bake in a preheated 250° oven for 2½–3 hours or until the meringues are firm to the touch. Carefully transfer to a wire rack and cool.

To make the curd, beat the eggs and yolk together and strain them into a heatproof bowl. Add the butter, sugar and lemon rind and juice. Pluck the tiny creamy flowers from the elderflower heads and add to the bowl. Put the bowl over a saucepan of simmering water and stir until the sugar dissolves and the butter melts. Cook, stirring from time to time (no need to stir continuously) as the curd thickens. The curd is thick enough when you can draw a line with your finger down the curd coating the back of the spoon. Allow to cool, then chill.

When ready to serve, whip the cream until stiff, then fold in the lemon and elderflower curd. Sandwich pairs of meringues together with generous amounts of the cream and curd mixture. Pile the meringues into a pyramid on a serving platter.

Pile the strawberries onto a platter. Dust with sugar. Have a bowl of more whipped cream and lemon and elderflower curd to serve with the strawberries.

COUNTRY LUNCH FOR 12

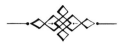

A country weekend lunch should consist of tasty, filling food, because those partaking of the lunch will have had plenty of exercise. They will also be cold and in need of warming from within.

Good thick soups and stews make ideal country lunches. The word stew often conjures up awful memories of school food, which is unfortunate because there is nothing nicer than a well-made stew. The one in the menu here is full of vegetables as well as a mixture of meat and game—in this case beef and squab—with plump parsley dumplings. This is old-fashioned food, and mashed or baked potatoes and pickled red cabbage are excellent accompaniments. Afterward, good cheese—a farm-house Cheddar and a Stilton, for example—with wholewheat rolls and apples, and a rich fruit cake will complete the satisfying and hearty meal. When your guests have had some sloe gin, cherry brandy or black currant brandy with their coffee at the end of lunch, they may not feel able to face an afternoon outdoors and may prefer to snooze for an hour by the fireside.

COUNTRY WEEKEND LUNCH FOR 12

BEEF STEW WITH PARSLEY DUMPLINGS

MASHED OR BAKED POTATOES
PICKLED RED CABBAGE

CHEESE BOARD
WHOLEWHEAT ROLLS
APPLES

RICH FRUIT AND GINGER CAKE

SUGGESTED WINE: A ROBUST RED, SUCH AS A POMEROL

Beef Stew with Parsley Dumplings

You can make the stew up to the addition of the dumplings 2 days in advance. Keep it, covered, in the refrigerator. Alternatively, make it 1–2 weeks ahead of time and freeze it. To reheat, bring it to a simmer on top of the stove, stirring occasionally, then add the dumplings. If you do not have a casserole large enough, make the stew in 2 or 3 casseroles and equally divide the dumplings between them.

4 tablespoons good bacon drippings or oil
6 lb chuck steak, cut into 1-inch chunks
2 teaspoons sugar
3 whole squab breasts, quartered
3 onions, thinly sliced
6 carrots, cut into $\frac{1}{4}$ inch thick slices
$\frac{1}{2}$ turnip, cut into 1 inch chunks
6 parsnips, cut into $\frac{1}{2}$ inch thick slices
$2\frac{1}{2}$ tablespoons wholewheat flour
$2\frac{1}{2}$ cups beef stock
$2\frac{1}{2}$ cups light beer
1 garlic clove, finely chopped
salt and pepper
PARSLEY DUMPLINGS
$1\frac{1}{2}$ cups self-rising flour
1 cup shredded suet
$\frac{1}{2}$ teaspoon salt
2 tablespoons finely chopped fresh parsley

Heat the drippings or oil in a large stew pan or casserole and brown the meat, a few pieces at a time, turning the pieces of meat over so that they brown evenly and well. Add the sugar. As the pieces of meat are browned, remove them from the pan and keep warm. Brown the pieces of squab breast and remove. Add the onions to the pan and cook, stirring occasionally, for 5 minutes, until soft but not browned. Add the carrots, turnip and parsnips and cook for a further 5 minutes, stirring to prevent sticking.

Sprinkle over the flour and cook for a couple of minutes, then gradually add the stock and beer, stirring all the time until boiling. Return the browned meat and squab breasts to the pan and add the garlic and seasoning. Cover tightly and cook in a preheated 350° oven for $1\frac{1}{2}$ hours.

Mix the ingredients for the dumplings together, then stir in enough cold water to bind the mixture. Divide into 24 equal portions and shape into balls.

Add the parsley dumplings to the stew, cover and cook for a further 30–35 minutes.

Beef Stew with Parsley Dumplings; Pickled Red Cabbage; Wholewheat Rolls

Pickled Red Cabbage

Pickled red cabbage makes a good accompaniment to a rich stew. Serve it from an earthenware bowl.

6–8 cups finely shredded red cabbage
salt
4 cups malt vinegar
$2\frac{1}{2}$ tablespoons pickling spice

Put the shredded cabbage into a bowl and sprinkle salt over it. Leave overnight.

Put the vinegar and pickling spice into a saucepan and bring to simmering point. Simmer for 30 minutes, then allow to cool completely.

The next day, rinse the cabbage and drain well, then pack it into jars. Pour the cooled spiced vinegar over the cabbage. Seal, label and store the jars in a cool, dry place.

Wholewheat Rolls

The rolls can be made the day before, but store closely covered to keep them beautifully fresh.
Makes about 24.

3 lb (10½ cups) wholewheat flour
1¼ teaspoons sugar
4 tablespoons active dry yeast
1½ teaspoons salt
1 tablespoon honey

Put the flour into a bowl in a warm place. Stir the sugar and yeast into 1½ cups tepid water. Leave in a warm place until frothy. Combine 3 cups tepid water with the salt and honey.

Make a well in the center of the flour and add the yeast and honey mixtures. Mix together, then turn out onto a floured work surface and knead well for 7–10 minutes.

Divide the dough in half, then each half in half again, and so on until you have 24 pieces of dough. This way you end up with equal-sized rolls!

Roll each piece of dough into a ball shape, and flatten it slightly with the palm of your hand. Put each roll on a baking sheet. Leave to rise, covered with a dishtowel, until the rolls have doubled in size.

Bake in a preheated 425° oven for 10–12 minutes, until the rolls are golden brown and sound hollow when you tap the bottoms. Cool on a wire rack in a warm place. (If you cool them in too cool a place they become tough and chewy.)

Rich Fruit and Ginger Cake

This can be made 2 or 3 weeks in advance and kept in an airtight tin. It improves with keeping.
Makes 23 cm (9 inch) cake.

½ lb (2 sticks) unsalted butter
1⅓ cups firmly packed brown sugar
4 large eggs, beaten
1¼ cups all-purpose flour
1¼ cups wholewheat flour
grated rind and juice of 1 orange
grated rind and juice of 1 lemon
2 teaspoons ground ginger
½ teaspoon freshly grated nutmeg
1¼ teaspoons apple pie spice
1¼ cups (6 oz) golden raisins
1¼ cups (6 oz) raisins
2¼ cups (12 oz) currants
¾ cup chopped mixed candied peel
6 pieces of preserved ginger, drained of syrup and chopped
¾ cup halved glacé cherries
¾ cup slivered almonds, toasted

Grease a deep 9-inch cake pan and line the bottom and sides with baking parchment paper.

Beat the butter until creamy, then gradually add the sugar, beating until the mixture is fluffy. Beat in some of the beaten eggs, then some of the flours. Continue adding the eggs and flours until all is incorporated. Beat in the orange and lemon rinds and juices and the spices. Mix in all the fruits, preserved ginger and the toasted almonds.

Put the cake batter into the prepared pan. Bake in a preheated 350° oven for 25–30 minutes, then reduce the heat to 300° and bake for a further 2 hours.

Leave the cake to cool in its pan, before storing it in an airtight tin or container.

Sloe Gin

I don't like gin, and yet sloe gin is one of my favorite things. It makes a wonderful drink in the winter; you prepare it during the previous autumn. A bottle of sloe gin makes a wonderful Christmas present. You can buy sloe gin, but it is not nearly as good as homemade and it tends to be too sweet.

1 lb sloes
5 cups gin
⅔ cup sugar
2 drops almond extract

Prick the sloes all over with a fork and put them into a glass jar or plastic container. Pour the gin over the sloes and stir in the sugar and almond extract. Cover tightly and store, stirring occasionally, for 4 months before drinking.

Rich Fruit and Ginger Cake; Sloe Gin

AFTER-THEATER SUPPER FOR 4-6

Entertaining friends at supper after the theater needs careful thought, because when you get home it will be quite late and you will all be hungry. The last thing you will want to do is to cook, and the last thing your friends will want to do is to sit, drinks in hands, waiting ravenously for food to appear!

The following menu is both simple and delicious, while being very convenient to prepare, needing only the minimum of cooking when you return from the theater. The two sauces for serving with the pasta main course contrast well with each other. One is a tomato sauce with pesto, which is a Genovese sauce made from basil and pine nuts. Pesto is readily available from good delicatessens— if you don't make your own! The other sauce is creamy and full of mushrooms, both cultivated and wild. With or after the pasta, there is a salad of mixed greens and fresh herbs, with garlic croûtons. A simple fruit compôte, served with crisp, buttery almond and cinnamon cookies completes the repast. Have ready a coffee tray, with regular and decaffeinated coffee, which many people prefer after a late supper.

AFTER-THEATER SUPPER FOR 4—6

GREEN FETTUCCINE
WITH
TOMATO AND PESTO SAUCE
AND
MUSHROOM, LEMON AND PARSLEY SAUCE

MIXED SALAD

NECTARINE AND RASPBERRY SALAD

ALMOND AND CINNAMON COOKIES

SUGGESTED WINE: A LIGHT RED, SUCH AS A
VALPOLICELLA

Green Fettuccine with Two Sauces

The pasta I like best is green fettuccine, thin flat ribbons. Buy it freshly made if possible, because it is nicest. But if you don't live near a pasta-making shop, buy the dried sort from a good delicatessen. For the mushroom, lemon and parsley sauce, if you cannot get chanterelles, cèpes or other edible fungi, treble the amount of cultivated mushrooms. Prepare both sauces, ready for reheating, in the afternoon.

1–1½ lb fresh green fettuccine
1 tablespoon olive oil
freshly grated Parmesan cheese, to serve
TOMATO AND PESTO SAUCE
4 tablespoons olive oil
2 onions, chopped
1 celery stalk, chopped
2 lb ripe tomatoes, quartered,
or two 16-oz cans tomatoes
1 large garlic clove, chopped
½ teaspoon sugar
salt and pepper
2 tablespoons bottled or homemade pesto
MUSHROOM, LEMON AND PARSLEY SAUCE
1 tablespoon oil
6 tablespoons unsalted butter
2 cups sliced mushrooms
½ lb fresh chanterelles, halved or sliced
½ lb fresh cèpes, stalks removed and sliced
2½ cups heavy cream
grated rind of 1 lemon
salt and pepper
1–2 tablespoons finely chopped fresh parsley

To make the tomato and pesto sauce, heat the oil in a saucepan, add the onions and cook over a moderate heat for 4–5 minutes, stirring occasionally, until soft and translucent. Add the celery and tomatoes and simmer for 20 minutes. Add the garlic, sugar and seasoning. Purée the sauce in a blender or food processor, then press through a sieve back into the saucepan. Stir in the pesto. Reheat to serve.

For the mushroom, lemon and parsley sauce, heat the oil and butter in a frying pan. Add the mushrooms, chanterelles and cèpes and cook for about 5 minutes, stirring occasionally to make sure the mushrooms cook as evenly as possible. Pour on the cream, and stir in the lemon rind and seasoning. Simmer for 2–3 minutes, then set aside ready to reheat. Just before serving, stir in the parsley.

Cook the pasta in a large saucepan of boiling water for about 3 minutes or until just tender. To test, fish out a strand of pasta with a fork and bite it or pinch between two fingernails. Drain well and toss with the oil. Serve immediately, with the hot sauces and Parmesan.

Almond and Cinnamon Cookies; Nectarine and Raspberry Salad

Mixed Salad

Make the croûtons and dressing in the afternoon. Prepare the salad greens and have them in their bowl, covered in the refrigerator ready to be dressed just before serving.

2 heads radicchio
1 small head chicory
several leaves of rocket (arugula)
fresh spinach leaves
few nasturtium leaves, if available
chopped fresh herbs, e.g., applemint, chives, parsley, chervil
DRESSING
1 teaspoon dry mustard
$\frac{1}{2}$ teaspoon sugar
salt and pepper
1 tablespoon white wine vinegar
2 tablespoons olive oil
GARLIC CROÛTONS
2 slices wholewheat or white bread
1 tablespoon unsalted butter
2 tablespoons olive or sunflower oil
2 garlic cloves, skinned

To make the garlic croûtons, remove the crusts from the bread and cut the slices into tiny cubes. Heat the butter and oil in a frying pan. Add the bread cubes and garlic and fry until the croûtons are golden brown all over. Drain on paper towels. Discard the garlic.

Tear all the salad leaves into pieces approximately the same size, and mix together in a bowl with the herbs.

Combine the dressing ingredients in a screw-top jar and shake well.

Just before serving, shake the dressing again and pour over the salad. Toss well and sprinkle with the croûtons.

Nectarine and Raspberry Salad

Prepare the salad and keep it, tightly covered with plastic wrap, in a cool place. Boysenberries or loganberries may replace the raspberries.

6 nectarines, peeled, pitted and sliced
1 lb raspberries
2 tablespoons sugar

Mix the slices of nectarine, the raspberries and sugar together in a glass or china serving bowl.

Almond and Cinnamon Cookies

Bake the cookies several days ahead, if more convenient, and store them in an airtight tin. Before leaving for the theater, arrange the cookies on a plate and cover with plastic wrap.
Makes 12–16 cookies.

8 tablespoons (1 stick) unsalted butter
$\frac{2}{3}$ cup sugar
$\frac{3}{4}$ cup (4 oz) ground almonds
$1\frac{1}{4}$ teaspoons ground cinnamon

Beat together the butter and sugar until the mixture is fluffy. Beat in the ground almonds and cinnamon. Put in teaspoonfuls on a baking sheet. Bake in a preheated 275° oven for 45 minutes–1 hour. Cool on a wire rack.

SUMMER SUPPER FOR 6

There really is nothing nicer than having a few friends around for supper, informally, served in the kitchen. There is an automatically relaxed atmosphere at an informal supper party, and you can be quite adventurous with the food. In this menu, the first course is an avocado-filled pie, with an unusual base of wholewheat breadcrumbs, almonds and garlic. This has a lovely crunchy texture, which contrasts well with the smooth avocado filling. The surface of the pie is covered with chopped tomatoes, parsley and chives, so it looks attractive, and tastes divine! Fat, juicy shrimp make a perfect main course for this informal supper party. They are served in a piquant dressing, with homemade wholewheat bread to mop up the delicious juices. To accompany the shrimp there are 3 salads—a combination of green beans and broad beans; crunchy snow peas; and fennel in a lemon dressing. Dessert is a fresh raspberry iced cream served with a simple raspberry sauce.

SUMMER SUPPER FOR 6

AVOCADO PIE WITH GARLIC CRUST

JUMBO SHRIMP IN PIQUANT DRESSING

WHOLEWHEAT BREAD

SNOW PEAS

FENNEL SALAD WITH LEMON DRESSING

GREEN BEAN SALAD

CRUSHED RASPBERRY ICED CREAM
WITH
RASPBERRY SAUCE

SUGGESTED WINE: A DRY WHITE BURGUNDY OR
SOAVE

Avocado Pie with Garlic Crust

The crust for this unusual pie can be baked the day before the party, if more convenient. However, the filling may discolor if left too long before serving, so finish the pie on the day you serve it.

$\frac{1}{4}$ cup white wine
4 teaspoons unflavored gelatin
2 large avocados
juice of 1 lemon
dash of Tabasco
dash of Worcestershire sauce
salt and pepper
1 tablespoon olive or sunflower oil
1 teaspoon wine vinegar
$\frac{1}{2}$ teaspoon sugar
6 tomatoes, skinned, seeded and chopped
finely chopped fresh parsley and chives, for garnish
GARLIC CRUST
3 cups fresh wholewheat breadcrumbs
$\frac{1}{2}-\frac{3}{4}$ cup (2–3 oz) slivered almonds
pinch of dried thyme, or fresh thyme sprig
6 tablespoons unsalted butter, melted
2 garlic cloves, finely chopped
salt and pepper

To make the crust, mix together the breadcrumbs, almonds, thyme, butter, garlic and seasoning. Press over the bottom and sides of a 9-inch flan or quiche dish. Bake in a preheated 400° oven for 12–15 minutes, until golden brown and crisp-looking. Allow to cool.

Put the wine into a small saucepan and sprinkle the gelatin over. Heat gently, stirring, until the gelatin has dissolved completely.

Halve and pit the avocados. Scrape all the flesh out of the avocado skins and put in a blender or food processor. Be sure to scrape all the dark green flesh from the inside of the skins. Add the wine and gelatin mixture, the lemon juice, Tabasco and Worcestershire sauces and seasoning. Blend until smooth. Pour this avocado mixture into the cooled pie crust, and leave in a cool place until the filling is set.

Mix together the oil, vinegar, sugar and seasoning. Stir in the chopped tomatoes. Spread in the center of the avocado filling. Sprinkle the tomatoes with parsley and chives. Serve cut into slices on the same day as the pie is made.

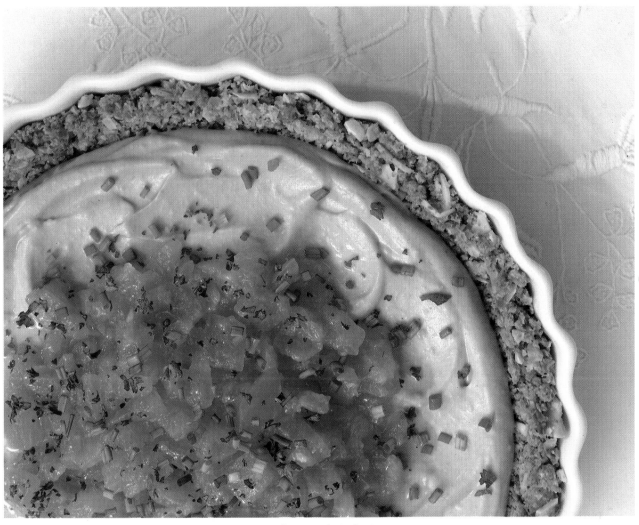

Avocado Pie with Garlic Crust

Jumbo Shrimp in Piquant Dressing

◆━◆━◆

Shrimp need very little cooking—they can so easily become overcooked and mushy—and they are very filling, so you don't need much more than 5 per person as a main course. The whole dish can be prepared in the morning and kept covered in a cool place for serving that evening.

about 6 lb jumbo shrimp, in their shells
DRESSING
½ onion, very finely chopped
6 tablespoons olive oil
3 tablespoons white wine
dash of Tabasco sauce
juice of ½ lemon
salt and pepper
1 tablespoon finely chopped fresh parsley

Half fill a very large saucepan with water and bring to a boil. Put half the shrimp into the boiling water and cook for 3–4 minutes.

Using a slotted spoon, scoop the shrimp out of the water. Let the water boil again, then put the remaining shrimp in and cook for 3–4 minutes. Drain these. Allow the shrimp to cool slightly, then when cool enough to handle, peel them.

Put the ingredients for the dressing, except the parsley, into a saucepan and bring to simmering point. Simmer for about 5 minutes.

Pour the dressing over the peeled shrimp. Mix well together, then mix in the parsley. Put in a serving dish and keep cool until you are ready to serve.

Mixed Grain Bread

This bread has a coarse nutty texture and the combination of flours makes it wonderfully moist. The bread freezes very well.
Makes three loaves.

4 tablespoons active dry yeast
½ tablespoon sugar
5 cups wholewheat or graham flour
1 cup wheat germ
1½ cups rolled oats
1 tablespoon honey
½ tablespoon salt

Stir the yeast and sugar into 1½ cups tepid water. Leave in a warm place for 15–20 minutes, until the yeast mixture is frothy.

Put the flour, wheat germ and rolled oats into a large mixing bowl and put the bowl in a warm place (the warmer all the ingredients are when they come together the quicker they will rise).

Stir the honey and salt into 3 cups hot water until the honey has melted and the salt dissolved.

Make a well in the center of the flour mixture and add the yeast and honey mixtures. Mix to form a dough, then knead on a floured surface for 7–10 minutes. Knead really well. (We usually have the radio on in the kitchen, and I measure the kneading time by listening to 3 records! It seems to help the kneading, which is quite hard work.)

Divide the dough into 3 equal portions and place in 3 oiled 8 × 4½ × 3-inch loaf pans. Cover and leave in a warm place to rise until the dough has at least doubled in size.

Bake in a preheated 400° oven for 20–25 minutes. To test if the bread is cooked, turn a loaf out of its pan and tap it on the bottom—it should sound hollow.

Cool on a wire rack in a warm place—if you cool the loaves in a cold place they tend to become tough.

Snow Peas

Snow peas, or sugar snap peas as they are sometimes known, are as good eaten cold, as a salad, as hot. They need no dressing. Their attraction lies both in their fresh flavor, and in their satisfying crunchy texture.

1 lb snow peas

Trim the very ends of each pea pod. Put them into a saucepan and pour on boiling water to a depth of about 1 inch. Cover tightly and bring the water back to a boil. Simmer for 2 minutes, then drain. Tip the peas into a serving bowl and cool.

Fennel Salad with Lemon Dressing

This is a deliciously crunchy salad. The lemony dressing complements perfectly the aniseed flavor of the fennel. I like to decorate this salad with fronds from the top of the fennel. Prepare the salad several hours in advance.

2 large fennel bulbs
DRESSING
1 teaspoon sugar
½ teaspoon salt
pepper
finely grated rind and juice of 1 lemon
3 tablespoons sunflower or olive oil

Put all the dressing ingredients in a screw-top jar and shake well. Pour the dressing into a mixing bowl.

Trim any brown outside bits and feathery fronds off the fennel. Cut each bulb into sticks, about ¼ inch thick and 2 inches long. Toss the sticks of fennel in the dressing, then arrange on a serving plate. Decorate the salad with feathery fronds of the fennel for an attractive garnish.

Green Bean Salad

In this bean salad, thin green beans are combined with tiny new broad beans in their pods, which are quite delicious when the broad beans are young. You can substitute lima beans if broad beans are not available. The dressing contains chopped scallions, which gives the salad a bit of a kick. The salad can be prepared several hours in advance.

1 lb green beans, end trimmed and cut into 2-inch lengths
½ lb new broad beans in their pods, ends trimmed and cut into 2-inch lengths
DRESSING
3 scallions, thinly sliced
2 tablespoons olive or sunflower oil
1 tablespoon wine vinegar
1 teaspoon sugar
½ teaspoon salt
½ teaspoon dry mustard
pepper

Put all the beans into a saucepan. Pour on boiling water to a depth of about 1 inch. Cover the pan with a lid and bring the water back to boiling point. Simmer for 2 minutes, then drain.

Mix all the dressing ingredients together. Taste and adjust the seasoning, if necessary. Add the dressing to the beans and toss together.

Put the dressed beans into a large serving bowl. Cover and set aside to cool until ready to serve.

Crushed Raspberry Iced Cream with Raspberry Sauce

—— ◆—◆ ——

This iced cream is very quick and simple to make. The raspberries are cooked for a short time first, which changes their flavor—it brings to mind the heavenly smell of raspberries cooking for jam. I like to serve a simple raspberry sauce with this iced cream. The jewel bright color of the sauce looks lovely against the creamy pink of the iced cream, and the flavor of both sauce and iced cream together is sublime. Both iced cream and sauce can be made a day or more before the party.

$1\frac{1}{2}$ lb raspberries
$1\frac{1}{4}$ cups heavy cream
4 large eggs, separated
$2\frac{1}{4}$ cups confectioners' sugar, sifted
SAUCE
1 lb raspberries
$1\frac{1}{2}$ cups confectioners' sugar

Put the raspberries into a saucepan over a moderate heat and cook for about 5 minutes, until the juices begin to run. Remove from the heat and set aside to cool at room temperature.

Whip the cream until thick but not stiff. Set aside.

Beat the egg yolks with 2 tablespoons of the confectioners' sugar, until the mixture is pale and thick.

Beat the egg whites until stiff, then gradually add the remaining confectioners' sugar, beating all the time.

With a slotted spoon, scoop the cooled raspberries from the saucepan and add them to the whipped cream. Then fold the raspberry cream into the yolk mixture. Finally, fold in the meringue mixture. Carefully pour into a freezerproof container, cover and freeze until the ice cream is solid.

To make the sauce, purée the raspberries and sugar in a blender or food processor. Sieve the sauce to remove the seeds, then chill.

About 45 minutes before serving, transfer the iced cream to the refrigerator to allow it to soften.

Crushed Raspberry Iced Cream with Raspberry Sauce

WINTER AFTERNOON TEA FOR 6-8

Tea is essentially a British meal, but it is being copied all around the world, and I am happy to say that afternoon tea is coming into its own once more. I'm sure this is because of the sorts of things one eats at tea-time. Summer time teas with thinly cut cucumber sandwiches are divine. There is nothing nicer, however, than tea set out by a blazing fire in the winter time, with the curtains drawn against the chill darkness outside and your family and friends gathered to enjoy all the delicious baked goods.

Most children particularly like cinnamon toast fingers which are simply made with finger shapes of bread, crusts removed, spread liberally with butter and sprinkled with a mixture of sugar and cinnamon before broiling until golden.

WINTER AFTERNOON TEA FOR 6–8

CHEESE SCONES
AND
SCOTTISH PANCAKES
WITH
RASPBERRY OR STRAWBERRY JAM

CINNAMON TOAST FINGERS

WALNUT AND APRICOT TEABREAD WITH LEMON ICING

VANILLA SPONGE WITH VANILLA BUTTERCREAM AND RASPBERRY JAM

VERY STICKY CHOCOLATE CAKE WITH FUDGE ICING

GOLDEN RAISIN COOKIES

CRISP GINGER COOKIES

CREAM-FILLED VANILLA MERINGUES

Cheese Scones

I like cheese scones served hot, with raspberry or strawberry jam.
Makes about 10.

2⅓ cups self-rising flour
½ teaspoon salt
1¼ teaspoons baking powder
1¼ teaspoons dry mustard
1 cup grated sharp Cheddar cheese
1 large egg
1½ cups milk

Sift the flour, salt, baking powder and mustard into a bowl. Stir in the cheese. Lightly beat the egg and milk together and add. Mix well, knead for 1 minute. Pat out the scone mixture on a floured work surface to a thickness of about 1 inch. Stamp out 2-inch rounds, or cut out triangles, and put them on a baking sheet. Bake in a preheated 425° oven for 12–15 minutes, until the scones are risen and golden. Serve warm with butter.

Scottish Pancakes

In England these are called drop scones. Whatever you call them, they are an essential part of a tea-table, and are loved by all who eat them. The batter can be prepared in the morning. To measure the corn syrup, dip the spoon in very hot water first.
Makes about 12.

1¾ cups all-purpose flour
1 teaspoon cream of tartar
½ teaspoon baking soda
pinch of salt
1 egg
1 tablespoon light corn syrup
1¼–1½ cups milk

Sift the flour, cream of tartar, baking soda and salt into a mixing bowl. Beat in the egg, corn syrup and milk. Cover with a dishtowel and leave for 1 hour.

Grease the surface of a griddle or frying pan and heat it. Spoon on the batter in fairly large spoonfuls. When bubbles appear evenly over the surface of each pancake, turn them over. Cook until golden brown. Keep warm on a wire rack while you cook the rest. Serve warm.

Cinnamon Toast Fingers; Scottish Pancakes

Vanilla Sponge with Vanilla Buttercream and Raspberry Jam

This is one of the favorite cakes which appears on our tea-table. It (along with the chocolate cake) is always requested before going-back-to-school, or as a birthday cake. The lightest sponge cake is filled with a fluffy vanilla-flavored buttercream and raspberry jam, and the top of the cake is dusted with confectioners' sugar. For our tea party it makes a perfect contrast to the dark, moist chocolate cake. An alternative is to flavor the cake with the grated rind of 1 lemon, and fill it with homemade lemon curd and whipped cream. The cake will freeze very well if cooled quickly and frozen immediately. You can fill it 2 or 3 hours before serving. Makes 20 cm (8 inch) cake.

3 large eggs
$\frac{1}{2}$ cup sugar
few drops of vanilla extract
$\frac{2}{3}$ cup self-rising flour, sifted twice
1 cup raspberry jam
sifted confectioners' sugar, to dredge
BUTTERCREAM
8 tablespoons (1 stick) unsalted butter
$1\frac{1}{2}$ cups confectioners' sugar, sifted
few drops of vanilla extract

Butter two 8-inch layer-cake pans and line the bottom of each pan with baking parchment paper.

Break the eggs into a large mixing bowl, and beat them together. Gradually add the sugar and vanilla extract, beating until the mixture is very thick, almost white in color and mousse-like in texture. This will take about 7 minutes. To test if the mixture is thick enough, stop beating and lift the beater out, trailing a squiggle of the mixture over the surface. If it sits on top, the mixture is thick enough; if it vanishes into the mixture, continue beating! Sift the flour over the mixture. Using a metal spoon, fold the flour quickly and thoroughly into the egg mixture.

Divide between the prepared cake pans, and bake in a preheated 350° oven for about 20 minutes, until the cakes are golden brown on top and just beginning to shrink from the sides of the pan. Turn out onto wire racks to cool.

To make the buttercream, beat the butter until creamy and gradually add the confectioners' sugar, beating until the buttercream is pale and fluffy. Beat in the vanilla extract.

Put one cake layer on a serving plate and spread it with the buttercream. Cover the buttercream with the raspberry jam, then put the second cake layer on top. Dredge confectioners' sugar over the surface of the cake. This cake is easier to cut with a serrated knife.

Very Sticky Chocolate Cake with Fudge Icing

This cake fulfills all that I require in a chocolate cake. I am something of a connoisseur on such chocolatey things as cakes and sauces and this is the best! It will keep for 2 or 3 days in an airtight container.

12 tablespoons ($1\frac{1}{2}$ sticks) unsalted butter
$1\frac{1}{2}$ cups dark brown sugar
$1\frac{1}{2}$ cups sweetened cocoa powder
6 tablespoons self-rising flour
4 large eggs
few drops of vanilla extract
walnut halves or crystallized rose petals, to decorate
BUTTERCREAM
8 tablespoons (1 stick) unsalted butter
$1\frac{1}{2}$ cups confectioners' sugar, sifted
1 tablespoon cocoa powder, sifted
CHOCOLATE FUDGE ICING
4 tablespoons unsalted butter
$\frac{1}{3}$ cup granulated sugar
$2\frac{1}{4}$ cups confectioners' sugar
$2\frac{1}{2}$ tablespoons cocoa powder

Butter a round 9-inch × 4-inch deep cake pan and line the bottom with baking parchment paper.

To make the cake, put the butter in a mixing bowl and beat well, gradually adding the sugar. Beat until the mixture is light and fluffy. Sift the sweetened cocoa and flour together. Beat 1 egg into the butter mixture, then beat in some of the cocoa and flour mixture. Beat in another egg, and so on until the eggs and flour mixture are all incorporated. Beat in the vanilla extract.

Spoon and scrape the mixture into the prepared cake pan. Bake in a preheated 350° oven for 45 minutes.

Test the cake, before you take it out of the oven, by sticking in a skewer and if it comes out smeared with gooey cake don't worry: this cake is meant to be like that. If you continue to cook it until a skewer comes out clean, the cake will be drier and not nearly so good! Cool for 1 minute in the pan, then turn out onto a wire rack to cool completely.

To make the buttercream, beat the butter, gradually adding the confectioners' sugar and cocoa. Beat all together well until light and fluffy.

When the cake is cold, cut into 2 layers using a serrated knife. Spread the buttercream over the bottom layer and cover with the top layer.

To make the icing, put the butter, granulated sugar and 6 tablespoons water in a saucepan over a moderate heat. Heat until the butter has melted and the sugar dissolved, then bring to a boil and boil fast for 4–5 minutes. Sift the confectioners' sugar and cocoa into a mixing bowl. Gradually beat in the buttery sugar syrup, to make a smooth thick icing. Spread the icing over the top and sides of the cake. Decorate.

Walnut and Apricot Teabread with Lemon Icing

This teabread is nicest eaten the day it is made, but it freezes very well so you could make two and keep one in the freezer.
Makes 1 kg (2 lb) loaf.

$1\frac{3}{4}$ cups all-purpose flour
$2\frac{1}{2}$ teaspoons baking powder
$1\frac{1}{4}$ teaspoons ground cinnamon
4 tablespoons dark brown sugar
1 cup (4 oz) chopped walnuts
3 oz dried apricots, soaked in water for 1 hour, drained and cut in half
3 tablespoons light corn syrup
$\frac{3}{4}$ cup milk
1 egg, beaten
$\frac{1}{4}$ cup (1 oz) chopped walnuts (optional)
LEMON ICING
5 tablespoons confectioners' sugar, sifted
1 tablespoon hot lemon juice

Butter a $8\frac{1}{2} \times 4\frac{1}{4} \times 2\frac{3}{4}$-inch loaf pan and line the bottom with baking parchment paper.

Sift the flour, baking powder and cinnamon into a mixing bowl. Add the sugar, walnuts and apricots. Put the corn syrup into a saucepan and pour in the milk. Heat together until the syrup has melted into the milk. Beat the syrupy milk into the flour mixture, then the egg.

Scrape the mixture into the prepared loaf pan and bake in a preheated 325° oven for about $1\frac{1}{4}$ hours, until a knife inserted into the center of the loaf comes out clean. Cool in the pan for several minutes, then turn out onto a wire rack to cool completely.

To make the icing, mix together the confectioners' sugar and lemon juice, beating until the icing is smooth. Cover the top of the teabread with icing, letting it trickle down the sides. Decorate with chopped walnuts.

Golden Raisin Cookies

These cookies don't sound particularly exciting, but they are among the most delicious cookies I've come across. They are crisp and buttery, and keep very well for 2 or 3 days when stored in an airtight tin.
Makes 12–16.

8 tablespoons (1 stick) unsalted butter
$\frac{2}{3}$ cup sugar
1 tablespoon light corn syrup
$1\frac{1}{3}$ cups self-rising flour
$\frac{1}{2}$ teaspoon baking soda
$\frac{1}{4}$ cup (2 oz) golden raisins

Beat the butter with the sugar and corn syrup until fluffy, then beat in the flour and baking soda. Mix in the raisins. Roll the dough into walnut-sized balls and arrange on greased baking sheets.

Bake in a preheated 375° oven for 15 minutes. Let set for a few minutes, then lift off the baking sheets with a long metal spatula and cool on a wire rack.

Crisp Ginger Cookies

These don't take a second to make, and are very good. They keep very well in an airtight tin.
Makes 12–16.

8 tablespoons (1 stick) unsalted butter
$\frac{2}{3}$ cup sugar
$\frac{3}{4}$ cup self-rising flour
$2\frac{1}{4}$ teaspoons ground ginger

Beat the butter until creamy and gradually beat in the sugar. When the mixture is light and fluffy, sift in the flour and ginger and beat well. Roll the mixture into walnut-sized balls and put them on a baking sheet.

Bake in a preheated 300° oven for 1 hour, until golden brown. Leave to cool for a couple of minutes on the baking sheet, then gently lift the cookies off onto a wire rack to cool completely.

Cream Filled Vanilla Meringues

A dish of meringues, piled into a pyramid, looks very pretty on a tea-table. For a tea party make the meringues smaller than you would for a dinner party dessert. They are very convenient for a tea party, because they can be made a few days in advance and stored in an airtight tin. Fill them with vanilla-flavored sweetened whipped cream shortly before serving. You will need about 1 cup of cream.
Makes about 18 pairs.

3 egg whites
1 scant cup sugar

Line a baking sheet with baking parchment paper.

Beat the egg whites until they are stiff, then very gradually add the sugar, beating continuously, until very stiff and glossy. Fill a pastry bag with the mixture, and using a wide star tube, pipe meringues about $1\frac{1}{2}$ inches in diameter onto the prepared baking sheet. Bake in a preheated 225° oven for $2\frac{1}{2}$–3 hours. Cool on a wire rack.

FORMAL ENTERTAINING

Formal entertaining is often entertaining on a large scale, and in this chapter there are menus for three such occasions—a Cocktail Party for 40, a Garden Party for 25, and a Coffee Morning for 15. There are, of course, many other reasons for formal entertaining. Special events call for a formal party—events such as a birthday, or an anniversary celebrated with friends. But there doesn't have to be any reason at all. You may just feel like making a special effort, setting the table with your finest cloth, polishing the silver and making sure that your glasses are gleaming. I always love the chance to do lots of flowers.

If you have invited people to your house for the first time, people that you don't know very well or perhaps business colleagues, you may feel more inclined to have them to a formal dinner rather than to a more intimate informal supper in the kitchen.

We have lots of friends who are considerably older than ourselves, and whenever any of them come to lunch or dinner I tend to make it a fairly formal occasion, really out of respect for their age.

In this chapter there are menus suggested to help and inspire you for any and all of these occasions.

Cocktail Party for 40 (see page 102)

SPRING LUNCH FOR 6

This delicious menu is the essence of spring. It consists of courses which are all light—a contrast to the game and root vegetables of the winter months. The first course is a creamy, delicate green timbale of snow peas, served with a garnish of crunchy snow pea strips. To follow the timbales there is salmon tartare—tiny cubes of fresh salmon marinated in a lime dressing, a wonderful flavor combination. The main course is roast lamb, with a herb-scented sauce, served with a platter of lightly steamed tiny new vegetables. The assortment of baby vegetables is a decoration in itself. For dessert, there is young, new rhubarb, poached in a fruity dry white wine, and served with a foamy orange sabayon sauce.

Warm Snow Pea Timbales

All the snow peas can be prepared for cooking, and the snow pea and egg yolk purée completed several hours in advance—in the morning for dinner that night. The snow pea timbales can be kept warm for up to half an hour before being turned out.

1 lb snow peas, trimmed and cut into strips lengthwise
2 eggs, separated
salt and white pepper
1 cup heavy cream, whipped

Reserve about one-quarter of the snow peas. Cook the remainder in boiling salted water for about 6 minutes or until tender. Drain well, then purée in a blender or food processor with the egg yolks. Pour into a bowl. Add seasoning and fold in the cream. Beat the egg whites until stiff but not dry, then fold into the snow pea cream.

Divide the mixture between 6 buttered dariole molds. Place the dishes in a roasting pan and surround with boiling water to reach $\frac{3}{4}$ the way up the molds. Bake in a preheated 350° oven for about 15 minutes, until risen and lightly set.

Meanwhile, cook the reserved snow peas in boiling salted water for 2–3 minutes, until tender but still crisp. Drain well and keep hot.

Leave the snow pea timbales to stand for about 2–3 minutes before turning out onto warmed plates. Arrange with the reserved snow peas around and serve.

SPRING LUNCH FOR 6

WARM SNOW PEA TIMBALES

SALMON TARTARE

LAMB WITH THYME AND ROSEMARY
PLATTER OF STEAMED BABY VEGETABLES

WINE-POACHED RHUBARB
WITH ORANGE SABAYON SAUCE

SUGGESTED WINES: A VERY DRY WHITE WINE—FOR EXAMPLE A MUSCADET—WITH THE FIRST AND SECOND COURSES; A MATURE, FRUITY CLARET OR CALIFORNIA CABERNET SAUVIGNON WITH THE LAMB

Warm Snow Pea Timbales

Lamb with Thyme and Rosemary

Ideally, the lamb should be carved just before serving, and this should be possible with just 6 diners. However, if you are single-handed cook cum host/hostess, it may be more convenient for you to carve the meat just before you and your guests sit down to eat the first course. In this case, reform the loins and wrap them in foil to keep warm.

6 tablespoons unsalted butter, diced
2 or 3 boned loins of lamb, depending on size, to give a total weight of about 4 lb
salt and pepper
small fresh rosemary sprig
fresh thyme sprig
3 cups chicken stock (see page 181)
2 cups full-bodied dry white wine
2 shallots, finely chopped
small fresh thyme and rosemary sprigs, for garnish

Heat 2 tablespoons of the butter in a large frying pan. Add the lamb and sear evenly. Transfer to a roasting pan. Season and spoon over the cooking juices from the frying pan. Roast in a preheated 425° oven for 10–15 minutes.

Meanwhile, simmer the rosemary and thyme sprigs in the stock.

Transfer the lamb to a warmed platter, cover and keep warm. Add the wine to the roasting pan and stir to mix with the sediment. Add the shallots and boil until the liquid is reduced to about 5 tablespoons. Stir in the stock, with the herbs, and continue boiling to reduce to about 1½ cups.

Strain the sauce into a saucepan and reheat gently. Over a low heat swirl in the remaining butter. Season and keep warm but do not allow to boil.

Cut the lamb into 24 neat slices. Divide the sauce between 6 warmed plates. Place the lamb on top and garnish each plate with small sprigs of fresh thyme and rosemary.

Alternatively, the lamb can be left whole and carved at the table, with the sauce served separately.

Salmon Tartare

1¼ lb salmon fillet, skinned and well chilled
very fine strips of cucumber, skinned, blanched red pepper strips and fresh coriander leaves, for garnish
DRESSING
1 tablespoon olive oil
4 tablespoons lime juice
1 tablespoon finely chopped shallot
fresh lemon thyme sprig
½ small fresh tarragon sprig
1 tablespoon crushed black peppercorns
sea salt

Shake the dressing ingredients together in a screw-top jar, then leave for 12 hours.

Make sure all the bones have been removed from the salmon—use tweezers to take out any stray ones. With a very sharp flexible-blade knife, cut the fish into slices about ⅛ inch thick. Stack the slices and cut cleanly into approximately ⅛ inch strips, then cut across the strips to make ⅛-inch cubes. Carefully transfer the cubes to a chilled bowl.

Shake the dressing, then strain off 3 tablespoons and mix gently but thoroughly with the salmon. Cover and chill for at least 45 minutes.

Carefully lift the salmon from the liquid with a slotted spoon and form into round mounds in the center of small, cold plates. Garnish with strips of cucumber and red pepper and coriander leaves.

Trim the carrots down to small neat shapes, leaving the tops intact. Cut and trim the zucchini until they resemble torpedoes, leaving the skin on. Trim the turnips, leaving the tops on.

Place the carrots in the top part of a steamer and place over boiling water. Cover and cook for 1 minute. Add the turnips and broad beans and cook for 30 seconds. Add the green beans and cook for 1½ minutes. Add the zucchini and cook for a final 2 minutes.

Squeeze the broad beans gently between the thumb and first finger so that the tender centers pop out.

Arrange the vegetables on a large plate or 6 small ones. Serve accompanied by melted butter.

Wine-poached Rhubarb with Orange Sabayon Sauce

Cook the rhubarb the day before your party, then cover and refrigerate.

1½ lb young rhubarb, cut into 1½-inch lengths
about ½ cup sugar
½ cup fruity dry white wine, e.g., Alsace Riesling
3 tablespoons honey or rosehip syrup
SAUCE
5 egg yolks
½ cup sugar
6 tablespoons orange liqueur, such as Cointreau

Layer the rhubarb and sugar in a large ovenproof casserole. Pour the wine over. Cover and cook in a preheated 325° oven for 20–30 minutes, until the rhubarb is tender but still retains its shape.

Carefully lift out the rhubarb with a slotted spoon and place in a serving dish. Pour the juices into a saucepan, stir in the honey and boil until reduced and syrupy. Pour over the rhubarb. Leave to cool, then cover and chill.

Beat the egg yolks, sugar and liqueur together in a bowl placed over a saucepan of hot water, until the sauce is thick and creamy. Remove from the heat, place the bowl in cold water and beat constantly until the sauce cools to lukewarm.

Serve the sauce warm with the cold rhubarb. Alternatively, beat the sauce until cold and serve cold, within 45 minutes to 1 hour of making. If the sauce separates, it can be beaten again but will not be quite as light.

Wine-poached Rhubarb with Orange Sabayon Sauce

Platter of Steamed Baby Vegetables

You can use any tiny, new vegetables you like for this attractive platter to accompany the lamb. Serve the melted butter in a small jug in the middle of the platter, and flavor the butter with finely chopped parsley and chives, if you like.

12 small young carrots with tops, scrubbed
12 small zucchini, about 1 inch in diameter
12 baby turnips with tops, scrubbed
12 oz shelled young broad beans
12 oz green beans, cut into 2-inch lengths
melted unsalted butter, for serving

SUMMER LUNCH FOR 8

This is a perfect menu for a summer lunch. If you have an enclosed porch or patio it would make the ideal setting in which to serve the exotic, subtly flavored food on this most elegant menu. The first course is perfectly cooked asparagus, served with a hollandaise sauce unusually flavored with coriander. The main course is a selection of fish and shellfish, which have been steamed over white wine and herbs. The seafood is served with a rich butter and wine sauce, made using the lobster shells. Suitable accompaniments for the seafood are new potatoes and a salad of greens, such as mâche, purslane, Boston or bibb lettuce and dandelion leaves. The dessert is a delicately flavored iced rose petal soufflé.

SUMMER LUNCH FOR 8

ASPARAGUS WITH CORIANDER HOLLANDAISE SAUCE

PLATTER OF FISH AND SHELLFISH

NEW POTATOES

TOSSED GREEN SALAD

ICED ROSE PETAL SOUFFLÉS

SUGGESTED WINES: A STRONG DRY ROSÉ, SUCH AS TAVEL, WITH THE FIRST COURSE; A DRY WHITE, SUCH AS A GOOD FRENCH CHABLIS OR CHARDONNAY FROM CALIFORNIA OR AUSTRALIA, WITH THE SEAFOOD

Asparagus with Coriander Hollandaise Sauce

This luxurious first course is lifted by the unusual addition of coriander to the hollandaise. The asparagus can be prepared for cooking and the coriander seeds toasted some time ahead.

$1\frac{3}{4}$ lb asparagus, stems scraped
salt
1 tablespoon lemon juice
SAUCE
3 tablespoons coriander seeds, crushed and lightly toasted
$\frac{1}{2}$ lb (2 sticks) unsalted butter, diced
3 tablespoons lemon juice
$1\frac{1}{2}$ tablespoons white wine vinegar
4 egg yolks
pinch of sugar
GARNISH
long fine strips of orange and lemon rind, blanched and knotted
fresh chervil or parsley sprigs

Gently warm the coriander seeds in the butter until the butter just begins to bubble. Remove from the heat, cover and leave to infuse for 20 minutes.

Tie the asparagus into 4 equal bundles. Stand them in a large saucepan of boiling salted water, to which the lemon juice has been added, packing foil around them if necessary so that they stand upright. The tips should be out of the water. Cover with a lid or dome of foil and cook gently for 7–10 minutes, until tender, depending on the size of the spears.

Meanwhile, bring the lemon juice and vinegar for the sauce to boiling point. Gently reheat the coriander butter until just beginning to foam. Briefly blend the egg yolks, sugar and a pinch of salt in a blender, then, with the motor running, slowly pour in the lemon juice and vinegar mixture. When it has all been absorbed, slowly pour in the coriander butter, with the motor still running.

Drain the asparagus well and arrange on warmed plates. Place a small pool of sauce on each plate. Garnish with fine strips of orange and lemon rind and sprigs of chervil.

Alternatively, the asparagus can be piled onto one large, warmed plate and the sauce served in a warmed bowl for the guests to help themselves. Garnish as above.

Platter of Fish and Shellfish

You can use whatever fish you like, or what is available to you where you live, but try to provide a variety of different types. Firm-fleshed white fish is better than softer fish such as sole or flounder. You can prepare the steaming broth and the base liquid for the sauce the day before your party, to save time on the actual day.

8 pieces skinned turbot fillet, about 2 oz each
8 pieces skinned sea bass fillet, about 2 oz each
claw and tail meat from 4 freshly cooked lobsters, about 1¼ lb each
8 pieces skinned monkfish fillet, about 3 oz each
8 scallops
fresh chervil or parsley and lemon balm or mint sprigs and peeled lime segments, for garnish
STEAMING BROTH
1 shallot, finely chopped
¾ cup medium-bodied dry white wine
½ cup fish stock (see page 181)
2 sprigs fresh lemon balm or mint
3 large sprigs fresh chervil or parsley
1 bay leaf, broken
salt and pepper
SAUCE
3 tablespoons olive oil
2 lobster shells, crushed and pounded
3 shallots, finely chopped
2 young carrots, finely chopped
4 tablespoons whiskey
5 fresh parsley stems
10 green peppercorns
2 bay leaves, broken
2 cups fish stock (see page 181)
1 cup medium-bodied dry white wine
½ lb (2 sticks) unsalted butter, diced
salt and white pepper

For the sauce, heat the oil in a saucepan, add the lobster shells and cook, stirring occasionally, for 5 minutes. Stir in the shallots and carrot, and cook gently, stirring occasionally, until the shallots are softened. Stir in the whiskey and set alight. When the flames have died down, stir in the parsley stems, peppercorns, bay leaves, stock and wine. Cover and simmer for 20–25 minutes.

Strain the liquid, pressing down well on the vegetables to extract as much liquid from them as possible. Measure the liquid—there should be about 1½ cups. If insufficiently reduced, boil down further. Set aside.

Put the ingredients for the steaming broth into the bottom of a steamer or a large saucepan and bring to a boil. Place the turbot in the steaming basket, place over the broth and cover. Steam for 30 seconds. Add the sea bass and steam for 1 minute, then add the lobster and monkfish and steam for 2 minutes longer. Add the scallops and steam for a final 30 seconds. Remove from the heat but keep covered.

Over a very low heat, gradually beat the butter into the sauce liquid, making sure each piece is fully incorporated before adding the next. Season and keep warm over a very low heat. Do not allow to boil.

Arrange the fish and shellfish on a large warmed platter and garnish with sprigs of chervil and lemon balm and lime segments. Serve with the sauce in a warmed sauce-bowl.

Iced Rose Petal Soufflés

An attractive recipe for rose gardeners, which illustrates how roses taste as good as they smell. You can either make individual soufflés or one large one. Do not make more than 2 or 3 days before your party.

2 oz well-scented rose petals, dried
⅔ cup sugar
7 oz cream cheese
scant ½ cup crème fraîche
4 egg whites
few drops of rose water (optional)
small rose petals, to decorate

Tie a collar of double thickness wax paper around 8 individual soufflé or ramekin dishes.

Mix the rose petals with the sugar in a blender or food processor until the petals are reduced to very small pieces. Blend the cream cheese and crème fraîche together. Beat the egg whites until stiff but not dry. Taste and add a few drops of rose water to increase the flavor, if necessary. Gently fold the egg whites into the cream cheese mixture with the sugared rose petals.

Divide the mixture between the dishes. Freeze until firm, then cover the tops.

About 25 minutes before serving, carefully remove the collars from the soufflés. Leave the soufflés in the refrigerator until required.

Serve decorated with small rose petals.

Platter of Fish and Shellfish

SUMMER DINNER FOR 4

Each course of this menu for special friends is exquisite in its detail and flavor, or combination of flavors. The first course is scallops, poached in wine with shallots, and served with a vermouth sauce. The scallops are presented with a nest of fine homemade pasta flavored with that most exotic of all spices, saffron. The main course is tenderloin of veal, with a luxurious champagne sauce, and simply steamed zucchini to accompany it. To follow, fresh soft summer cheeses are offered with oat crackers. For dessert there are fresh strawberry mousses, set in heart-shaped molds.

SUMMER DINNER FOR 4

SCALLOPS WITH VERMOUTH SAUCE

SAFFRON PASTA

TENDERLOIN OF VEAL WITH CHAMPAGNE SAUCE
AND ZUCCHINI

PLATTER OF FRESH SOFT SUMMER CHEESES

OAT CRACKERS

STRAWBERRY MOUSSES

SUGGESTED WINES: A MEDIUM SWEET WHITE WINE,
SUCH AS CROZES HERMITAGE BLANC, WITH THE
SCALLOPS; A CALIFORNIA CHARDONNAY WITH THE
VEAL; DEMI-SEC CHAMPAGNE WITH THE DESSERT

Scallops with Vermouth Sauce

Make the pasta in the morning, ready to cook in the evening.

12 large or 16 small scallops
8 tablespoons (1 stick) unsalted butter
3 tablespoons finely chopped shallots
$\frac{2}{3}$ cup medium-bodied dry white wine
salt and white pepper
$1\frac{1}{4}$ cups fish stock (see page 181)
$\frac{1}{2}$ cup dry vermouth
hot, freshly cooked saffron pasta (see below)

Cut the scallops in half horizontally if they are large.

Heat 2 tablespoons butter in a frying pan, add the shallots, cover and cook over a low heat, shaking the pan occasionally, until the shallots are softened. Pour in the wine, season and bring to simmering point. Add the scallops and poach gently for 1 minute. Turn the scallops over and poach for a further 30 seconds. Using a slotted spoon, transfer the scallops to a warmed plate and keep hot.

Bring the liquid back to a boil and reduce to a syrupy glaze. Stir in the stock and boil to reduce to $\frac{2}{3}$ cup. Stir in the vermouth and simmer for 2–3 minutes.

Strain the sauce into a clean saucepan and reheat gently. Gradually swirl in the remaining butter, cut into small pieces, over a low heat. Season.

Divide the saffron pasta between warmed plates and arrange the scallops next to it. Spoon the vermouth sauce over and serve.

Saffron Pasta

1 cup + 3 tablespoons all-purpose flour
salt
$\frac{1}{2}$ teaspoon saffron threads,
dissolved in 1 teaspoon warm water
2 eggs
1 tablespoon oil

Sift the flour and salt into a large bowl and make a well in the center. Lightly beat the saffron liquid with the eggs and pour into the well. Gradually draw the flour into the liquids using a fork. Mix to a smooth paste, adding a little more warm water if necessary.

Turn the paste onto a well-floured surface and knead well for about 5 minutes until smooth, almost elastic and no longer sticky. Wrap in a damp cloth and leave to "relax" for 30 minutes.

Roll out the dough on a well-floured surface, using a well-floured rolling pin, to about 15 inches square, turning it frequently to ensure that it does not stick. Leave to dry out for about 10–20 minutes, until it begins to look leathery.

Fold the pasta in half, then in half again in the same direction. Cut across the pasta with a sharp knife to make ¼-inch wide strips. Carefully unfold the strips, then leave to dry for a further 10–20 minutes.

Cook in a large saucepan of boiling salted water, to which the oil has been added, for 1–2 minutes until just tender. Drain and rinse under hot running water. Drain again well and serve hot.

Tenderloin of Veal with Champagne Sauce and Zucchini

Prepare the caramelized strips of lemon rind the day before the party, but take care not to brown them as they cook. The zucchini can be made ready for cooking in the morning.

thinly pared rind of 3 lemons, cut into fine strips
1 tablespoon sugar
12 tablespoons (1½ sticks) unsalted butter
1½ lb tenderloin or boneless loin roast of veal
salt and white pepper
2 cups champagne
1¼ cups veal stock
4–6 zucchini, cut lengthwise into thin slices
fresh chervil or parsley sprigs, for garnish

Put the strips of lemon rind into a saucepan of boiling water and boil for 1 minute. Drain and refresh under cold running water.

Dissolve the sugar in 6 tablespoons water. Add the lemon rind strips and boil until the liquid has evaporated and the lemon rind is caramelized. Remove from the heat immediately as the lemon must not brown. Set aside.

Heat 4 tablespoons of the butter in a heavy flameproof casserole in which the veal will just fit. Add the veal and sear evenly all over. Season, then transfer to a preheated 425° oven. Roast for 15 minutes: the veal will remain pink in the center.

Transfer the veal to a warmed plate, cover and keep warm. Tip any excess fat from the casserole, then stir in the wine, dislodging any sediment. Bring to a boil and reduce to 6 tablespoons. Stir in the stock and boil to reduce to ¾ cup.

Meanwhile, steam the zucchini for about 2 minutes, until tender but still crisp.

Strain the sauce into a clean saucepan and reheat gently. Over a low heat, gradually beat in the remaining butter, cut into small pieces, making sure each piece is fully incorporated before adding the next. Season and keep warm over a low heat. Do not allow the sauce to boil.

Carve the veal into neat slices. Spoon the sauce over 4 warmed plates. Place the veal on top and arrange the zucchini slices neatly around. Garnish with the caramelized lemon rind strips and sprigs of chervil.

Strawberry Mousses

The mousses, in their heart-shaped molds, can be made the day before the party and kept, covered, in the refrigerator.

1 lb strawberries, hulled
1 tablespoon unflavored gelatin
⅔ cup sugar
2 teaspoons lemon juice
1 cup heavy cream
2 egg whites
DECORATION
sliced strawberries
Cognac
fresh mint leaves, cut into strips

Purée the strawberries, then pass through a sieve to remove the seeds. Dissolve the gelatin in a little of the purée in a small bowl placed over a saucepan of hot water. Remove from the heat and allow to cool slightly, then blend with the remaining purée. Add half the sugar and lemon juice to taste.

Whip the cream and fold into the purée. Beat the egg whites until stiff but not dry, then gradually beat in half the remaining sugar. Add the rest of the sugar and beat until stiff. Fold into the purée.

Divide equally between 4 lightly oiled heart-shaped molds and leave to set in a cold place. Cover loosely when set.

For the decoration, sprinkle the sliced strawberries with a little Cognac and mint and chill.

Unmold the mousses onto cold plates and decorate with the strawberries sprinkled with Cognac and mint.

Strawberry Mousses; Oat Crackers with Cheese

Oat Crackers

———————◆———————

Make 2 or 3 days in advance of the party.
Makes 8–10.

1 cup + 3 tablespoons oatmeal
$\frac{1}{3}$ cup + 1 tablespoon all-purpose flour
1 teaspoon baking powder
pinch of salt
4 tablespoons unsalted butter, melted
oatmeal for sprinkling

Mix the oatmeal, flour, baking powder and salt together in a bowl and make a well in the center. Pour the butter into the well, then mix all the ingredients together with a fork, adding sufficient cold water to give a stiff dough.

Roll out the dough on a surface sprinkled with oatmeal, using a rolling pin that has been sprinkled with oatmeal. Cut out circles of dough with a floured 3-inch cutter and carefully transfer to a greased baking sheet. Bake in a preheated 350° oven for about 30 minutes, until lightly colored. Leave to set for a few minutes on the baking sheet, then transfer to a wire rack to cool.

WINTER LUNCH FOR 6

In the Winter a formal party is often better planned for lunchtime rather than for dinner, chiefly because of the weather. If you live in rural areas the last thing you want is for your guests to sit anxiously through the meal wondering if the forecast snow has in fact fallen while they have been enjoying your cooking. If you invite your guests to lunch, there may well be snow, but a drive home in daylight is not so hazardous.

This lunch menu is full of delicious surprises, yet much of it can be prepared in advance, so you won't have to spend the morning slaving in the kitchen before your guests arrive! The first course is broiled jumbo shrimp given a touch of piquancy with cayenne and lemon juice. They are served with a buttery tomato sauce. The main course of beef tenderloin has a creamy horseradish sauce, and is garnished with foil-baked shallots. The vegetable accompaniments are purposely simple, to complement the beef and its sauce. The dessert is a rich yet light concoction of sweet cookies sandwiching a filling of almond custard.

Jumbo Shrimp with Concassé Tomatoes

The tomatoes can be skinned, seeded and diced the day before the party. Keep them in the refrigerator, in a covered container.

1 shallot, finely chopped
$\frac{1}{2}$ cup medium dry white wine
18 raw jumbo or Gulf shrimp, in their shell
$1\frac{1}{2}$ tablespoons lemon juice
sea or kosher salt
cayenne
3 tablespoons unsalted butter, melted
2 large tomatoes, skinned, seeded and diced
6 tablespoons cold unsalted butter, diced
finely chopped fresh chives, for garnish

Simmer the shallot in the wine in a small saucepan until most of the liquid has evaporated.

Meanwhile, toss the shrimp in the lemon juice, seasoned with sea salt and cayenne pepper. Brush with the melted butter and broil for 2–3 minutes, turning frequently.

Gently warm the tomatoes in a small saucepan until their juices are reduced.

Gradually beat the diced butter into the wine mixture, making sure each piece is completely incorporated before adding the next. Season with salt and a pinch of cayenne.

Divide the butter sauce among 6 warmed plates. Remove the tomatoes from the saucepan with a slotted spoon, allowing any excess moisture to drain, and place in the sauce. Place 3 shrimp to the side of each plate. Sprinkle a few chives over the sauce and serve.

WINTER LUNCH FOR 6

JUMBO SHRIMP WITH CONCASSÉ TOMATOES

BEEF TENDERLOIN WITH HORSERADISH AND SHALLOTS

CREAMED POTATOES

GLAZED CARROTS

STEAMED BROCCOLI

CLEMENTINE COOKIES WITH APRICOT SAUCE

SUGGESTED WINES: DRY WHITE FRENCH BORDEAUX OR CALIFORNIA SAUVIGNON WITH THE FIRST COURSE; A FINE FRENCH BURGUNDY OR CALIFORNIA PINOT NOIR WITH THE BEEF

Beef Tenderloin with Horseradish and Shallots

The day before the lunch party, trim the shallots, ready to bake in foil the next day. You can also prepare the sauce up to the addition of the cream.

4 tablespoons unsalted butter
3-lb beef tenderloin roast
salt and pepper
12 equal-sized shallots, unpeeled but tops trimmed
1 carrot, chopped
1 small onion, chopped
1 small celery stalk, chopped
$\frac{1}{4}$ cup peeled and shredded fresh horseradish root,
or prepared horseradish, drained
3 tablespoons Cognac
2 cups beef stock
$\frac{3}{4}$ cup heavy cream
fresh parsley sprigs, for garnish

Melt half of the butter in a roasting pan on top of the stove, add the beef and sear evenly all over. Season, then transfer to a preheated 425° oven. Roast for 45–50 minutes (the beef will be rare).

Meanwhile, place the shallots in a piece of foil, season well and fold the foil over to make a tight parcel. Bake in the oven with the beef for 20–30 minutes, until tender.

When the beef is ready, remove it to a warmed plate, cover and keep warm.

Heat the remaining butter in a saucepan, add the carrot, onion, celery and horseradish and cook, stirring frequently, until browned. Drain off the surplus fat, then stir in the Cognac and set alight. When the flames have died down, stir in the beef stock and boil until reduced by about two-thirds. Strain the sauce and measure it— there should be about $\frac{1}{2}$ cup. Pour into a clean saucepan and boil to reduce further if necessary, then stir in the cream and bubble until thickened to a light sauce consistency. Check the seasoning and keep warm over a low heat.

Cut the beef into 6 individual pieces or into slices. Cut the shallots in half. Spoon the sauce over the base of a warmed serving platter and place the beef on top. Garnish with sprigs of parsley.

Beef Tenderloin with Horseradish and Shallots

Clementine Cookies with Apricot Sauce

◆━◆

The cookies and filling can be made a day or two ahead; store the cookies in an airtight tin. The apricot sauce can also be made a day or two in advance of the party, and kept in a covered container in the refrigerator. Makes 6 pairs.

$\frac{2}{3}$ cup all-purpose flour
pinch of salt
2 egg whites, very lightly beaten
1 cup confectioners' sugar, sifted
$4\frac{1}{2}$ tablespoons unsalted butter, melted
FILLING
5 tablespoons milk
$\frac{1}{2}$ teaspoon cornstarch
1 egg yolk
$2\frac{1}{2}$–3 tablespoons sugar
drop of vanilla extract
2 teaspoons Cognac
2 tablespoons ground almonds
$\frac{2}{3}$ cup heavy cream, whipped
6–9 clementines or tangerines, peeled and any pits removed
APRICOT SAUCE
$\frac{1}{3}$ cup sugar
$1\frac{1}{2}$ cups dried apricots, soaked overnight
squeeze of lemon juice

Mix the flour, salt, egg whites and confectioners' sugar together, then stir in the melted butter. Spoon the mixture in 12 equal rounds, spaced a little way apart, on two baking sheets lined with greased wax paper.

Bake in a preheated 350° oven for about 10 minutes, until a light golden color. Cool on a wire rack.

Heat the milk to boiling point. Blend the cornstarch with the egg yolk, then stir in the hot milk. Pour into a clean saucepan and cook over a low heat, stirring constantly until the sauce thickens. Remove from the heat and stir in the sugar, vanilla extract, Cognac and ground almonds. Cover the surface of the filling closely with plastic wrap and leave to cool. When cold, fold in the whipped cream.

For the sauce, dissolve the sugar in about 4 tablespoons of water. Add the drained apricots and lemon juice, cover and simmer until soft. Purée in a blender or food processor, or pass through a sieve. Boil down further if the purée is too liquid, then leave to cool. Chill.

To assemble the dessert, place 6 of the cookies on 6 cold plates. Cover with the filling, then top this with clementine or tangerine segments. Place the remaining cookies on top and dredge with confectioners' sugar.

A decorative pattern can be created in the confectioners' sugar by placing a red hot skewer briefly on it a number of times. Dust any surplus sugar from the plates. Spoon the apricot sauce around the cookies.

WINTER DINNER FOR 8

Ithink that one of the nicest forms of entertaining is a small dinner party. With the table beautifully set with gleaming silver and glistening crystal, and plenty of candlelight, the stage is set for a perfect evening. Here is a menu to fit the occasion. The first course of oyster and watercress tarts is luxurious and yet simple to make. It is followed by a tarragon chicken consommé—an elegant soup, full of flavor. The main course is loin of venison, garnished with apples poached in Calvados and cranberries. The venison has a sauce made from reduced game stock. To accompany the venison there is a purée of celeriac, a vegetable which beautifully complements game dishes of all sorts. To complete the repast there is an amaretti bavarois, a creamy confection with a contrasting crunch of brandy-soaked amaretti cookies, served with a tangy orange sauce.

WINTER DINNER FOR 8

OYSTER AND WATERCRESS TARTS

TARRAGON CONSOMMÉ

LOIN OF VENISON
WITH CRANBERRIES AND GLAZED APPLES

CELERIAC PURÉE

AMARETTI BAVAROIS WITH ORANGE SAUCE

SUGGESTED WINES: A DRY WHITE, SUCH AS A
CHABLIS, WITH THE FIRST COURSE; A RICH
HERMITAGE OR CHATEAUNEUF DU PAPE WITH THE
VENISON; WITH THE DESSERT MUSCAT DE BEAUMES
DE VENISE

Oyster and Watercress Tarts

The watercress purée can be made the day before the dinner party, and kept in a cool place. The oysters can be removed from their shells, and the shells lined with filo pastry in the morning to save time in the evening. Keep the pastry tightly covered to prevent it drying out.

12 oz young watercress, thick stalks removed
salt
lemon juice
¾ cup heavy cream or crème fraîche
18 oysters, unshucked
about 4 tablespoons unsalted butter, melted
3 sheets of filo pastry

Cook the watercress in a little boiling salted water, to which a squeeze of lemon juice has been added, for 2–3 minutes. Drain well. Purée the watercress with the cream or crème fraîche, then transfer to a small heavy-based saucepan.

Open the oyster shells and carefully remove the oysters. Brush the deep shells with melted butter. Arrange on 1 or 2 baking sheets.

Stack the sheets of filo pastry, brushing between them with melted butter. Cut the stack into 18 squares, each 2½–3 inches on all sides.

Line each oyster shell with a stacked square of pastry and brush the top with melted butter. Bake in a preheated 400° oven for 5–8 minutes.

Meanwhile, gently warm the watercress purée. Add a squeeze of lemon juice to the remaining melted butter.

Divide the watercress purée among the filo shells. Place the raw oysters on top and brush them lightly with the lemon butter. Serve 3 per person.

Tarragon Consommé

The consommé can be clarified the day before the party—in fact, it is better made in advance, because this allows all the fat to rise to the surface, where it can be lifted off easily. Flavor the consommé with the tarragon only 1–2 hours before serving.

7½ cups chicken stock (see page 181)
1½ cups ground chicken meat
2 leeks, fairly thinly sliced
2 celery stalks, fairly thinly sliced
2 carrots, fairly thinly sliced
2 shallots, diced
2 egg whites, lightly beaten
2 egg shells, crushed
3 tablespoons finely chopped fresh tarragon or
1½ tablespoons dried
shapes cut from lemon rind, for garnish

Tarragon Consommé

Bring the stock to a boil. Mix the chicken and vegetables together in a large saucepan, then mix in the egg whites and shells. Gradually pour in the stock, beating all the time, then bring to a boil, still beating.

Immediately when boiling point is reached, stop beating. Lower the heat and simmer very gently for 1 hour.

Carefully make a small hole in the scum on the surface of the liquid. Without disturbing the scum, ladle the liquid out into a sieve lined with muslin or cheesecloth. Leave the strained, clarified liquid to become cold, then carefully lift the fat from the surface.

Put the tarragon into a mortar. Bring a scant cup of the consommé to a boil, then gradually pour it onto the tarragon, pounding it well with the pestle. Cover and leave to infuse for 10 minutes.

Mix the tarragon liquid and tarragon with the remaining consommé. Heat gently to boiling point, and then ladle into warm soup bowls. Cut the shapes from the lemon rind and then float these shapes on top of the consommé.

Loin of Venison with Cranberries and Glazed Apples

The venison stock can be made at least 2 days before the party, and kept in a cool place. Cook the cranberries a day or two in advance, and drain them of their liquid on the morning of the party, ready for garnishing the venison along with the apples, that evening.

two 1½-lb loins of venison, bones and trimmings reserved
3 carrots, chopped
2 celery stalks, chopped
3 small leeks, chopped
16 juniper berries, crushed
pared rind of 1 orange
bouquet garni of 3 fresh thyme sprigs, 1 fresh rosemary sprig, 1 bay leaf and 6 fresh parsley stalks tied together
salt and pepper
1 bottle fruity red wine
8 tablespoons (1 stick) butter
1 cup cranberries
½ cup sugar
¼ cup Calvados or applejack
¼ cup dry muscat wine
3 crisp green apples, cored and sliced

Put the venison bones and trimmings in a roasting pan and brown under a hot broiler. Add the vegetables and brown these lightly. Tip the bones and vegetables into a large saucepan and add the juniper berries, orange rind, bouquet garni and seasoning.

Stir half of the red wine into the roasting pan and bring to a boil, stirring to mix in the sediment. Pour this wine into the saucepan and add 5¼ cups water. Bring to a boil, skimming the scum from the surface, and simmer for about 2¼ hours, skimming occasionally.

Leave to cool, then remove the fat from the surface. Strain the stock, pressing down well to extract as much liquid from the vegetables and flavorings as possible, but do not press the vegetables through the sieve. Stir the remaining red wine into the stock and boil this sauce until reduced to 3 cups.

Heat half of the butter in a roasting pan, add the loins of venison and sear evenly all over. Transfer to a preheated 425° oven and roast for 15–20 minutes; they will remain pink inside.

Meanwhile, put the cranberries into a saucepan and pour ⅓ cup of boiling water over. Cover and leave to soak for 5 minutes. Bring to simmering point and simmer for 3 minutes. Remove from the heat and leave for 5 minutes, then stir in 3 tablespoons of the sugar. Set aside.

Remove the venison from the roasting pan to a carving board, cover and keep warm.

Heat the Calvados and muscat wine in a saucepan to simmering point. Stir in the remaining sugar, then add the apples. Lower the heat and poach for about

Loin of Venison with Cranberries and Glazed Apples; Celeriac Purée

3 minutes. Remove from the heat.

Gently reheat the sauce and gradually swirl in the remaining butter, cut into small pieces. Season. Keep warm, but do not allow the sauce to boil.

Cut each loin of venison into 12 or 16 slices. Spoon the sauce over a large, warmed platter and place the venison on top. Remove the cranberries and apples from their liquid with a slotted spoon. Use to garnish the serving platter. Serve sliced with some cranberries and apples and the sauce spooned around.

Amaretti Bavarois

Make the sauce the day before the party, and keep it in a cool place. The custard for the bavarois can also be made the day before, but make the bavarois in the morning for dinner that night—don't be tempted to complete the bavarois a day ahead, because it will soften the amaretti cookies, and one of their attractions—along with their flavor—is their slight crunch through the smooth creaminess of the bavarois.

1 vanilla bean
2 cups milk
1 cup sugar
6 egg yolks
2 oz amaretti cookies (about 10), roughly broken up
$\frac{1}{4}$ cup peach brandy
4 teaspoons unflavored gelatin
2 cups heavy cream
very fine strips of orange rind, blanched, to decorate
SAUCE
$1\frac{1}{4}$ cups orange juice
2 tablespoons grated orange rind
1 cup sugar
about 1 tablespoon lemon juice

Gently heat the vanilla bean in the milk to simmering point. Remove from the heat, cover and leave to infuse for 20 minutes. Remove the vanilla bean.

Beat the sugar and egg yolks together in a bowl placed over a saucepan of hot water. Bring the milk to a boil and gradually pour onto the egg yolks, stirring constantly. Cook over gently simmering water, stirring constantly, until the custard is thick enough to coat the back of the spoon.

Strain the custard into a mixing bowl. Cover the surface closely with plastic wrap or wax paper and leave to cool.

Put the amaretti into a bowl, sprinkle the peach brandy over and leave to soak for 30–45 minutes.

Dissolve the gelatin in 4 tablespoons water in a small bowl placed over a saucepan of hot water. Leave the gelatin to cool slightly, then stir in a little of the custard. Pour this mixture into the remaining custard and stir well. Leave in a cool place until almost setting.

Whip the cream and fold into the custard. Half-fill 8 individual damp molds with the custard. Divide the amaretti among the molds, piling them in the center, then cover with the remaining custard. Chill until set.

To prepare the sauce, gently heat the orange juice, rind and sugar, stirring until the sugar has dissolved. Simmer until reduced to a light sauce-like consistency. Pour into a bowl and leave to cool, then chill.

Unmold the bavarois onto cold plates. Taste the sauce and add sufficient lemon juice to "lift" the flavor. Spoon around the bavarois. Decorate the tops of the bavarois with fine strips of orange rind.

Celeriac Purée

The purée can be prepared in advance and kept covered in the refrigerator. To serve, place the purée in a bowl over a saucepan of hot water and reheat, stirring frequently.

2 lb celeriac, peeled and chopped
salt and white pepper
2 cups milk
3 tablespoons unsalted butter
3 tablespoons heavy cream

Cook the celeriac in simmering salted milk for 6 minutes, or until tender. Drain the celeriac well, reserving the milk. Purée the celeriac in a blender or food processor.

Heat the butter in a non-stick saucepan and stir in the celeriac purée, then heat, stirring constantly to drive off excess moisture. Beat in the cream and enough of the reserved milk to give a creamy consistency. Add seasoning to taste.

GARDEN PARTY FOR 20

A garden party such as this could well be a special celebration party—a birthday, perhaps, or an anniversary, or it would make a perfect menu for a small wedding lunch or dinner reception. The buffet consists of: slices of tender beef tenderloin with green peppercorns set in a wine aspic; chicken breasts cooked in muscat wine, garnished with poached fresh apricots given just a hint of cinnamon; a very pretty terrine of layered sole, smoked salmon and spinach, served with 2 delicious sauces—a fresh tomato and herb cream, and a sorrel and lettuce mayonnaise; and 3 contrasting salads—bulgur, lychee and kumquat salad, a mixed lettuce salad in a creamy dressing, and a crunchy salad of zucchini, celery and apple. There are 2 desserts—a geranium leaf cream served with summer fruits, and a passion fruit cake.

GARDEN PARTY FOR 20

CHICKEN BREASTS IN MUSCAT WINE WITH APRICOTS

SLICES OF BEEF IN WINE ASPIC

MIXED LETTUCE SALAD
ZUCCHINI, CELERY AND APPLE SALAD

SOLE AND SMOKED SALMON TERRINE
TOMATO SAUCE
SORREL AND LETTUCE MAYONNAISE

BULGUR, LYCHEE AND KUMQUAT SALAD

LEMON BARLEY WATER

PASSION FRUIT CAKE

GERANIUM CREAM WITH RED SUMMER FRUITS

SUGGESTED DRINKS: GIN AND HOMEMADE LEMON BARLEY WATER COCKTAILS OR CHAMPAGNE BEFOREHAND; A GEWÜRTZTRAMINER, OR A CALIFORNIA CHENIN BLANC WITH THE BUFFET

Chicken Breasts in Muscat Wine with Apricots

For convenience, start this recipe 2 days before the party. Finish off the dish the day before the party and keep it in the refrigerator overnight. If you do not have a casserole large enough, use 2 or 3.

2 bottles of dry Alsatian muscat wine
3 large shallots, finely chopped
about 8 fresh thyme sprigs
2 bay leaves, torn in half
1 tablespoon finely chopped lemon rind
salt and pepper
20 chicken breast halves (on the bone)
$\frac{1}{2}$ cup sugar
2 cinnamon sticks
4 lb ripe apricots, halved and pitted
fresh chervil or parsley sprigs, for garnish

Boil $3\frac{3}{4}$ cups of the wine in a large casserole until reduced to 5 tablespoons. Pour in the remaining wine and add the shallots, herbs, lemon rind and seasoning. Add the chicken breasts, skin side down. Bring just to boiling point, then cover tightly and transfer to a preheated 325° oven. Cook for 45–50 minutes, turning the chicken over after 20 minutes and then again after a further 20 minutes. Leave the chicken to cool in the liquid.

Drain the chicken, reserving the liquid. Discard the skin, and remove the breasts from the bones in one piece. Remove any fat from the surface of the liquid. Return the breasts to the liquid, cover and refrigerate overnight.

The next day, the liquid should have jelled slightly. Remove any remaining fat from the surface. Lift out the chicken breasts and set aside. Warm the liquid slightly, then pour it through a sieve lined with muslin or cheesecloth.

Reserve about $\frac{2}{3}$ cup of the liquid and put the remainder in a saucepan. Add the sugar. Heat, stirring, until the sugar has dissolved, then add the cinnamon sticks and bring to a boil. Lower the heat and add about one-third of the apricots. They should be covered by the liquid. Poach the fruit for about 5 minutes. Transfer to a bowl using a slotted spoon. Poach the remaining apricots in the same way and add to the bowl.

Pour the liquid over the apricots and leave to cool, moving the apricots around from time to time, if necessary, so that they are equally soaked. Cover and chill.

Carve the chicken breasts into thin slices. Arrange the slices in fan shapes on one or two large, cold platters. Brush the slices lightly with the reserved liquid.

Remove the apricots from their liquid using a slotted spoon and arrange them on and around the chicken, cutting some of the apricot halves in half again. Garnish the platter with sprigs of chervil.

Slices of Beef in Wine Aspic

These savory beef aspics can be made entirely the day before the party, and kept in the refrigerator. Depending on the weather, unmold 1–2 hours before serving; if the weather is very hot, leave the unmolding until as late as possible.

3 tablespoons oil
4-lb beef tenderloin roast, tied into a neat cylindrical shape
3 cups lightly jellied veal stock
1½ cups medium-bodied red wine
1½ cups sercial (dry) Madeira
2 small bay leaves, torn
fresh parsley sprig
small fresh rosemary sprig
2½ teaspoons unflavored gelatin
3 tablespoons green peppercorns
chicory or lettuce and fresh herb leaves or small sprigs,
for garnish

Heat the oil in a roasting pan on top of the stove, add the beef and sear evenly all over. Transfer to a preheated 425° oven and roast for 45–60 minutes (the beef will be rare). Using tongs, transfer the beef to a cooling rack with a baking tray placed underneath. Leave to cool completely. When cold, cut the beef into ½–¾-inch thick slices.

Boil the stock, wine and Madeira with the herbs until reduced by half.

Dissolve the gelatin in 1½ tablespoons of water in a bowl placed over a saucepan of hot water. Remove the bowl from the saucepan. Remove the herbs from the reduced liquid and slowly stir the liquid into the gelatin.

Spoon a thin layer of this aspic over the bottom of ramekins or other similar small dishes, one for each slice of beef. Chill until set. Keep the remaining aspic liquid at room temperature.

Place about ½ teaspoon green peppercorns in the center of each dish on the layer of aspic. Carefully place a slice of beef on top. Spoon in sufficient aspic to surround and just cover each slice. Chill until set.

Arrange a fine bed of shredded chicory on cold plates. Unmold the beef aspics onto the plates and garnish with leaves or small sprigs of fresh herbs.

Mixed Lettuce Salad

For the salad here, 3 kinds of lettuce are dressed with a mixture of cream, Meaux or Dijon mustard and lemon juice. Almonds add a subtle crunch. The dressing can be made 1 or 2 days ahead, and stored in a screw-top jar in the refrigerator. The lettuce can be washed and shredded the evening before, and kept in a plastic bag in the refrigerator. Toss with the dressing just before serving.

1 head iceberg lettuce, shredded
1 medium head romaine lettuce, shredded
1 head Bibb or Boston lettuce, shredded
6 tablespoons (1½ oz) slivered almonds, lightly toasted
DRESSING
1⅓ cups heavy cream
2 tablespoons Meaux or Dijon mustard
½ cup lemon juice
salt and pepper

Blend the cream into the mustard, then add the lemon juice and seasoning. Cover and keep cool.

Toss the lettuce together and put into one or two cold salad bowls.

Stir the dressing and pour over the lettuce. Toss lightly, then sprinkle the nuts over. Toss again very briefly and serve at once.

Zucchini, Celery and Apple Salad

The dressing for this crunchy, refreshing salad can be made a day ahead, and kept in the refrigerator. If you like, the zucchini and celery can be steamed briefly and cooled, rather than being used raw in the salad.

2½ lb small zucchini, thinly sliced (about 7 or 8 cups)
10 celery stalks, thinly sliced
4 large crisp green apples, cored and chopped
DRESSING
1¼ cups thick plain yogurt
¾ cup lemon juice
3 tablespoons finely grated lemon rind
½ cup Dijon mustard
3 tablespoons chopped fresh thyme or 1½ tablespoons dried
salt and pepper

Make the dressing by blending the yogurt, lemon juice and rind and mustard together. Stir in the thyme and seasoning. Cover and chill.

Toss the salad ingredients together. Pour the dressing over and toss again lightly.

93

Sole and Smoked Salmon Terrine

This terrine will serve 8–10 people, so make 2. It looks most attractive, with its creamy white exterior, its pale pink layer, and core of dark green spinach purée. Make the terrines the day before the party and keep in the refrigerator.

$1\frac{1}{4}$ lb sole fillets, skinned
1 tablespoon lemon juice
salt and white pepper
2 egg whites
$\frac{2}{3}$ cup heavy cream
$2\frac{1}{2}$ cups shredded young spinach leaves
SMOKED SALMON CREAM
6 oz smoked salmon
lemon juice
1 medium egg white
$\frac{1}{3}$ cup crème fraîche or heavy cream
cayenne
GARNISH
red and green peppers, cucumber skin, lemon rind and very small watercress sprigs

Purée the sole in a blender or food processor. Add the lemon juice and salt and then the egg whites. For a really smooth terrine, pass the mixture through a fine sieve. Return it to the blender or food processor bowl. With the motor running, very gradually pour in the cream. Season with pepper. Chill for at least 1 hour.

Purée the smoked salmon in a blender or food processor. Add a squeeze of lemon juice and then the egg white. Pass through a fine sieve as for the sole, then return to the blender or food processor. With the motor running, gradually pour in the crème fraîche or cream. Season with cayenne. Chill for about 1 hour.

Cook the spinach with 1 tablespoon water until wilted. Drain well, then rinse in cold running water. Drain well again, pressing down on the spinach to extract as much water as possible. Purée and season.

For the garnish, broil the peppers until they are soft and the skins are charred all over. Allow to cool, then peel the peppers. Remove the core and seeds. Cut the peppers into decorative shapes. Arrange the pepper shapes, cucumber skin and lemon rind in an attractive pattern on the bottom of a lightly oiled 10×4-inch terrine.

Carefully cover the bottom and sides of the terrine with about two-thirds of the sole mixture. Leave an open channel in the center. Place about half of the smoked salmon mixture in the channel, then cover the salmon with the spinach purée. Cover with the remaining smoked salmon mixture and cover this with the re-

Sole and Smoked Salmon Terrine; Mixed Lettuce Salad; Sorrel and Lettuce Mayonnaise

maining sole mixture. Cover with greased wax paper.

Put the terrine into a roasting pan. Surround with boiling water and bake in a preheated 325° oven for about 50 minutes, until just set in the center. Remove the terrine from the oven and leave to cool. Drain off any excess cooking liquid.

Carefully unmold the terrine onto a cold plate. Garnish the plate with very small sprigs of watercress.

Tomato Sauce

This creamy tomato sauce is not cooked, so it has a lovely fresh flavor. You can make this the day before. It will keep very well, covered, in the refrigerator.

3 lb large tomatoes, skinned, seeded and diced
6 tablespoons cream cheese
$\frac{1}{2}$ cup sour cream
4 teaspoons Dijon mustard
3 tablespoons lemon juice
5 tablespoons finely chopped fresh parsley
4 tablespoons finely chopped fresh tarragon
salt and pepper
few drops of Tabasco sauce

Leave the tomatoes between several thicknesses of paper towels to remove excess moisture. Do this in batches.

Beat the cream cheese, sour cream and mustard together, then gradually stir in the lemon juice. Add the herbs and seasoning, then the tomatoes. Cover and chill.

Sorrel and Lettuce Mayonnaise

This sauce has a delicate flavor, and can be made a day or more in advance.

$\frac{1}{2}$ cup shredded iceberg lettuce
$\frac{1}{2}$ cup shredded small sorrel leaves
salt and pepper
1 egg, at room temperature
$\frac{1}{2}$ teaspoon mustard powder
3 tablespoons lemon juice
$1\frac{1}{4}$ cups olive oil

Cook the lettuce and sorrel with 3 tablespoons water for about 4 minutes until the sorrel has wilted. The lettuce will remain quite crisp. Drain well, season and cool.

Blend the egg with the mustard powder and lemon juice in a blender or food processor. With the motor running, pour in the oil in a slow steady stream. Transfer to a bowl and season. Fold in the sorrel and lettuce.

Bulgur, Lychee and Kumquat Salad

◆━●━◆

This is a most unusual salad, but oh so good, with its contrast not only of flavors but also of textures. Its minty dressing complements all the ingredients. The bulgur can be soaked and cooked in advance, and the dressing made the day before.

1¼ lb (4 cups) bulgur
salt
10 fresh lychees, peeled, halved and pitted,
or drained canned lychees
10 oz kumquats, quartered and seeded
¼ cup finely chopped scallions
mint leaves, for garnish
DRESSING
4¾ tablespoons white wine vinegar
¾ cup olive oil
¼ cup finely chopped fresh mint
salt and pepper
scant 1 teaspoon Dijon mustard

Soak the bulgur in 4 pints boiling salted water for about 30 minutes, until tender and the water has been absorbed. Rinse in cold running water and squeeze dry with the hands. Shake all the ingredients for the dressing together in a screw-top jar.

Cut some of the lychee halves in half, some into thirds. Cut some of the kumquat quarters in half or into smaller pieces, depending on size.

Toss the bulgur, lychees, kumquats and scallions together. Shake the dressing again, pour over the salad and toss together. Cover and chill lightly.

Serve garnished with mint leaves.

Lemon Barley Water

◆━●━◆

This popular summer libation can be made up to a week before the party.

½ cup pearl barley
pared rind of 4 large lemons, in long strips
⅔ cup sugar or to taste

Put the barley and lemon rind into a large saucepan. Pour 2½ quarts of boiling water over. Return to a boil, then lower the heat, cover the saucepan and simmer for 1¼–1½ hours, until the barley is soft.

Remove from the heat and leave to cool for about 15 minutes, then strain the liquid. Stir in the lemon juice and add sugar to taste. Leave to cool completely, then cover and refrigerate. Serve diluted to taste with cold water (or gin or dry vermouth) and ice cubes.

Passion Fruit Cake

◆━●━◆

This layered cake, with its exotic passion fruit filling, will serve 8–10, so for 20 guests, make 2 cakes. If you like, you can make the cakes well in advance and freeze them, then on the day of the party you just need to fill and ice them and decorate with pistachio nuts.
Makes 23 cm (9 inch) cake.

4 eggs, separated
⅔ cup sugar
⅔ cup self-rising flour
pinch of salt
2 tablespoons unsalted butter, melted
PASSION FRUIT CREAM
12 oz cream cheese
5 tablespoons plain yogurt
few drops of orange flower water
1½ tablespoons confectioners' sugar
5 ripe passion fruit, halved
DECORATION
⅔ cup heavy cream, lightly whipped
1 cup (3–4 oz) chopped shelled pistachio nuts
shelled pistachio nuts, to decorate

Beat the egg yolks and sugar together until thick and pale. Sift the flour and salt over and fold in lightly. Beat the egg whites until stiff but not dry, then lightly fold into the yolk mixture. Trickle the butter over and carefully fold in.

Turn the batter into a greased and lined 9-inch loose-bottomed deep cake pan. Bake in a preheated 350° oven for 25–35 minutes, until risen, and springy to the touch when lightly pressed in the center.

Leave to cool slightly in the pan, then turn out onto a wire rack covered with a dishtowel. Remove the lining paper and leave to cool completely.

For the passion fruit cream, mix the cream cheese, yogurt, orange flower water and confectioners' sugar together. Stir in the passion fruit flesh.

Cut the cake into 3 equal layers. Spread about one-third of the passion fruit cream over the bottom layer. Place the second layer gently on top and cover with another one-third of the passion fruit cream, not taking it right to the edge. Spread the remaining passion fruit cream over the top cake layer, not taking it right to the edge, and gently place this on top of the cake.

Reserving a little of the whipped cream for piping around the top of the cake, spread the remainder over the sides of the cake. Coat the sides with the chopped pistachio nuts.

Spoon the reserved cream into a pastry bag fitted with a small star tube and pipe a border around the top edge of the cake. Decorate with the pistachio nuts.

Geranium Cream with Red Summer Fruits; Passion Fruit Cake

Geranium Cream with Red Summer Fruits

This rich cream, which is a mixture of heavy cream and fresh cream cheese, is delicately scented with geranium leaves. If you can't obtain them, the creamy mixture will taste just as good without. The red summer fruits served with it look beautiful, with their jewel-like colors surrounding the white cream. Make the geranium cream 2 days before the party.

$1\frac{1}{4}$ cups heavy cream
6 sweet geranium leaves, bruised
2 lb cream cheese
1 cup sugar or to taste
3 lb red summer fruits, such as raspberries, wild strawberries, small strawberries and red currants, chilled
sugar, for serving

Gently heat the cream with the geranium leaves in the top of a double boiler, or in a bowl placed over a saucepan of hot water, for 10–15 minutes, until it just reaches simmering point. Do not allow it to boil. Remove from the heat, cover and leave to cool.

Strain the cream, then gradually stir it into the cheese, stirring until smooth. Rinse the geranium leaves, dry them and stir into the cream mixture. Cover and leave in a cool place for 12 hours.

Remove the geranium leaves and stir in sugar to taste. Spoon the cream into a mound on a cold decorative plate. Spoon the fruits around. Serve sugar for sprinkling over the fruits separately.

97

COFFEE MORNING FOR 15

A coffee morning can be just a gathering of friends—perhaps with the purpose of introducing someone who is new to your neighborhood—or it can be part of a fund-raising venture. A coffee morning is a pleasant way of raising money for any charity, be it local or national.

After your guests have eaten the goodies on this coffee morning menu, one thing is quite certain—they won't be able to eat any lunch! There are warm apple pancakes, spread with cinnamon butter; a moist orange curd cake (similar to a cheesecake); a dried fruit loaf, scented with orange honey, rum and spices, and thinly iced with a glacé icing; rich butter cookies, some with a Cognac icing, little cheesey shortbreads made with Parmesan; and a 3-layer almond and Marsala cake. With a choice of 2 or more coffees to drink, this is a veritable morning feast, and it is guaranteed that all who attend this coffee morning will certainly enjoy every mouthful!

There is quite a lot that can be prepared on days before the coffee morning, to save you from having to make an exceptionally early start in order to get everything done.

COFFEE MORNING FOR 15

ALMOND AND MARSALA CAKE

SCENTED FRUIT LOAF

APPLE PANCAKES WITH CINNAMON BUTTER

ORANGE CURD CAKE

BUTTER COOKIES

PARMESAN SHORTBREAD

SELECTION OF COFFEES

Almond and Marsala Cake

This is a rich, delicious 3-layer cake. The cake can be made 2 or 3 weeks ahead and kept in the freezer; the filling and icing can be made the day before. The night before, thaw the cake, then fill and ice it about 2 hours before your guests are expected.
Makes 25×10 cm (10×4 inch) loaf.

3 eggs, separated
$\frac{1}{2}$ cup sugar
$\frac{1}{3}$ cup self-rising flour
pinch of salt
$\frac{2}{3}$ cup ground almonds
4 tablespoons unsalted butter, melted
4 tablespoons Marsala
toasted slivered almonds, to decorate
FILLING
$\frac{1}{3}$ cup sugar
$\frac{1}{2}$ cup unblanched almonds
$1\frac{1}{4}$ cups cottage cheese, sieved
2 tablespoons heavy cream
ICING
$\frac{3}{4}$ cup (6 oz) cream cheese
$1\frac{1}{4}$ cups confectioners' sugar, or to taste
vanilla extract

Beat the egg yolks with the sugar until thick and pale. Carefully fold in the flour, salt, ground almonds, butter and Marsala until just evenly blended. Beat the egg whites until stiff but not dry, then fold into the batter.

Turn into a 10×4-inch loaf pan lined with greased wax paper. Bake in a preheated 350° oven for about 45 minutes.

Leave the cake to cool in the pan for a few minutes, then turn it out onto a wire rack. Leave it to cool a few minutes more, then carefully remove the lining paper. Leave to cool completely.

To make the filling, heat the sugar in a small heavy saucepan, stirring until it has melted. Stir in the nuts and continue to cook, stirring, until the mixture turns golden brown. Pour onto an oiled, cold surface and leave to cool and harden. Break up this praline and grind to a coarse powder in a blender or food processor. Chill.

Beat the cottage cheese and cream together, then stir in the praline. To make the icing, beat the cheese and sugar together, and add vanilla extract to taste. Chill.

Cut the cake into 3 equal layers. Place the bottom layer on a serving plate. Spread half the filling over. Cover with the middle layer and spread this with the remaining filling. Put the top layer in place. Spread the icing over the top and sides of the cake.

Press toasted slivered almonds around the bottom and around the top of the cake. Refrigerate the cake for about 1 hour. Keep the cake cool until ready to serve.

Almond and Marsala Cake; Butter Cookies; Parmesan Shortbread

Scented Fruit Loaf

This can be made the day before and kept in an airtight container in a cool place. If possible, ice it on the morning.

FILLING

4 oz ($\frac{2}{3}$ cup) dried apples, chopped
4 oz ($\frac{2}{3}$ cup) dried peaches, chopped
4 oz ($\frac{2}{3}$ cup) dried pears, chopped
4 oz ($\frac{2}{3}$ cup) dried apricots, chopped
2 tablespoons orange or other scented honey
4 tablespoons dark rum
3 tablespoons lemon juice
1$\frac{1}{2}$ teaspoons grated lemon rind
1$\frac{1}{2}$ teaspoons grated orange rind
$\frac{1}{4}$ teaspoon ground cardamom
$\frac{1}{2}$ teaspoon ground coriander

DOUGH

$\frac{1}{2}$ cup milk
3 tablespoons unsalted butter, chopped
$\frac{1}{3}$ cup sugar
2 tablespoons active dry yeast
2 egg yolks, beaten
about 1$\frac{2}{3}$ cups all-purpose flour
large pinch of salt
1 teaspoon grated lemon rind
glacé icing (see page 101) and 3 tablespoons slivered almonds (optional), to decorate

Bring 2 cups of water to a boil in a heavy-based saucepan. Add the dried fruits and simmer until they are very soft, stirring frequently. Stir in the honey, rum, lemon juice, fruit rinds and spices. Simmer, stirring frequently, until the liquid has been absorbed. Leave to cool.

For the dough, gently warm the milk with the butter and sugar until the butter has melted and the sugar dissolves. Leave to cool until the mixture feels just warm to the fingertips, then stir in the yeast until dissolved.

Sift the flour and salt into a bowl. Make a well in the center. Pour the egg yolks into the well followed by the yeast mixture. Add the lemon rind. Gradually draw the dry ingredients into the liquids to give a smooth dough.

Beat well for 3–4 minutes, then turn onto a lightly floured surface and knead for 3–4 minutes. Transfer the dough to a lightly oiled bowl, cover with lightly oiled plastic wrap and leave to rise in a warm place until doubled in size.

Punch the dough down and knead for 2–3 minutes, then press out into a large rectangle, about $\frac{1}{2}$ inch thick. Spread the fruit filling over the dough, leaving a narrow border clear around the edges. Dampen the edges and roll up the dough like a jelly roll. Press the edges firmly together to seal.

Transfer the roll to a large buttered baking sheet, placing the seam underneath, and forming the roll into a horse-shoe shape if necessary. Cover with oiled plastic wrap and leave to rise in a warm place until puffy.

Bake in a preheated 350° oven for about 20–25 minutes, until golden and the loaf sounds hollow when tapped on the bottom. Transfer to a wire rack and cool to lukewarm.

Brush the loaf with glacé icing, allowing it to trickle down the sides. Sprinkle with nuts, if used. Leave to cool and set.

Almond Pancakes with Cinnamon Butter

Prepare the cinnamon butter 2 or 3 days in advance and keep it, covered, in the refrigerator. The batter may be made the evening before the coffee morning; stir and add the grated apple just before cooking the pancakes.

$\frac{2}{3}$ cup all-purpose flour
pinch of salt
1$\frac{1}{2}$ teaspoons baking powder
2 tablespoons light brown sugar
2 tablespoons unsalted butter, melted
1 egg, beaten
$\frac{1}{2}$ cup milk
1 teaspoon lemon juice
1 small crisp apple
butter for greasing

CINNAMON BUTTER

8 tablespoons (1 stick) unsalted butter
$\frac{1}{3}$ cup granulated sugar
$\frac{1}{3}$ cup light brown sugar
4 teaspoons ground cinnamon

To make the butter, beat all the ingredients together. Spoon into pots, level the surface, cover with plastic wrap and refrigerate. Remove from the refrigerator at least 30 minutes before serving.

Mix the flour, salt, baking powder and sugar together in a bowl. Make a well in the center. Mix the butter, egg, milk and lemon juice together and pour into the well in the dry ingredients. Gradually draw the dry ingredients into the liquid to make a smooth thick batter. Grate in the apple.

Butter a griddle or large heavy-bottomed, preferably non-stick, frying pan. Place over a moderate heat. Drop 3 or 4 small spoonsful of the batter onto the griddle or frying pan, keeping the pancakes well apart, and spread each one out slightly with the back of the spoon. Cook for 2–3 minutes until bubbles appear on the surface, then turn each one over with a long metal spatula and cook the other side for about 2 minutes.

Keep the pancakes warm between 2 dishtowels while cooking the remaining pancakes in the same way.

Serve warm, with the cinnamon butter.

Orange Curd Cake

This cake can be made the day before the coffee morning, and kept covered in a cool place.
Makes 23 cm (9 inch) cake.

1 lb ricotta cheese, sieved
1 cup sugar
2 tablespoons semolina
4 eggs, separated
3 tablespoons orange juice
2 teaspoons finely grated orange rind
$\frac{1}{4}$ cup chopped candied peel

Beat the cheese, sugar, semolina, egg yolks and orange juice and rind together. Stir in the peel. Beat the egg whites until stiff but not dry, then carefully fold into the cheese mixture until just evenly blended.

Spoon into a greased 9-inch loose-bottomed deep cake pan. Bake in a preheated 350° oven for 30–35 minutes, until just set in the center.

Leave the cake to cool slightly in the pan before removing it, still on the base of the pan. Carefully slide the cake from the base onto a wire rack covered by a sheet of wax paper, so that it remains the right way up. Leave to cool.

Butter Cookies

These cookies can be made 3 or 4 days in advance. Ice them on the morning of the party.
Makes 15–20.

1$\frac{1}{3}$ cups all-purpose flour
pinch of salt
$\frac{1}{4}$ teaspoon baking powder
1$\frac{1}{2}$ teaspoons ground cardamom
12 tablespoons (1$\frac{1}{2}$ sticks) unsalted butter, diced
1 scant cup confectioners' sugar
$\frac{1}{2}$ teaspoon vanilla extract
GLACÉ ICING WITH COGNAC
$\frac{2}{3}$ cup confectioners' sugar
2–3 teaspoons Cognac

Sift the flour, salt, baking powder and cardamom into a bowl. Rub in the butter until the mixture resembles breadcrumbs. Sift the confectioners' sugar over, then gently stir in. Sprinkle the vanilla extract over, then press the ingredients together to make a smooth dough. Cover and chill for at least 3 hours.

Roll out the dough on a lightly floured surface, using a lightly floured rolling pin, to about $\frac{1}{4}$ inch thick. Cut into rounds with a floured 2-inch fluted cutter. Transfer to baking sheets, leaving about $\frac{1}{2}$ inch space around each.

Bake in a preheated 375° oven for about 12 minutes,

until lightly golden. Leave to set on the baking sheets for a few minutes, then transfer the cookies to a wire rack and leave to cool.

Sift the confectioners' sugar and mix to a smooth consistency with about 1 tablespoon cold water and the Cognac. Spread a thin layer of glacé icing over the tops of half of the cookies. Leave to set.

Parmesan Shortbread

These rich crackers can be made the day before the coffee morning—or made several days before and stored in an airtight container.
Makes about 15.

$\frac{2}{3}$ cup all-purpose flour
pinch of salt
pinch of cayenne
8 tablespoons (1 stick) unsalted butter, diced
$\frac{3}{4}$ cup freshly grated Parmesan cheese
1 egg yolk
egg yolk beaten with a little milk, for glazing
sesame seeds, poppy seeds and salt crystals

Mix the flour, salt and cayenne together. Add the butter, then rub in until the mixture resembles breadcrumbs. Stir in the cheese. Bind the mixture to a dough with the egg yolk, adding a little water if too dry. Cover with plastic wrap and chill for 30 minutes.

Roll out the dough on a lightly floured surface, using a lightly floured rolling pin, to about $\frac{1}{2}$ inch thick. Cut into rounds with a 1$\frac{1}{4}$-inch cookie cutter. Transfer to baking sheets.

Brush the tops of the rounds with the egg yolk glaze and sprinkle with sesame seeds, poppy seeds or salt. Bake in a preheated 325° oven for about 30 minutes, until light golden.

Leave to cool on the baking sheets for a few minutes before transferring to a wire rack to cool completely.

101

COCKTAIL PARTY FOR 40

A cocktail party is an excellent way to entertain a lot of your friends all at once. Also, it is an ideal occasion to introduce new people to your circle. A cocktail party should be more than just drinks, with bowls of peanuts and potato chips. On the menu for this cocktail party there is a whole host of delectable cocktail eats, which will almost render dinner totally unnecessary for any of your guests! There are spicy clams, coated in a white wine batter and deep fried; there are oat-coated slices of goat's cheese broiled and served warm; eggs stuffed with a purée of artichokes; a caper and cheese mousse wrapped in lettuce on slices of rye bread; slices of homemade basil sausage in saffron brioche, with a lemony sauce; pinwheels of raw beef spread with a mustard cream; a selection of tartlets with pastry flavored to complement the fillings of smoked salmon, broccoli and tomato; and little nibbles of warm toasted chick peas and flavored black and green olives.

COCKTAIL PARTY FOR 40

CLAM FRITTERS

BROILED OAT-COATED CHÈVRE

EGGS WITH ARTICHOKE FILLING

LETTUCE AND CHEESE MOUSSE ROLLS ON RYE

BASIL SAUSAGE IN SAFFRON BRIOCHE WITH LEMON SAUCE

ROLLS OF BEEF WITH MUSTARD CREAM

SELECTION OF TARTLETS

TOASTED CHICK PEAS

FLAVORED OLIVES

SUGGESTED DRINKS: PUNCH AND A SELECTION OF COCKTAILS

Clam Fritters

Make the batter the day before the party, but add the egg white just before frying. The evening before, the clams may be removed from their shells, and kept with the liquid in a covered container in the refrigerator.

$\frac{3}{4}$ cup all-purpose flour
pinch of salt
1 egg, separated
$\frac{2}{3}$ cup medium-bodied dry white wine
40 small clams
about 2 tablespoons anchovy paste
vegetable oil for deep frying
lemon wedges and scallions, for garnish

Sift the flour and salt into a bowl. Make a well in the center and add the egg yolk followed by the wine. Gradually draw the dry ingredients into the liquids to make a smooth batter. Beat well for 1–2 minutes, then cover and leave for at least 30 minutes.

Open the clams (reserve their liquid for fish stock) and remove them from their shells. Drain on paper towels. Spread a little anchovy paste over each.

Beat the egg white until stiff, then fold into the batter. Lightly but evenly coat the clams in batter. Deep-fry, in batches, at 375° for 2–2$\frac{1}{2}$ minutes, turning each fritter over during cooking so that it becomes an even, light golden brown. Check the temperature of the fat in between batches. Drain the fritters on paper towels.

Serve hot, garnished with small lemon wedges and scallions with the green parts tied into knots.

Broiled Oat-Coated Chèvre

Slice the goat's cheeses and coat them, ready for cooking, the day before the party. They will then be ready to pop under the hot broiler just before serving.

5 log-shaped goat's cheeses (Bûcheron), about 4 oz each, rinded
1–1$\frac{1}{2}$ cups fresh breadcrumbs
$\frac{1}{3}$–$\frac{1}{2}$ cup oatmeal
salt and pepper
5–6 eggs, beaten
watercress sprigs or radicchio leaves, for garnish

Cut the cheeses into slices about $\frac{1}{4}$ inch thick.

Mix the breadcrumbs, oatmeal and seasoning together. Dip each slice of cheese into the eggs and drain well, then coat with the crumb mixture. Put on a wire rack and chill.

Broil about 4 minutes, turning once, until puffed.

Broiled Oat-Coated Chèvre; Clam Fritters

Eggs with Artichoke Filling

Cook the artichokes and the eggs the day before the party. Then on the morning of the party, prepare the stuffing, stuff the eggs and arrange them on their serving plates. Keep, covered, in a cool place.

6 fleshy globe artichokes, trimmed
salt and pepper
lemon juice
20 small eggs
6 tablespoons heavy cream
40 small fresh chervil or parsley sprigs, for garnish

Cook the artichokes in boiling salted water, to which a squeeze of lemon juice has been added, for 35–40 minutes, until tender. Leave the artichokes to drain upside-down.

Meanwhile, put the eggs in simmering water, bring to a boil then simmer for about 6 minutes so they are soft boiled. Cool immediately in cold running water.

Remove the leaves from the artichokes and scrape the flesh from the base of the leaves into a blender or food processor. Remove and discard the choke. Chop the base or heart and add to the blender.

Shell the eggs and slice them in half lengthwise. Carefully remove the yolks and put into the blender. Add the cream, a squeeze of lemon juice and seasoning. Purée the ingredients together.

Spoon the purée into a pastry bag fitted with a small star tube. Arrange the egg white halves on serving plates and pipe the purée into the cavities. Garnish the top of each egg half with a small sprig of chervil.

Lettuce and Cheese Mousse Rolls on Rye

Make the cheese and lettuce rolls the evening before the party and store, covered, in the refrigerator. On the afternoon, slice the rolls and arrange on the bread. Cover and keep cool until serving.

5 teaspoons unflavored gelatin
1½ cups cottage cheese, sieved
1½ cups thick plain yogurt
celery salt
pepper
2½ egg whites
3 tablespoons capers, chopped
5 medium-size inner iceberg lettuce leaves
butter for spreading (optional)
thinly sliced medium rye bread, crusts removed, cut into 40
1¼-inch squares

Dissolve the gelatin in 1½ tablespoons water in a small bowl placed over a saucepan of hot water. Remove from the heat and leave to cool slightly.

Mix the cottage cheese and yogurt together. Purée in a blender until completely smooth. Stir a little into the gelatin, then mix into the remaining cheese mixture. Season and leave in a cold place until beginning to set.

Beat the egg whites until stiff but not dry. Fold into the cheese mixture with the capers.

Trim the stalks from the lettuce leaves, if necessary, and divide the cheese mixture among them. Spread it out smoothly and evenly over the lettuce. Roll up each lettuce leaf. Place seam-side down on a plate and chill.

With a sharp knife, cut each lettuce roll crosswise into 8 slices. Thinly butter the bread, if liked. Place a slice of cheese-filled lettuce roll on each square of bread.

Basil Sausage in Saffron Brioche

The sausages can be made a day or two before the party and kept in the refrigerator. The saffron brioche really has to be made on the day of the party, but it is so delicious it is well worth the effort—there won't be a slice of this left over!
Make the lemon sauce the day before the party, and keep in a covered bowl in the refrigerator.

3 oz pork fatback
4 oz boned shoulder of veal
2 oz lean boneless pork
4 tablespoons finely chopped fresh basil or 2 tablespoons dried
2 tablespoons gin
2 eggs
1 teaspoon salt
1 teaspoon pepper
about 2½ quarts chicken stock (see page 181)
1 egg white, lightly beaten
1 egg yolk, beaten with 2 tablespoons milk, for glazing
BRIOCHE
1 teaspoon saffron powder
1½ tablespoons warm milk
¾ cup all-purpose flour
1 teaspoon sugar
1 package active dry yeast
½ teaspoon salt
1½ eggs, lightly beaten
8 tablespoons (1 stick) unsalted butter, chopped

Grind the fat and meats together, using the coarse blade of a grinder, then pass half the mixture through the fine blade. Mix both the mixtures together with the basil, gin, eggs and seasoning. Add more egg, if necessary, to give a moist but not loose mixture. Check the seasoning by frying a small piece of the mixture and then tasting it.

Form the meat mixture into 2 sausages, each about 10 inches long, and wrap in a double thickness of muslin or cheesecloth. Twist the ends of the cloth around, like a firecracker, and tie them securely with string.

Bring sufficient stock to cover the sausages to simmering point in a large saucepan or a fish cooker. Lower in the sausages and simmer gently, turning the sausages frequently, for about 10–15 minutes, until the juices run clear when the sausages are pierced through to the center.

Leave the sausages to cool for 30 minutes in the stock, then drain and leave to cool completely.

For the brioche, stir the saffron into the milk and leave for 15 minutes. Stir the flour, sugar, yeast and salt together in a large bowl and make a well in the center. Mix the saffron liquid with the eggs and pour into the well. Gradually draw the dry ingredients into the liquids and beat very well for about 3 minutes to give a smooth dough. Gradually beat in the butter and continue beating until the dough is smooth and elastic.

Turn the dough onto a floured surface and knead well for 4–5 minutes, until firm. Put the dough into a clean bowl, cover and leave to rise in a warm place until doubled in size—about $1\frac{1}{2}$ hours. Punch the dough down. Press the dough out to a rectangle that is slightly longer than the sausages and wide enough to enclose them individually. Smoothly cut the rectangle of dough in half lengthwise.

Remove the cheesecloth from the sausages. Brush the sausages and the surface of the dough with beaten egg white. Place the sausages lengthwise in the center of the dough rectangles. Roll the dough around the sausages, pressing the edges—particularly at the ends—together well to seal them. If necessary, brush the edges with more egg white to make sure they are sealed.

Place with the seams underneath on a large buttered baking sheet. Cover loosely and leave to rise in a warm place for 25–30 minutes, until risen and puffy.

Brush the dough lightly with the egg yolk glaze and make a few holes in the top with a fork. Bake in a preheated 375° oven for 20–35 minutes, until golden. Leave to cool on a wire rack.

Serve sliced, accompanied by lemon sauce.

Lemon Sauce

3 egg yolks
3 tablespoons olive oil
5 teaspoons lemon juice
salt and pepper
$\frac{1}{2}$ teaspoon chive mustard or Dijon mustard
$\frac{1}{2}$ cup ricotta cheese
$1\frac{1}{4}$ cups plain yogurt

Mix the egg yolks, oil, lemon juice, seasoning and mustard together in a saucepan. Gradually stir in the cheese and yogurt. Cook over a low heat, stirring constantly, until the sauce thickens.

Remove from the heat, pour into a bowl and leave to cool. Cover and refrigerate until ready to serve.

Rolls of Beef with Mustard Cream

Prepare the beef rolls on the morning of the party. Slice the rolls and garnish them about an hour before serving; keep them, covered, at cool room temperature.

$\frac{1}{2}$-lb piece of tenderloin beef
6 tablespoons sour cream
$2\frac{1}{4}$ teaspoons Dijon mustard
salt and pepper
small, or small pieces of, colorful raw vegetables, for garnish

Place the beef in the freezer to firm up for about $1\frac{1}{2}$ hours. (This slight freezing makes it easier to slice thinly.)

Meanwhile, mix the sour cream, mustard and seasoning together.

With a very sharp knife, or a meat slicing machine, cut the beef into *very* thin slices. Spread the slices with the mustard cream and roll them up firmly across their width. Cover the rolls and chill them.

With a sharp knife, cut the beef rolls crosswise into $\frac{1}{2}$–$\frac{3}{4}$-inch thick slices. If necessary, secure the slices with halves of wooden toothpicks; trim the toothpicks so they do not protrude too much.

Arrange the slices on cold plates and garnish with small, or small pieces of, colorful raw vegetables.

Selection of Tartlets

Make the flavored tartlet cases the day before the party and store in an airtight tin. You can also make the fillings for the smoked salmon tartlets and tomato tartlets the day before the party, but the broccoli filling is best made on the day.

PASTRY

10 tablespoons unsalted butter
$\frac{2}{3}$ cup (5 oz) cream cheese
1 cup + 3 tablespoons all-purpose flour
pinch of salt
1 egg yolk
scant $\frac{1}{2}$ teaspoon fennel seeds, chopped
pinch of grated nutmeg
$\frac{1}{2}$ teaspoon finely chopped fresh thyme or $\frac{1}{4}$ teaspoon dried

SMOKED SALMON FILLING

$\frac{1}{4}$ cup (2 oz) cream cheese
3 tablespoons heavy cream
1 small egg, beaten
$\frac{1}{2}$ teaspoon all-purpose flour
salt and white pepper
squeeze of lemon juice
2 oz smoked salmon, chopped
fresh chervil or fennel sprigs, for garnish

BROCCOLI FILLING

6 oz broccoli
salt and pepper
squeeze of lemon juice
3 oz cream cheese

TOMATO FILLING

3 tablespoons olive oil
1 garlic clove, crushed
$\frac{1}{2}$ cup finely chopped onion
1 lb beefsteak tomatoes, skinned, seeded and chopped
5 tablespoons finely chopped fresh parsley
1 tablespoon finely chopped fresh oregano or 2 teaspoons dried
salt and pepper
$\frac{1}{2}$ red pepper
7 stuffed olives, sliced

For the pastry, beat the butter and cheese together until softened. Sift the flour and salt over and quickly mix into the fats, adding the egg yolk to make a dough.

Divide the mixture into three portions. Work the fennel seeds into one portion, the nutmeg into another, and the thyme into the last portion. Cover and chill well.

Roll out the pieces of dough thinly on a lightly floured surface, using a lightly floured rolling pin. Cut each piece into rounds using a $2\frac{1}{2}$-inch cutter. Use the rounds to line 12 tartlet pans, easing the dough down well into the shape of the pan. Chill for 30 minutes.

Prick the bases, line with wax paper and weigh down with baking beans. Bake in a preheated 400° oven for 6 minutes. Remove the beans and paper and bake for a further 5 minutes. Leave to cool for a few minutes, then remove the pastry cases from the pans and cool completely on a wire rack.

To make the smoked salmon tartlets, beat the cream cheese and heavy cream together, then beat in the egg. Blend a little of the mixture into the flour, then stir back into the remaining mixture. Season and add a squeeze of lemon juice.

Return the fennel-flavored pastry cases to the tartlet pans. Divide the salmon between them and cover with the cheese mixture. Bake in a preheated 350° oven for 5–8 minutes, until lightly set. Leave to cool slightly, then remove from the pans again and carefully transfer to a wire rack to cool completely. Serve garnished with sprigs of chervil or fennel.

For the broccoli tartlets, cut away and discard any woody parts from the broccoli stalks. Cut off the heads and divide into small florets. Roughly chop the stalks. Cook the broccoli in boiling salted water, to which a squeeze of lemon juice has been added, until tender. The florets will take only 30 seconds. Drain well and refresh under cold running water, then dry on paper towels.

Purée the broccoli stalks with the cream cheese. Season. Divide between the nutmeg-flavored tartlet cases and place the broccoli florets on top.

For the tomato tartlets, heat the oil in a saucepan, add the garlic and cook gently, stirring occasionally, for 1 minute. Add the onion and cook, stirring occasionally, until softened. Stir in the chopped tomato and cook, stirring occasionally, until reduced to a thick pulp.

Remove from the heat and stir in the parsley and oregano. Season and divide between the thyme-flavored tartlet cases.

Broil the red pepper until it is soft and charred on all sides. Allow to cool, then peel off the skin. Remove the core and seeds, and cut the pepper into fine strips.

Garnish with strips of red pepper and slices of olive.

Toasted Chick Peas

These nibbles can be made 2 or 3 days in advance and stored in a screw-top jar. Warm up before serving.

2 tablespoons olive oil
2 garlic cloves, crushed
$1\frac{1}{2}$ lb cooked or drained canned chick peas
salt

Heat half the oil in a heavy frying pan over a low heat. Add 1 garlic clove and half the chick peas and cook, stirring frequently but gently, for 5 minutes. Sprinkle with salt and stir again, then transfer to a roasting pan. Repeat with the remaining oil, garlic, chick peas and more salt.

Spread the chick peas out evenly in the roasting pan. Toast in a preheated 400° oven for about 10 minutes, turning twice, until lightly colored. Serve warm.

Selection of Tartlets

Flavored Olives

These subtly flavored olives are prepared 1–2 weeks before the party. To serve, drain them and pile up in small dishes.

CARDAMOM AND ORANGE BLACK OLIVES
1 lb good quality black olives
pared rind of 1 small orange, cut into long strips
1 tablespoon cardamom seeds, bruised but not crushed
olive oil to cover
LEMON AND FENNEL GREEN OLIVES
1 lb good quality green olives
1 large lemon, thinly sliced
scant 1 teaspoon fennel seeds
olive oil to cover

For the black olives, make 2 or 3 slits in each olive with the point of a small sharp knife. Rinse well under cold running water and drain on paper towels.

Layer the olives, orange rind and cardamom seeds in a glass jar. Pour in sufficient oil to cover the olives completely. Seal the jars and keep in a cool place for 1–2 weeks.

For the green olives, make 2 or 3 slits in each olive, then layer in a glass jar with slices of lemon and fennel seeds. Add sufficient oil to cover the olives. Seal and keep in a cool, dark place for at least a week before serving.

Punch

This delicious punch makes a refreshing alternative to plain white wine.

5 pints cold Lapsang Souchong tea
2½ cups Cointreau
twelve bottles of champagne
ice cubes
sliced oranges, sliced limes and fresh borage flowers, to decorate

Mix the tea and Cointreau together in a large punch bowl. Cover and chill.

Add the champagne at the last minute, just before your guests arrive. Finish with ice cubes, orange and lime slices and borage.

TRADITIONAL CELEBRATIONS

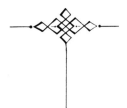

In this chapter we have menu suggestions for celebrations that only happen once in a lifetime—occasions such as a Christening, Twenty-First Birthday and Silver Wedding Anniversary—as well as celebrations which occur annually, such as Christmas, New Year's Eve and Easter. These also include a romantic St. Valentine's Day dinner for two and a St. Andrew's Night Dinner—celebrated by those of Scottish descent all over the world on November 30th. Then there are those less formal occasions that are just as traditional—a Harvest Supper, Thanksgiving Dinner and a Children's Party.

As part of the menus, we make suggestions for wines suitable to drink with the food. These are only suggestions, intended to be guidelines for those who, like me, spend ages racking their brains trying to think not only of what to cook but also of what to drink with it when it's cooked.

Silver Wedding for 30 (see page 110)

SILVER WEDDING FOR 30

This very special occasion warrants a luxurious feast, and those guests invited to celebrate the Silver Wedding will feel extremely pleased to share this buffet dinner.

For an occasion as special as this, the table decorations must be special too. To carry through the silver theme, silvery-green foliage such as eucalyptus, Lambs' Ears, Stachys and Fresh Honesty could be mixed with gray Senecio and white flowers. There are people who don't like white flowers, but I think they are lovely. Alternatively, the silvery-green and gray foliage could be arranged in sprays on white tablecloths.

SILVER WEDDING FOR 30

SEAFOOD PLATTER
WITH

SPICY TOMATO AND ONION SAUCE

SWEET AND SOUR SAUCE

TARRAGON MAYONNAISE

SOUR CREAM AND LEMON SAUCE

DARK RYE BREAD

STANDING RIB ROAST WITH MANGO AND
HORSERADISH SAUCE

GLAZED HAM WITH MUSTARD SAUCE

CUCUMBER AND FENNEL SALAD

BROCCOLI AND ASPARAGUS SALAD

CURRIED NEW POTATO SALAD

GREEN SALAD

RUM BAVAROIS WITH CHERRY SAUCE

SILVER WEDDING CAKE (SEE PAGE 186)

SUGGESTED WINES: CHAMPAGNE BEFORE THE
MEAL, AND WITH THE SILVER WEDDING CAKE AT
THE END; ICED AQUAVIT WITH THE FIRST COURSE.
ALTERNATIVELY, POUILLY FUMÉ OR SANCERRE AS
APERITIF AND WITH THE FIRST COURSE. A FINE
RED, SUCH AS A BURGUNDY, WITH THE BEEF

Seafood Platter

The following selection of seafoods may be made more elaborate with the addition of freshly cooked lobster and crab, and oysters on the half shell—when in season. Cook the squid and mussels the day before. Make the tarragon mayonnaise, spicy tomato and onion sauce, and sweet and sour sauce the day before. Also, slice the smoked salmon, if necessary, and cook the shrimp and crayfish if using fresh ones.

2 lb smoked mackerel fillet with peppercorns, or smoked trout
fillet or sturgeon fillet
4 lb peeled cooked shrimp, thawed if frozen
2 lb soused, marinated or pickled herrings, drained
2 lb smoked salmon, thinly sliced
4 lb sliced dark rye bread
butter curls
30 cooked crayfish or langoustines, in their shells
2 bottles of aquavit, well chilled in freezer
MARINATED SQUID
6 lb small squid, cleaned thoroughly
1 cup olive oil
2 large onions, finely chopped
8 garlic cloves, crushed
salt and pepper
juice of 2 lemons
6 tablespoons finely chopped fresh parsley
STEAMED MUSSELS
8 lb mussels in their shells, scrubbed (discard any that are not
tightly closed)
$1\frac{1}{4}$ cups dry white wine
few fresh parsley sprigs
2 onions, thinly sliced
4 garlic cloves, crushed
2 bay leaves
few fresh thyme sprigs
SPICY TOMATO AND ONION SAUCE
1 tablespoon olive oil
2 large onions, finely chopped
2 fresh green chilies, seeded and chopped
$1\frac{1}{2}$ lb canned tomatoes
2 garlic cloves, crushed
2 tablespoons red wine vinegar
salt
1 teaspoon sugar
SWEET AND SOUR SAUCE
$\frac{2}{3}$ cup fresh orange juice
2 tablespoons tomato paste
$\frac{1}{4}$ cup white wine vinegar
3 tablespoons clear honey
1 teaspoon paprika
few drops of Tabasco
1 garlic clove, crushed
salt and pepper

TARRAGON MAYONNAISE
$\frac{1}{4}$ cup white wine vinegar
2 teaspoons dried tarragon
2 large egg yolks
1 teaspoon mustard powder
salt and pepper
$1\frac{1}{4}$ cups olive oil
1 tablespoon lemon juice
SOUR CREAM AND LEMON SAUCE
$1\frac{1}{4}$ cups sour cream
finely grated rind and juice of 1 lemon
2 teaspoons Dijon mustard
salt and pepper
GARNISH
finely chopped fresh parsley
watercress
capers
chopped fresh dill
3 large red onions, thinly sliced
30 lemon wedges
fresh parsley sprigs

To prepare the squid, cut the bodies into rings about $\frac{3}{4}$ inch thick, cut the flaps or wings into strips, and leave the tentacles whole.

Heat 4 tablespoons of the olive oil in a very large saucepan, or use two saucepans. Add the onions and a quarter of the garlic and fry gently for 5 minutes, until softened but not browned. Add the prepared squid and season well. Cover the pan(s) with a tightly fitting lid and cook the squid gently until it gives off its pink juices, then continue to cook the squid in its own juices for about 20–25 minutes, until very tender. Transfer the squid to a very large mixing bowl, cover and allow to cool. Refrigerate the squid until well chilled, or overnight.

Drain off all of the juices from the squid into a saucepan. Bring the juices to a boil and boil gently until they are reduced to about $\frac{1}{4}$ cup. Allow to cool.

Put the lemon juice into a large mixing bowl with the remaining garlic and seasoning and stir well until the salt dissolves. Beat in the remaining olive oil, squid juices and parsley. Add the squid to the dressing and mix. Cover and refrigerate at least 3 hours before serving.

To prepare the mussels, put them into two large saucepans and add half of the white wine to each pan. Divide the remaining ingredients between the two pans. Cover the saucepans tightly and cook over a high heat for 3–5 minutes, until the mussels are all open. Shake the pans frequently to ensure even cooking. Pour the mussels into colanders placed over mixing bowls and leave to drain and cool. (Discard any mussels that have remained closed.)

Put the mussels into clean bowls. Strain the mussel liquid through clean cheesecloth to free it of any grit, then pour it over the mussels. Cover the bowls with plastic wrap and refrigerate until ready to serve.

To make the spicy tomato and onion sauce, heat the oil in a saucepan and add the onions and chilies. Fry gently for about 5 minutes, until softened but not browned. Meanwhile, drain the tomatoes and reserve the juice. Cut the tomatoes in half and remove the seeds, then roughly chop the flesh. Add the chopped tomatoes, tomato juice, garlic, vinegar, salt and sugar to the onions and chilies. Bring to a boil, then reduce the heat, cover and simmer for 25–30 minutes. Allow to cool, then purée in a blender or food processor or press through a nylon sieve. Pour the sauce into a serving bowl, cover and refrigerate until ready to serve.

To make the sweet and sour sauce, put all of the ingredients into a saucepan and stir well. Bring to a boil, then reduce the heat and simmer gently for about 20 minutes, until slightly thickened and mellow in flavor. Allow to cool, then pour into a serving bowl. Cover and refrigerate until ready to serve.

To make the tarragon mayonnaise, put the vinegar and tarragon into a small saucepan. Bring to a boil, then boil gently until reduced to about 1 tablespoon. Cool. Put the egg yolks into a medium-size mixing bowl with the mustard powder, seasoning and the tarragon vinegar (including the tarragon). Gradually whisk in the olive oil in a very slow trickle, using a wire whisk or an electric beater, until the mayonnaise begins to thicken, then the oil may be added a little more quickly. When all of the oil has been added, whisk in the lemon juice, adding a little more to suit your own taste if liked. Spoon the mayonnaise into a serving bowl and cover closely with plastic wrap. Refrigerate until ready to serve.

To make the sour cream and lemon sauce, mix the sour cream with the lemon rind and juice, mustard and seasoning. Pour into a serving bowl, cover and refrigerate until ready to serve.

To serve, pile the mussels in a large serving bowl. Pour the squid and its marinade into a deep serving platter, and sprinkle with chopped parsley. Cut the mackerel (or trout or sturgeon) into small pieces and arrange them neatly on a large serving platter; garnish with watercress and a sprinkling of capers. Put the shrimp into a large serving dish and sprinkle with chopped dill. Cut the herrings into small pieces and arrange them attractively on a large serving platter: scatter with red onion rings and chopped parsley. Arrange the smoked salmon on a large platter and garnish with lemon wedges and sprigs of parsley.

Place the bowl of mussels, raised on a stand, on the table, then arrange the platters of fish, the sauces, the rye bread and small dishes of butter curls neatly around it. Drape the crayfish over the edge of the bowl containing the mussels. Serve with iced Aquavit presented in chilled schnapps or shot glasses.

Standing Rib Roast with Mango and Horseradish Sauce

———— ◆●◆ ————

Cook the beef the day before the party, putting it in the refrigerator when it has cooled completely. Take it out of the refrigerator at least 2 hours before serving, to allow it to come to room temperature. Make the mango and horseradish sauce a day ahead, and keep it in a covered container in the refrigerator.

12-lb standing rib roast of beef, chined
2 tablespoons olive oil
salt and pepper
finely chopped fresh parsley, for garnish
MANGO AND HORSERADISH SAUCE
1 ripe mango
1 cup heavy cream
¼ cup prepared white horseradish
2 tablespoons finely chopped fresh parsley

Wipe the beef well with paper towels. Stand the roast in a large roasting pan, fat side uppermost. Rub the meat all over with the olive oil, then season well.

Roast the beef in a preheated 425° oven for 1 hour, then reduce the oven temperature to 375° and continue roasting for a further 1½ hours, basting the beef frequently during cooking with its drippings.

Remove the beef from the oven and allow to cool, then cover loosely with foil and refrigerate overnight.

To make the mango and horseradish sauce, carefully peel the mango and cut the flesh away from the pit. Chop the mango flesh into small pieces. Whip the cream until thick. Mix the mango, horseradish, cream and parsley together, then spoon into a serving bowl. Cover and refrigerate until ready to serve.

To serve the beef, carefully cut away the feather bones from the meat with a sharp knife, if the butcher has not already done this. Leave the rib bones still attached. Trim off as much fat as is possible from the meat, leaving behind just a thin layer. Cover the fat with a thin layer of finely chopped parsley—this gives a very attractive appearance. Place the beef on a board, rib bones down. Carve into thin slices down to the bones, freeing the meat from the bones with the knife held horizontally against the bones. Serve with the sauce.

Glazed Ham with Mustard Sauce

———— ◆●◆ ————

Prepare the ham a day in advance, keeping it in the refrigerator overnight, but, like the beef, remember to take it out of the refrigerator a couple of hours before serving to let it come to room temperature; food loses some of its flavor if it is served too cold. The mustard sauce can be made about 1 hour before serving and kept in a covered container in the refrigerator. If you cover your dishes with plastic wrap you can write in felt tip pen straight on to the wrap to remind yourself which dish holds savory sauces and which holds plain whipped cream!

12-lb cooked whole ham, on the bone
16 oz can of pineapple rings
½–⅔ cup glacé cherries, halved
cloves
1 cup clear honey
1 cup light brown sugar
MUSTARD SAUCE
¼ cup mustard powder
1 cup mayonnaise
½ cup sour cream

Carefully remove the skin from the ham. Score the fat deeply with an attractive diamond pattern.

Drain the pineapple rings, reserving the juice. Cut each pineapple ring equally into six. Decorate the ham attractively with the pineapple pieces and the cherries, securing them to the fat with cloves.

Place the decorated ham in a large roasting pan and carefully spoon the honey evenly all over it. Sprinkle the sugar evenly all over the honey, reserving about 3 tablespoons. Spoon about 4 tablespoons of the pineapple juice over the sugar and honey.

Bake the ham in a preheated 425° oven for about 45 minutes, basting it frequently with the sugar and honey mixture, until it is nicely glazed but not overbrowned. Remove the ham from the oven and sprinkle evenly with the reserved sugar. Allow to cool, then cover loosely with foil and refrigerate until ready to serve.

To make the mustard sauce, blend the mustard powder with ¼ cup of cold water until smooth. Cover and allow to stand for about 15 minutes. Mix the mustard, mayonnaise and sour cream together until smooth. Pour into a serving bowl, cover and refrigerate until serving.

To serve, place the ham on a stand, or a board, and decorate the end of the bone with a ham frill. Serve in slices with the sauce.

Glazed Ham with Mustard Sauce; Green Salad

Cucumber and Fennel Salad

You can salt and drain the cucumber a day in advance of the party. The whole salad can be prepared entirely several hours before serving, and kept in a cool place.

4 large cucumbers
salt and pepper
2 whole fennel bulbs, cut into fine shreds
2 bunches of scallions, finely chopped
$3\frac{1}{2}$ cups plain yogurt

Thinly peel the cucumbers, cut them in half lengthwise and scoop out the seeds. Cut the cucumber halves crosswise into slices about $\frac{1}{4}$ inch thick. Put the slices into a large mixing bowl and sprinkle lightly with salt. Cover and let stand for at least 1 hour (the salt extracts the excess water, and crisps the cucumber). Rinse the cucumber and drain well in a colander or pat dry with paper towels.

Put the cucumber, fennel and chopped scallions into a large salad bowl. Add the yogurt and seasoning. Mix together until well mixed. Cover the salad and refrigerate until ready to serve.

113

Broccoli and Asparagus Salad

The peppers, broccoli and asparagus can all be cooked the day before the party, and the dressing made, thereby saving you quite a lot of work on the actual day. Beat up the dressing again just before adding the vegetables.

4 red peppers
2 green peppers
3 lb broccoli
2 lb asparagus
salt and pepper
3 tablespoons red wine vinegar
2 teaspoons Dijon mustard
4 garlic cloves, crushed
$\frac{2}{3}$ cup olive oil

Put the peppers on a rack in a broiler pan, and cook under a hot broiler until they are very soft and the skins are charred, turning them frequently during cooking. Remove the peppers from the pan to a bowl and allow to cool.

Peel the stalks of the broccoli up to the heads. Remove the heads and cut them into small florets. Cut the stalks into thin slices, on a slant.

Trim the asparagus spears and scrape the stalks, using a potato peeler, up to the tips. Cook the asparagus in boiling salted water for 3–5 minutes, depending on the thickness of the spears, until they are only just tender. Remove the asparagus from the water to a colander, then refresh them under a cold tap. Drain the asparagus very well on paper towels.

Cut the tips off the asparagus spears and set them aside. Slice the asparagus stalks thinly, on a slant.

Cook the broccoli in the same boiling water for 2–3 minutes, until it too is only just tender. Drain the broccoli well in a colander and refresh it under a cold tap. Drain very well.

Peel the cooked peppers, retaining any juices, and remove the core and seeds. Cut the peppers into long, thin strips.

Put the vinegar into a large salad bowl with the mustard, garlic and seasoning and stir well until the salt dissolves. Beat in the olive oil and the reserved juices from the peppers.

Just before serving, add the broccoli, sliced asparagus stalks and pepper strips to the dressing and mix lightly together. Garnish with the reserved asparagus tips and serve.

Silver Wedding Cake (page 186)

Curried New Potato Salad

This salad can be made entirely a day, or even 2 days, before the party, but add the parsley garnish at the last minute. Keep the salad in its serving bowl, covered, in the refrigerator. Remove 1–2 hours before serving.

5 lb small new potatoes
5 teaspoons white wine vinegar
1 teaspoon mustard powder
3 garlic cloves, crushed
salt and pepper
6 tablespoons olive oil
$3\frac{1}{2}$ cups mayonnaise
3 tablespoons mild curry powder
chopped fresh parsley, for garnish

Cook the potatoes in boiling salted water until they are just tender. Drain well and allow to cool. Cut larger potatoes into thick slices.

Put the vinegar into a large mixing bowl with the mustard, garlic and seasoning and stir until the salt dissolves. Beat in the olive oil. Add the cooled potatoes to the dressing and mix together gently until the potatoes are well coated with the dressing.

Mix the mayonnaise and curry powder together. Pour over the potatoes and carefully fold together well.

Spoon the salad into a large serving bowl and sprinkle with parsley. Cover and refrigerate until ready to serve.

Green Salad

Hard-boil the eggs the day before the party. Make the basic vinaigrette dressing 2 or 3 days in advance, but add the eggs and herbs on the day. Wash and tear the lettuce into shreds a couple of days before the party, keeping it in a plastic bag in the refrigerator. Put a piece of paper towel in the bag too—this helps to prevent the lettuce from discoloring.

2 tablespoons white wine vinegar
2 teaspoons Dijon mustard
4 garlic cloves, crushed
salt and pepper
$\frac{1}{2}$ cup olive oil
6 hard-boiled eggs, finely chopped
6 tablespoons finely chopped fresh parsley
3 tablespoons snipped fresh chives
2 heads iceberg, romaine, Boston or bibb lettuce, shredded

Put the vinegar into a large salad bowl with the mustard, garlic and seasoning and stir until the salt dissolves. Beat in the olive oil. Add the chopped eggs, parsley and chives and mix well. Just before serving, add the lettuce to the dressing and toss lightly together.

Rum Bavarois with Fresh Cherry Sauce

Make the bavarois and the cherry sauce the day before the party. You will need to make four bavarois to serve 30 people, but this quantity of cherry sauce is plenty for 30. A microwave oven can be used to speed up the making of the custard for the bavarois.

BAVAROIS (makes one)
$2\frac{1}{2}$ cups milk
1 vanilla bean, split lengthwise
12 large egg yolks
$\frac{1}{2}$ cup sugar
8 teaspoons unflavored gelatin
$2\frac{1}{2}$ cups heavy cream
3 tablespoons dark rum

CHERRY SAUCE
3 lb dark cherries, pitted and thawed if frozen
$\frac{2}{3}$ cup sugar
3 tablespoons arrowroot
3 tablespoons kirsch

DECORATION
$2\frac{1}{2}$ cups heavy cream
1 teaspoon vanilla extract
1 tablespoon sugar
1 lb fresh dark cherries, with stalks left on

To make the bavarois, put the milk into a saucepan with the vanilla bean and bring almost to a boil. Remove from the heat, cover and leave to infuse for 5 minutes. Remove the vanilla bean.

Put the egg yolks and sugar into a heatproof mixing bowl, and beat lightly together. Beat in the hot milk. Place the bowl over a large saucepan of hot, but not boiling, water. Stir the custard, over a low heat, until it is thick enough to coat the back of the wooden spoon thinly. Immediately when the custard thickens, strain it through a fine nylon sieve into a clean large mixing bowl.

Put 6 tablespoons of cold water into a small mixing bowl and sprinkle the gelatin evenly over the surface.

Allow to soak for a few minutes until the gelatin swells and turns opaque. Add the softened gelatin to the hot custard, and stir well until completely dissolved. Allow the custard to cool until it is only just cold—do not allow it to set. Stir the custard frequently while it is cooling to prevent a skin from forming.

Whip the cream with the rum until it will hold soft peaks. Carefully fold the cream and the custard together, until no trace of white remains. Pour the custard mixture into a 5-pint ring mold or angel cake pan. Cover the mold with plastic wrap to prevent the delicately flavored bavarois from absorbing flavors from other foods and refrigerate until set. Make three more bavarois in the same way.

To make the cherry sauce, put 1 lb of the cherries into a saucepan with $1\frac{1}{4}$ cups of water and the sugar. Cover and cook gently for about 30 minutes, until the cherries are very soft. Purée the cooked cherries and their juice in a blender or food processor. Strain the purée through a nylon sieve into a clean saucepan. Dissolve the arrowroot in 4 tablespoons of cold water and stir it into the cherry purée. Bring to a boil, stirring all the time until the sauce thickens and clears. Reduce the heat and cook gently for about 3 minutes, stirring constantly. Stir the remaining cherries into the sauce and cook for about 10 minutes longer until they are only just soft. (If using frozen cherries, remove the sauce from the heat and stir in the cherries—there is no need for further cooking.)

Pour the cherry sauce into a large bowl and stir in the kirsch. Cover the surface of the sauce with plastic wrap to prevent a skin forming. Allow to cool, then refrigerate until quite cold.

To unmold the bavarois, dip the molds, one at a time, up to the rim in very hot water for 5 seconds. Remove from the water and dry the mold. Place a flat serving plate on top of the mold, then invert the mold and the plate together. Holding the plate and mold firmly together, shake sharply to free the bavarois. Carefully lift off the mold.

Whip the cream for the decoration with the vanilla extract and sugar until it is thick but not buttery. Put the cream into a pastry bag fitted with a medium-size star tube. Pipe cream around the base of each bavarois, then decorate with cherries. Keep refrigerated until serving.

THANKSGIVING DINNER FOR 12

Thanksgiving is celebrated in the United States on the fourth Thursday in November. It is also celebrated by expatriate Americans all over the world. Thanksgiving is a family time—children come home (with their own children) to be with their parents, and the generations enjoy together the holiday weekend that follows.

This dinner starts with a delicious punch. The golden roast turkey is stuffed with a chestnut and cornbread mixture, and garnished with pears filled with cranberry sauce. Sweet potatoes with pineapple, glazed onions with peas, and roast potatoes accompany the bird, providing delicious sweet and sour contrasts. To complete the feast comes a pumpkin cheesecake, with layers of orange and creamy white, garnished with green pistachio nuts. Later on, there are two sorts of pecan cookies to serve with coffee.

THANKSGIVING DINNER FOR 12

HOT CIDER CUP WITH BAKED APPLES

ROAST TURKEY WITH CHESTNUT AND CORNBREAD STUFFING

GARNISHED WITH PEAR HALVES FILLED WITH CRANBERRY SAUCE

SWEET POTATOES WITH PINEAPPLE

GLAZED ONIONS WITH PEAS

ROAST POTATOES

PUMPKIN CHEESECAKE

PECAN COOKIES

SUGGESTED WINE: A VERY GOOD DRY WHITE WINE WITH THE TURKEY. CHABLIS WOULD BE IDEAL, OR CALIFORNIA CHARDONNAY. FOR THE DESSERT A MUSCAT DESSERT WINE—MUSCAT DE BAUMES DE VENISE OR CALIFORNIA MUSCAT

Pecan Cookies

These can conveniently be made a couple of days in advance and stored in an airtight tin. Traditionally they are served at the end of the meal, but in England they can also be handed round with the pre-dinner drink.

PECAN COOKIES I
$\frac{2}{3}$ cup all-purpose flour
$\frac{1}{3}$ cup cornstarch
$\frac{3}{4}$ teaspoon baking powder
pinch of salt
2 teaspoons ground ginger
1 teaspoon apple pie spice
1 teaspoon ground cinnamon
$\frac{1}{2}$ cup (2 oz) finely chopped pecans
6 tablespoons unsalted butter
$\frac{1}{2}$ cup light brown sugar
3 tablespoons corn syrup
30 pecan halves, to decorate
PECAN COOKIES II
1 large egg white
$\frac{1}{4}$ cup sugar
$\frac{3}{4}$ cup (3 oz) finely ground pecans
small pieces of pecan, to decorate

To make Pecan Cookies I, lightly grease several baking sheets.

Sift the flour, cornstarch, baking powder, salt and the spices into a bowl. Stir in the chopped pecans.

Beat the butter with the sugars until very soft, light and fluffy. Beat in the corn syrup, then mix in the flour and nut mixture. Knead the dough very lightly on a floured surface until smooth.

Divide the dough into 30 walnut-sized pieces. Roll each one into a ball and place on the greased baking sheets, spacing the balls well apart. Flatten each ball of dough with a fork, then press a pecan half into the center of each one.

Bake in a preheated 350° oven for 15–20 minutes, until just lightly browned around the edges. Allow to cool slightly on the baking sheets, then remove with a long metal spatula to wire racks to cool completely.

To make Pecan Cookies II, line several baking sheets with rice paper.

Beat the egg white until it is very stiff, then fold in the sugar and the ground pecans. Put the mixture into a pastry bag fitted with a large star tube. Pipe stars of the mixture onto the rice paper, spacing them apart. Press a small piece of pecan into the center of each star.

Bake the cookies in a preheated 350° oven for 20 minutes, until firm. Allow to cool completely, then remove the cookies from the rice paper, tearing it away from the edges.

To serve, arrange both types of cookies together on a doily-lined plate or in a basket.

Hot Cider Cup with Baked Apples

Makes 4 quarts.

3 large apples, wiped and cored
4 quarts dry hard cider
6 cloves
6 whole allspice berries
2 teaspoons grated nutmeg
6-oz can frozen lemonade concentrate
6-oz can frozen orange juice concentrate
1 cup light brown sugar
To serve:
sugar
cinnamon sticks

Cut the apples in half crosswise and place them, cut side down, in an ovenproof dish. Bake in a preheated 350° oven for 10 minutes or until tender when tested with a fork.

Meanwhile, pour 2½ cups cider into a very large pan. Add the spices; cover and simmer for 10 minutes.

Add the remaining cider, undiluted fruit juice concentrates and brown sugar. Heat through without boiling, stirring occasionally.

Pour the mixture carefully into a large heated punch bowl.

Add the apples, skin side up, and sprinkle them with a little sugar.

Serve at once, ladling the punch into heatproof punch cups. Garnish each cup with a short cinnamon stick.

Roast Turkey with Chestnut and Cornbread Stuffing

If at all possible, get a fresh turkey, not a frozen one. The texture and flavor of a fresh bird is incomparable. Make the cornbread for the stuffing a few days before and store it in an airtight tin. Or make it well ahead and freeze it. The stuffing can be prepared a day ahead, but the turkey should not be stuffed until just before cooking. The giblet stock can be made up to 3 days in advance and kept in the refrigerator.

13-lb oven-ready turkey
6 tablespoons unsalted butter, softened
salt and pepper
pear halves filled with cranberry sauce (see page 120)
and watercress, for garnish

STUFFING
8 tablespoons (1 stick) unsalted butter
3 cups finely chopped onions
2 lb pork sausage
1 lb fresh or canned unsweetened chestnut purée
2 cups crumbled cornbread (see page 119), (or fresh white breadcrumbs)
3 tablespoons mixed dried herbs
4 tablespoons chopped fresh parsley
finely grated rind of 1 lemon
1 large egg, beaten
GRAVY
the giblets from the turkey
1 onion, roughly chopped
1 carrot, roughly chopped
1 bay leaf
fresh parsley sprig
fresh thyme sprig
1 garlic clove, unskinned
about 3 tablespoons flour
1 cup light cream or half-and-half

Wipe the turkey well, inside and out, with paper towels. Using a very small sharp knife, carefully remove the wishbone from the neck cavity—this will make carving easier.

To make the stuffing, melt the butter in a frying pan, then pour off half into a small bowl and set aside. Add the onions to the frying pan and cook very gently for about 10–15 minutes, until soft but not brown. Allow to cool.

Put all of the remaining ingredients for the stuffing into a large mixing bowl. Add the softened onions and the reserved butter, then season very well with salt and pepper. Knead the ingredients together until they are thoroughly blended. To test for seasoning, fry a little of the stuffing until cooked, then taste. Adjust the seasoning if necessary.

Stuff the neck end of the turkey with the stuffing, then truss the bird neatly. Place the turkey in a large roasting pan. Spread with the softened butter, then season well with salt and pepper. Cover the turkey with foil. Any remaining stuffing can be placed in a roasting pan and cooked for the final 30 minutes with the turkey.

Roast the turkey in the center of a preheated 375° oven for 3½–4 hours, removing the foil for the last hour to brown the skin. Baste the turkey frequently during cooking. Test the turkey for doneness by piercing the thighs at their thickest parts; if the juices run clear, the turkey is cooked (if the juices are pink, then continue cooking a little longer). Be sure to test both thighs; sometimes one side can be cooked before the other.

While the turkey is cooking, prepare the stock for the gravy. Put the giblets into a saucepan with the onion, carrot, herbs and garlic. Season well with salt and pepper. Bring slowly to a boil, then skim off any scum from the surface. Reduce the heat, partially cover the saucepan and simmer gently for about 2 hours. Strain the stock into a measuring cup and add water, if necessary, to yield 2½ cups.

Roast Turkey with Chestnut and Cornbread Stuffing; Pear Halves Filled with Cranberry Sauce

When the turkey is cooked, lift it carefully from the roasting pan onto a large serving dish. Loosely cover with foil and allow to stand for 30 minutes before carving.

To make the gravy, tilt the roasting pan and very carefully skim off all of the fat from the surface of the juices in the pan. Stir the flour into the juices left in the pan, using a wire whisk, then beat in the turkey stock. Bring the gravy to a boil, beating all the time until the gravy thickens. By this time the residue from the roasting pan will have dissolved into the gravy, so the gravy can be strained into a saucepan, for easier handling. Simmer the gravy gently for 15 minutes, to cook off the raw flour taste. Season the gravy with salt and pepper, then stir in the cream. Allow to heat through, but not to boil. Pour the gravy into a hot serving boat.

To serve the turkey, remove the trussing string, then garnish with pear halves filled with cranberry sauce, and watercress.

Cornbread

$1\frac{2}{3}$ cups cornmeal
$\frac{2}{3}$ cup all-purpose flour
1 teaspoon salt
1 tablespoon baking powder
12 tablespoons ($1\frac{1}{2}$ sticks) unsalted butter
2 large eggs, beaten
$1\frac{1}{4}$ cups milk

Grease and flour a loaf pan, about $9 \times 5 \times 2\frac{1}{2}$ inches.

Sift the cornmeal, flour, salt and baking powder into a mixing bowl. Rub in the butter until the mixture resembles fine breadcrumbs. Add the beaten eggs and the milk, and mix to a soft consistency.

Pour the mixture into the prepared loaf pan. Bake in the center of a preheated 400° oven for 40–45 minutes, until well risen, golden brown and firm to the touch. Carefully remove the cornbread from the pan onto a wire rack, and allow to cool.

Pear Halves Filled with Cranberry Sauce

You can make the cranberry sauce several days ahead, and cook the pears the day before. They can either be served around the roast turkey, or on a separate dish of their own.

1¾ cups sugar
thinly pared rind and juice of 3 lemons
6 large ripe, firm pears
½ lb fresh cranberries
4 teaspoons arrowroot
finely grated rind of 2 limes

Put 2½ cups of cold water into a saucepan with sugar and 1¼ cups lemon rind and juice. Heat slowly until the sugar dissolves, then bring to a boil. Boil gently for 10 minutes.

Peel the pears, leaving the stalks on. Very carefully cut each pear in half lengthwise, cutting right through the stalk, so that each half retains a stalk. Using a teaspoon, scoop out the core from each pear half.

Put the pear halves into the hot lemon syrup and cook very gently for about 20 minutes, until they are only just tender. Pour the pears and the syrup into a large bowl and allow to cool, then cover and refrigerate.

Put the cranberries and remaining sugar into a saucepan, with just enough cold water to cover them. Cover the saucepan and cook the cranberries gently for 15–20 minutes, until they pop and soften. Pour the cranberries into a nylon sieve placed over the mixing bowl, to drain off the juice.

Return the cranberry juice to the saucepan. Dissolve the arrowroot in a little cold water to make a smooth paste, then stir it into the cranberry juice. Bring to a boil, stirring all the time until the sauce thickens and clears. Stir the cranberries and lime rind into the sauce. Pour the cranberry sauce into a bowl and cover the surface closely with plastic wrap, to prevent a skin from forming. Allow to cool, then refrigerate.

To serve, lift the pear halves from the syrup with a slotted spoon, and drain them well on paper towels. Fill each pear half with cranberry sauce. Put any remaining sauce into a serving bowl and serve separately. Arrange the pears around the cooked turkey. Or, if the serving platter is too small, arrange them on a bed of redleaf lettuce on a separate dish.

Sweet Potatoes with Pineapple

The pineapple can be prepared and the sweet potatoes parboiled in the morning for dinner that evening. Roast potatoes, the third vegetable accompaniment, can also be peeled in the morning, ready for cooking; keep them covered with cold water to prevent discoloration.

1 medium-sized pineapple
3 lb sweet potatoes or yams
salt and pepper
12 tablespoons (1½ sticks) unsalted butter
chopped fresh parsley, for garnish

Cut away all of the skin from the pineapple, making sure to remove all of the little "eyes." Cut the pineapple into eight wedges lengthwise, then cut away the hard center core from each wedge. Cut the wedges into ½-inch thick triangular-shaped pieces. Cover and set aside until needed.

Peel the sweet potatoes and cut them into thick slices, immediately putting them into cold water in a large saucepan. Add 2 teaspoons of salt to the water and bring to a boil, then drain.

Melt the butter in a large ovenproof dish or roasting pan. Add the parboiled sweet potato slices to the dish and turn in the butter until well coated. Add seasoning.

Bake on the top shelf of the oven with the turkey, or in a second oven, preheated to 400°, for 30 minutes.

Add the pineapple pieces and baste well with butter. Continue cooking for about another 45 minutes, until the sweet potatoes are golden brown and tender.

Spoon the sweet potatoes and pineapple into a warmed serving dish and sprinkle with chopped parsley.

Glazed Onions with Peas

A quick way to skin tiny onions is to cover them with boiling water, leave for a minute and then drain them. Their skins will slip off easily, thereby saving you from flowing tears if you laboriously skin them! This preparation of the onions can be done in advance.

2 tablespoons olive oil
2 tablespoons unsalted butter
3 tablespoons sugar
2 lb small white onions, skinned
1½ lb frozen peas
salt and pepper

Heat the olive oil and the butter in a very large sauté pan or frying pan with a lid. Sprinkle the sugar into the pan, and heat gently until the sugar dissolves and turns a golden caramel color.

Add the onions to the pan and shake well until they

Pumpkin Cheesecake

are evenly coated with the caramel mixture. Cover the pan tightly, reduce the heat and cook very gently for 45 minutes to 1 hour, until the onions are tender yet still retain their shape. Shake the pan frequently to ensure even cooking.

Add the peas to the pan and cook for a further 20 minutes. Season well.

Pumpkin Cheesecake

The cheesecake can be prepared the day before Thanksgiving. Add the decoration shortly before serving.

4 cups diced pumpkin
$1\frac{1}{2}$ cups sugar
thinly pared rind and juice of 3 oranges
6 passion fruit
6 tablespoons unflavored gelatin
8 tablespoons (1 stick) unsalted butter
3 tablespoons corn syrup
12 oz ($4\frac{1}{2}$ cups) crushed graham crackers
4 large eggs, separated
finely grated rind of 3 lemons
$\frac{1}{4}$ cup lemon juice
$1\frac{1}{2}$ lb cream cheese
2 cups heavy cream
1 cup heavy cream, whipped, and a few skinned pistachio nuts, to decorate

Put the pumpkin into a large saucepan with $\frac{1}{2}$ cup of the sugar and the orange rind and juice. Cover the saucepan and cook the pumpkin gently for about 45 minutes, until it is very soft. Allow to cool slightly, then purée the pumpkin in a blender or food processor.

Cut each passion fruit in half and scoop out the seeds

into a nylon sieve placed over a small bowl. Work the seeds in the sieve with the back of a spoon until all of the juice is extracted into the bowl. Stir the juices into the pumpkin purée.

Put 3 tablespoons cold water into a small bowl and sprinkle 2 tablespoons of gelatin evenly over the surface. Allow to soak for a few minutes until the gelatin swells and turns opaque. Stand the bowl of gelatin in a pan of hot water until the gelatin dissolves and becomes very hot. Stir the gelatin into the pumpkin purée, then put the purée aside to cool.

Put the butter and corn syrup into a large saucepan and heat gently until the butter melts. Stir in the crushed graham crackers and mix well. Spread the mixture evenly over the bottom of a 12-inch springform pan, pressing gently to firm. Refrigerate the crumb crust while making the cheese mixture.

Beat the egg yolks with the remaining sugar and the lemon rind until the mixture is very thick, and will hold a ribbon trail for at least 5 seconds when the beater is lifted out. Gradually beat in the lemon juice.

Beat the cream cheese until it is very soft, then gradually beat in the lemon mixture.

Dissolve the remaining gelatin in 6 tablespoons of water, as above. Whip the cream until it will hold soft peaks. Beat the egg whites until stiff.

Mix the dissolved gelatin into the cheese and lemon mixture, then quickly fold in the cream, followed by the egg whites. Pour the mixture into the crumb crust. Refrigerate for at least 1 hour until set.

Remove the set cheesecake from the refrigerator, then very carefully pour the cold, but not yet set, pumpkin mixture on top. Smooth the surface. Refrigerate for at least 3 hours or preferably overnight, until well set.

To serve, carefully run a long metal spatula around the side of the cheesecake to loosen it from the pan, then gently remove the side of the pan. Place the cheesecake on a serving plate. Decorate with whipped cream and pistachio nuts. Refrigerate until ready to serve.

New Year's Eve Dinner for 12

There is no nicer way to welcome in the New Year than with your friends around you, enjoying a delicious dinner. A formal dinner, with champagne to drink beforehand and at midnight, is perfect for the occasion, with fireworks (weather permitting!) after dinner, to pass the time until midnight. Ask the tallest, darkest man present to cross the threshold of your front door with a piece of coal and a piece of bread at the very stroke of midnight. This Scottish tradition, called first-footing, which has spread worldwide, brings luck.

The dinner in this suggested menu is well balanced and each course distinctively delicious. The first course of scallop brochettes with saffron rice and a shrimp sauce makes an elegant beginning to the meal. The main course consists of wine-glazed roast loin of lamb, with apples coated with Cumberland sauce for garnish. This is followed by a plate of cheeses. The dessert is a champagne syllabub.

NEW YEAR'S EVE DINNER FOR 12

SCALLOP BROCHETTES WITH SHRIMP SAUCE

WINE-GLAZED ROAST LOIN OF LAMB

APPLES GLAZED WITH CUMBERLAND SAUCE

JULIENNED ZUCCHINI IN GARLIC BUTTER

CREAMED POTATO GRATIN

GREEN BEANS

CHEESE PLATTER

CHAMPAGNE SYLLABUB

SUGGESTED WINES: A WHITE BURGUNDY WITH THE FIRST COURSE, AND A FINE CLARET WITH THE LAMB. WITH THE CHEESES EITHER OLD TAWNY PORT OR AN OLD BURGUNDY

Scallop Brochettes with Shrimp Sauce

The scallops can be marinated up to a day in advance of the party, kept in a cool place.
The saffron rice can be cooked in the morning, ready to reheat for dinner that night. The shrimp sauce can also be made in the morning up to the point where the cream and shrimp are added to it.

SAFFRON RICE
$1\frac{1}{2}$ cups long grain rice
3 cups chicken stock (see page 181)
good pinch of saffron threads
salt and pepper
BROCHETTES
24 large or sea scallops, about 4 lb, well thawed if frozen
juice of 1 lemon
salt and pepper
4 tablespoons olive oil
1 tablespoon chopped fresh dill, or 2 teaspoons dried dill
SHRIMP SAUCE
3 tablespoons butter
$\frac{1}{3}$ cup all-purpose flour
$2\frac{1}{2}$ cups fish stock (see page 181)
5 tablespoons dry white wine
3 tablespoons heavy cream
1 lb cooked peeled shrimp

Put the rice into a large saucepan with the chicken stock, saffron and seasoning. Bring to a boil and stir, then reduce the heat, cover and simmer gently until the rice is cooked and all of the stock has been absorbed. Transfer the rice to a bowl. Allow to cool, then cover and set aside until needed.

Clean the scallops thoroughly, then pat dry with paper towels. Put the lemon juice into a large shallow dish, season well with salt and pepper and stir until the salt dissolves. Stir in the olive oil and dill. Add the scallops to the marinade and turn them until they are evenly coated. Cover and put in a cool place to marinate for about $1\frac{1}{2}$ hours.

About 30 minutes before serving, reheat the rice, covered, in a hot oven. Alternatively, the rice can be reheated in the microwave, at full power, for 3–4 minutes.

To make the shrimp sauce, melt the butter in a saucepan, then stir in the flour. Gradually stir in the fish stock. Bring the sauce to a boil, stirring all the time, then reduce the heat and simmer for about 20 minutes, stirring frequently. Season the sauce well with salt and pepper. Stir in the white wine and the cream. Add the shrimp to the sauce and heat gently for about 5 minutes, just until the shrimp are thoroughly heated through. Do not overcook the shrimp, as this will make them toughen.

Meanwhile, thread the scallops onto short skewers,

two to each skewer. Cook the scallop brochettes under a hot broiler for about 6–8 minutes, turning them halfway through cooking, and basting occasionally with the marinade. Do not overcook the scallops, as they too will toughen.

To serve, spoon a small bed of saffron rice onto twelve individual heated serving plates. Place the brochettes on top of the rice. Pour the shrimp sauce into a hot serving bowl or jug and serve immediately.

Wine-glazed Roast Loin of Lamb

To serve twelve people, you will need two boneless double loin roasts. Ask your butcher to leave two rib chop bones on one end, if possible, and to remove all of the fell, the thin skin that covers the fat. Your butcher should do this for you willingly, but be sure to give him advance warning.

The stuffing for the lamb can be made the day before New Year's Eve, and the lamb prepared with the stuffing in the morning ready for roasting for dinner that night. The Cumberland sauce for the garnish can be made at any time during the week between Christmas and New Year, thereby making the finishing touch of apples glazed with Cumberland sauce very quick to put together at the last minute.

2 boneless double loin roasts of lamb
5 tablespoons olive oil
salt and pepper
2 large garlic cloves, crushed
1 cup red wine
about 2 cups beef stock
3 tablespoons unsalted butter, softened
$\frac{1}{3}$ cup all-purpose flour
apples glazed with Cumberland sauce (see page 124) and chopped fresh parsley, for garnish
HERB STUFFING
$\frac{3}{4}$ cup chopped bacon
$\frac{1}{2}$ cup shredded suet
6 cups fresh white breadcrumbs
3 tablespoons chopped fresh parsley
6 tablespoons chopped mixed fresh herbs
2 tablespoons mixed dried herbs
grated rind of $1\frac{1}{2}$ lemons
3 eggs, beaten
salt and pepper

To prepare the stuffing, fry the bacon in its own fat without browning. Mix it with the suet, breadcrumbs, parsley, herbs, lemon rind, egg and seasoning.

Place the loins of lamb on the work surface, meat side up. Very carefully remove as much excess fat as possible. Sprinkle the meat with about 2 tablespoons of the olive oil. Season well with salt and pepper and rub the garlic all over the meat.

Place the herb stuffing neatly along the center of each loin. Bring the side flaps of the meat up and over the stuffing to enclose it completely. (Depending on how your butcher has trimmed the lamb, you may need to trim off about 2 inches from each flap. This outer edge can be rather fatty, and you only need sufficient to cover the stuffing securely.) Make sure that the flaps overlap each other. Tie the meat securely with thin string at 1-inch intervals all along the roasts. Turn the roasts over and rub the remaining olive oil all over the fat. Season well with salt and pepper.

Place the roasts in a very large roasting pan. (Should your pan not be quite large enough to take both roasts, you will have to use two pans.) Roast the lamb in the center of a preheated 425° oven for 45 minutes, then reduce the heat to 350° and continue roasting for about $1\frac{3}{4}$ hours.

After the lamb has been cooking for 1 hour, pour a scant cup of the wine over the roasts. Baste the lamb with the wine for the remaining cooking time. Cook until the lamb is tender and golden brown. (If you prefer your lamb to be slightly pink, cook for about 2 hours only.)

Lift the cooked lamb carefully from the roasting pan onto a large hot serving platter. Cover loosely with foil and allow to stand for about 20 minutes, while making the gravy.

Pour all of the juices from the roasting pan into a tall jug, stand the jug in cold water and set aside for about 10 minutes to allow the fat to rise to the surface. Pour a little more red wine into the roasting pan and bring it to a boil, stirring and scraping all of the residue from the bottom of the pan. Pour this into the jug with the other juices.

Carefully skim all of the fat from the surface of the pan juices, then add enough stock to make $3\frac{1}{2}$ cups. Pour into a saucepan. Bring to a boil, then reduce the heat to a simmer. Blend the softened butter and the flour together to make a paste, then beat it, a little at a time, into the simmering liquid. Increase the heat, and bring the gravy back to a boil. Boil for 2–3 minutes, then pour into a hot serving boat or jug.

To serve, remove all of the string from the lamb. Garnish with apples glazed with Cumberland sauce, and chopped parsley. Serve with the gravy.

Julienned Zucchini in Garlic Butter

I do love something garlicky with lamb, and these zucchini are ideal. They can be cooked in advance—in the morning for dinner that night, and then reheated before dinner, if liked. The green beans, to be served with the lamb, can also be prepared ready for cooking. Chill in a plastic bag.

4 lb zucchini
8 tablespoons (1 stick) unsalted butter
2 large garlic cloves, crushed
salt and pepper

Cut the zucchini into fine shreds or julienne. Alternatively, grate them coarsely. Put the shreds into a large colander and leave to drain for about 1 hour. During this time the excess liquid will drain away from the zucchini. Pat dry with paper towels.

Melt the butter in two large frying pans and add the garlic. Divide the zucchini evenly between the two pans and season well with salt and pepper. Cook the zucchini gently for about 20–25 minutes, until they are only just tender but still retain their shape. Do not allow the zucchini to brown or to overcook. Spoon the zucchini into a large warmed serving dish.

Creamed Potato Gratin

This potato dish goes very well with all roast meat and game, but especially so with lamb. The potatoes can be mashed and put into their dish, ready for baking, well in advance, but add the cream and cheese only just before putting the dish into the oven.

6 lb potatoes, peeled
salt and pepper
12 tablespoons (1½ sticks) unsalted butter
⅔ cup milk
⅔ cup heavy cream
¾ cup freshly grated Parmesan cheese

Cook the potatoes in boiling salted water until tender. Drain well and return to the pan. Mash the potatoes with a potato masher, then beat in the butter and milk to make a creamy mixture. Season well.

Pipe the potatoes into a large ovenproof dish.

Pour the cream evenly over the potatoes, then sprinkle with the grated cheese. About 1 hour before the lamb has finished cooking, put the potatoes into the oven, with the lamb, on the top shelf. After removing the lamb, the oven temperature can be increased to 425° to brown the top of the potatoes.

Apples Glazed with Cumberland Sauce

8 Rome Beauty or Northern Spy apples
6 tablespoons unsalted butter
CUMBERLAND SAUCE
1 lb (1⅓ cups) red currant jelly
thinly pared rind and juice of 2 lemons
thinly pared rind and juice of 2 oranges
1¼ cups red wine
2 tablespoons arrowroot

Put the red currant jelly into a saucepan with the lemon and orange rinds and juice and the red wine. Bring to a boil, then reduce the heat and simmer gently for 20 minutes. Remove the rinds from the saucepan with a slotted spoon.

Wine-glazed Roast Loin of Lamb; Apples Glazed with Cumberland Sauce; Julienned Zucchini in Garlic Butter

Champagne Syllabub

The caramelized fruit decoration can be made the previous day. The syllabub can be made in the afternoon and kept, with plastic wrap over each glass, in the refrigerator until dinner time.

4 large lemons
1 large orange
2 cups champagne
6 tablespoons Grand Marnier
$\frac{2}{3}$ cup sugar
$3\frac{1}{2}$ cups heavy cream
macaroons and langues de chat cookies, to serve
DECORATION
thinly pared rind of 1 small orange
thinly pared rind of 1 small lemon
thinly pared rind of 1 lime
$\frac{1}{2}$ cup sugar

Very thinly pare the rind from the lemons and the orange, taking care not to remove any of the white pith. Squeeze the juice from the fruit and strain it. Put the rinds and juice into a mixing bowl, then pour in the champagne and Grand Marnier. Add the sugar and stir well until dissolved. Cover and leave to soak for at least 8 hours. (The remaining champagne may be stoppered and refrigerated to be served later—to toast in the New Year or to make a Mimosa for the hostess while she is completing the dinner!)

To make the decoration, cut the orange, lemon and lime rind into very, very fine shreds. Put the shreds into a saucepan with the sugar and $\frac{2}{3}$ cup of cold water. Heat very gently until the sugar dissolves, then bring to a boil. Reduce the heat and cook gently until the shreds are very soft, and the sugar and water have reduced to a heavy syrup. Pour into a small bowl and cover. Allow to cool, then refrigerate until ready to serve.

Strain the champagne liquid into a large, well-chilled mixing bowl. Discard the lemon and orange rinds. Pour the cream, in a thin stream, into the bowl, beating all the time. Continue to beat until the mixture thickens and retains its shape—take care not to overbeat as the mixture will curdle. Spoon the syllabub into twelve 8 fl oz serving glasses. Cover the glasses with plastic wrap to prevent the syllabub from absorbing flavors from other foods in the refrigerator. Refrigerate until ready to serve.

Just before serving, decorate each syllabub with the caramelized orange, lemon and lime shreds. Serve with macaroons and langues de chat cookies, or any other light crisp cookie of your choice.

Dissolve the arrowroot in a little cold water to form a smooth paste, then stir it into the wine mixture. Bring back to a boil, stirring all the time, and boil until the sauce thickens and clears.

Pour the Cumberland sauce into a bowl and cover the surface closely with plastic wrap to prevent a skin from forming. Allow to cool, then refrigerate.

Peel, quarter and core the apples. If the apples are large, cut each quarter in half again.

Melt the butter in a large frying pan, add the apple pieces and cook them gently until they are very lightly browned and only just tender—take care to retain the shape of the apples. Lift the apples from the pan to a heatproof dish and keep warm.

Just before serving the lamb, spoon sufficient Cumberland sauce over the apples to glaze them evenly. Pour the rest of the sauce into a serving bowl, and serve separately with the lamb. Garnish the lamb with the glazed apples.

CHRISTENING PARTY FOR 20

A christening is a once-in-a-lifetime event that is remembered forever, both by the parents of the child and the invited friends and relations. The lunch menu suggested here is ideal for just such an occasion. There is a delicious appetizer to be eaten in the fingers with drinks before lunch—savory pastries called pirozhkis. These are served hot, so they are very warming—especially welcome if the day has been cold. The impressive main course is a galantine of chicken. It has to be made in advance, so it is very convenient and only requires a final garnish of watercress on the day of the christening. It is accompanied by four unusual and delicious salads—a mushroom and potato salad, an avocado, orange and cucumber salad, a tomato and snow pea salad and a tossed green salad. The dessert of choux swans, filled with Grand Marnier-flavored cream and strawberries, looks very pretty. Then there is the christening cake, at the end of lunch. Instructions for making the cake can be found on page 186.

CHRISTENING PARTY FOR 20

PIROZHKI

CHICKEN GALANTINES

MUSHROOM AND POTATO SALAD
AVOCADO, ORANGE AND CUCUMBER SALAD
TOMATO AND SNOW PEA SALAD
TOSSED GREEN SALAD

CHOUX SWANS
CHRISTENING CAKE (SEE PAGE 186)

SUGGESTED WINES: CHAMPAGNE BEFORE LUNCH
AND WITH THE CAKE; A GOOD DRY WHITE WINE,
SUCH AS A CHABLIS, WITH THE MAIN COURSE

Pirozhki

Pirozhki are little golden-brown half-moon-shaped pastry parcels, filled with a delicious mixture of mushrooms, beef and hard-boiled eggs. Prepare them the day before the Christening and put them on baking sheets ready for baking. If possible, ask someone to put them into the oven just before you come home from church, so that they are ready to serve to your guests with a glass of champagne.

FILLING
2 tablespoons unsalted butter
1 large onion, finely chopped
12 oz (3 cups) mushrooms, finely chopped
juice of $\frac{1}{2}$ lemon
3 tablespoons chopped fresh parsley
1 tablespoon olive oil
1 garlic clove, crushed
1 lb very lean ground round
3 hard-boiled eggs, finely chopped
salt and pepper
PASTRY
$5\frac{1}{4}$ cups all-purpose flour
1 teaspoon salt
12 oz (3 sticks) unsalted butter
3 large eggs, beaten with 2 tablespoons cold water
beaten egg for glazing

To make the filling, melt the butter in a large frying pan, add the onion and fry gently for about 5 minutes, until softened but not browned. Add the mushrooms to the onion and continue cooking for about another 10 minutes, until the mushrooms are softened. Stir in the lemon juice and parsley, then increase the heat and boil gently until almost all of the liquid in the pan has evaporated. Remove the mushroom mixture from the pan and set it aside.

Heat the oil in the frying pan, add the garlic and cook for a few seconds. Add the ground round and cook over a moderate heat, stirring all the time, until the beef changes color. Remove from the heat, then stir in the mushroom mixture, chopped eggs and seasoning. Cover and allow to cool.

To make the pastry, sift the flour and salt into a large mixing bowl. Rub in the butter until the mixture resembles fine breadcrumbs. Mix in the beaten eggs to form a stiff dough, adding more water if necessary. Knead the dough very lightly on a floured surface until smooth. Cut the dough into two equal pieces.

Roll out one piece of dough on a floured surface to about $\frac{1}{8}$ inch thick, then cut out small rounds using a $2\frac{3}{4}$-inch plain round pastry cutter. Remove the pastry trimmings, leaving the rounds on the surface.

Place a small teaspoonful of the filling in the center of each pastry round. Moisten the edges with water, then fold each round over in half to enclose the filling. Press the edges well together to seal. As they are shaped, place

Pirozhki

the pirozhki on baking sheets, cover with foil, and refrigerate. Repeat with the remaining pastry, re-rolling the trimmings, until all of the pastry and the filling is used up. You should have about 100 pirozhki.

If possible, set your oven to come on automatically at 425° and preheat while you are at church. On your return, brush the pirozhki with beaten egg and bake for 20–25 minutes, until golden brown. Allow to cool slightly, then remove the pirozhki from the baking sheets with a metal spatula and carefully pile them into napkin-lined baskets. Hand the pirozhki around with pre-lunch drinks.

Chicken Galantines

Start to prepare the galantines 3 days before they are to be served. The stock used to cook the chickens can be clarified and used to make the aspic.

two 6-lb chickens
6-lb duck
MARINADE
¼ cup dry white wine
2 tablespoons olive oil
1 teaspoon mixed dried herbs
salt and pepper
STOCK
wing tips and bones from the chickens and duck
2 large onions, roughly chopped
2 large carrots, roughly chopped
large fresh parsley sprig
fresh thyme sprig
4 garlic cloves, unskinned
1 bay leaf
salt and pepper
FORCEMEAT
1 lb very lean veal, roughly chopped
1 lb very lean pork, roughly chopped
1 lb pork fatback, roughly chopped
livers from the chickens and duck
3 large eggs, beaten
2 cups fresh white breadcrumbs
1 tablespoon mixed dried herbs
1 teaspoon ground allspice
¼ cup chopped fresh parsley
2 large onions, finely chopped and softened in 4 tablespoons
unsalted butter
4 tablespoons unsalted butter, melted
2 tablespoons brandy
salt and pepper
½ cup (2 oz) pistachio nuts, skinned
CHAUD-FROID SAUCE
4 tablespoons unsalted butter
¼ cup all-purpose flour
3½ cups milk
1 bay leaf
1 blade of mace
4 tablespoons unflavored gelatin
¼ cup heavy cream
⅔ cup mayonnaise
⅔ cup liquid aspic
salt and pepper
GLAZE AND DECORATION
1 quart liquid aspic
1 small red pepper
watercress

Three days before
Bone the chickens and the duck as follows:

Cut off the wing tips at the second joint; put these aside for the stock. Place one chicken, breast down, on a board and make a long cut right along the center of the back, down to the bone. Working on one side, carefully cut the meat away from the bones, using a small, very sharp knife. Keep the knife close to the bones as you work. Gradually work from the center of the back down over the rib cage and down to the tip of the breast bone, freeing the legs and wings at their joints as you come to them. Having completed one side, repeat with the other side, then remove the rib cage and the back bones. To remove the bones from the legs and the wings, simply scrape the meat away from the bones. Repeat with the second chicken and the duck.

Remove as many of the white sinews from the meat as possible. Put the chickens on a large plate, loosely cover with foil, and refrigerate.

Remove all of the meat from the duck and discard the skin and fat. Put the leg and thigh meat on a plate, loosely cover with foil and refrigerate.

Cut the duck breast meat into long strips about ½ inch square. Mix the ingredients for the marinade together in a shallow dish, add the duck strips and coat them well with the marinade. Cover and refrigerate.

To make the stock, put the wing tips from the chickens and duck into a large saucepan. Cover with cold water and bring slowly to a boil. As soon as the water boils, reduce the heat and skim off all of the scum that has risen to the surface. Add all of the remaining ingredients for the stock. Partially cover the pan and simmer gently for at least 3 hours. Strain the stock through a large cheesecloth-lined colander into a large clean bowl. Allow to cool, then refrigerate.

Two days before
Make the forcemeat. Finely grind the veal, pork and fatback in a food processor (in batches) with the duck leg and thigh meat and chicken and duck livers, grinding until very smooth. Alternatively, grind the meats very finely passing them through a grinder 2 or 3 times. Put the meat into a large mixing bowl and add the remaining ingredients for the forcemeat, except the pistachio nuts. Beat very well together until smooth. To test for seasoning, cook a little forcemeat in a frying pan, taste, adjust the seasoning.

Lay the boned chicken out flat on a work surface, skin-side down. Pull the legs and wings through to the surface and lay them out evenly. Season the chickens.

Divide the forcemeat equally into 6 portions. Place one-sixth of the forcemeat down the center of one of the chickens, then arrange one-quarter of the marinated duck strips on top. Scatter over one-quarter of the pistachio nuts. Place another sixth of the forcemeat on top of the nuts. Add another quarter of the duck strips and nuts, then cover with another sixth of the forcemeat. Repeat with the second chicken.

Enclose the forcemeat in each chicken by bringing the ends and sides firmly up and over the forcemeat to cover it completely. Sew up the seams with fine string. Wrap each chicken very tightly in a double thickness of cheesecloth and tie the ends tightly to secure.

Put the chickens into one large, or two smaller saucepans in which they fit comfortably. Skim the fat from the surface of the stock, then pour the stock over the chickens to cover them completely. Add a little cold water, if necessary, to ensure they are covered.

Bring the chickens to a boil, then reduce the heat, cover and simmer gently for 2 hours, turning them over after 1 hour. Remove the pan(s) from the heat and cool the chickens in the stock until lukewarm.

Remove the chickens from the stock. Re-tie the cheesecloth so that the chickens are tightly wrapped. Place each chicken on a large flat plate, then place a flat board on top of each one. Place some heavy weights, or cans of food, on top of the boards to compress the chickens. Refrigerate overnight.

The day before
Remove the chickens from their cheesecloth wrappings, and very carefully remove the string. Wipe each chicken with paper towels to remove any fat. Place the chickens on wire racks over large trays.

To make the chaud-froid sauce, melt the butter in a large saucepan and stir in the flour, then gradually stir in the milk. Add the bay leaf and mace. Bring the sauce to a boil, stirring all the time, then reduce the heat and simmer for 10–15 minutes. Remove from the heat.

Put 3 tablespoons cold water into a small bowl and sprinkle the gelatin evenly over the surface. Allow the gelatin to soak for a few minutes until it swells and becomes opaque. Add the gelatin to the hot sauce and stir until dissolved. Remove the bay leaf and mace. Stir the cream, mayonnaise and aspic into the sauce. Season. Allow the sauce to cool until it is thick enough to coat the back of a spoon quite thickly, stirring the sauce frequently to prevent a skin from forming.

Pour the sauce evenly over each chicken to coat completely. Refrigerate until the sauce sets.

Chill a little of the aspic until it becomes slightly thickened but not set. Broil the pepper until it is soft and the skin is charred all over. Cool. Peel off the skin, and remove the core and seeds. Cut some petal or flower shapes from the red pepper, using small truffle or gelée cutters. Select some well-shaped leaves from the watercress; they should be flat. Dip the leaves in the chilled aspic, then arrange them decoratively on the galantines. Dip the red pepper petals or flowers in the aspic, then arrange these on the galantines with the watercress leaves to resemble flowers. Refrigerate the galantines until the decoration is set firmly in place.

Chill the remaining aspic until it is on the point of setting, then spoon it carefully over the galantines to glaze them completely and evenly. Refrigerate overnight. Refrigerate the remaining aspic.

On the day
Carefully remove the galantines to large serving platters. Chop the remaining set aspic on wet wax paper with a wet knife, then arrange around the galantines. Garnish with watercress.

Mushroom and Potato Salad

———— •■• ————

This salad can be made the day before, and kept in a cool place or, covered, in the refrigerator. Sprinkle with parsley just before serving.

3 lb new potatoes, peeled
1 lb button mushrooms, thickly sliced
juice of 1 lemon
¼ cup chopped fresh chives
2½ cups sour cream
¼ cup mayonnaise
1 tablespoon Dijon mustard
salt and pepper
chopped fresh parsley, for garnish

Cook the potatoes in boiling salted water until tender, then drain well and allow to cool. Cut them into slices or dice, depending on their size. Put the mushrooms into a large mixing bowl, add the lemon juice and mix lightly together. Add the potatoes and chives.

Mix the sour cream with the mayonnaise, mustard and seasoning. Pour the dressing over the potatoes and mushrooms and mix gently together. Spoon into one or two serving dishes and sprinkle with chopped parsley.

Tomato and Snow Pea Salad

———— •■• ————

This salad has an attractive contrast in both color and texture. The snow peas can be cooked and the dressing made the day before. Assemble the salad on the morning of the party.

1 lb snow peas, preferably very small ones
salt and pepper
2 tablespoons red wine vinegar
3 garlic cloves, crushed
1 teaspoon Dijon mustard
6 tablespoons olive oil
2 tablespoons chopped fresh parsley
3 tablespoons chopped fresh basil
2 lb ripe but firm tomatoes, sliced

String the snow peas, if necessary. Blanch them in boiling salted water for 2 minutes, then pour them into a large colander and refresh under a cold tap. Drain very well. Dry the snow peas very thoroughly on clean dishtowels. If the snow peas are large, cut them into slices, cutting on a slant. Leave small ones whole.

Put the vinegar, garlic, mustard and seasoning into a mixing bowl and stir well until the salt dissolves. Beat in the olive oil. Stir in the parsley and basil.

Arrange the tomato slices and snow peas in attractive layers on a large serving dish, spooning the dressing over each layer.

129

Avocado, Orange and Cucumber Salad

This is a most decorative salad, with the cardamom giving an unexpected and delicious flavor. The cucumber and orange can be prepared well in advance, but not the avocado as it will tend to discolor if it is left too long.

2 large cucumbers
salt and pepper
5 oranges
4 large ripe but firm avocados
1 tablespoon white wine vinegar
1 teaspoon freshly ground cardamom
3 tablespoons olive oil
grated orange rind, for garnish

Peel the cucumbers, cut each one in half lengthwise and scoop out the seeds. Cut the cucumbers crosswise into $\frac{1}{4}$-inch thick slices. Put the slices into a mixing bowl and sprinkle lightly with salt, then cover and let stand for 1 hour (the salt extracts the excess water and crisps the cucumber).

Meanwhile, peel the oranges and cut them into segments, cutting between the connective tissue. Squeeze the remaining tissue over a bowl, to extract the juice. Cut the segments into smaller pieces and add them to the juice.

Cut each avocado in half and remove the pit, then carefully pull away the skin from each half. Cut the avocados into slices crosswise.

Thoroughly rinse and drain the cucumber on paper towels.

Put the vinegar, cardamom and seasoning into a salad bowl and stir well until the salt dissolves. Beat in the olive oil. Add the oranges, orange juice, avocados and cucumber to the dressing, and mix gently together . Garnish with grated orange rind.

Christening Cake (see page 186)

Choux Swans

Prepare the Choux Swans the day before and freeze them: they are baked frozen. If you want to make them well ahead of time, remove the frozen shapes from the baking sheets and pack them into freezer bags or boxes for storage. Make the custard for the filling the day before, and keep it in a covered container in the refrigerator. Do not fill and assemble the swans too far in advance of serving as they will become soggy.

CHOUX PASTRY
3 cups water
18 tablespoons (2 sticks + 2 tablespoons) unsalted butter
$2\frac{1}{3}$ cups all-purpose flour
9 large eggs, beaten
FILLING AND DECORATION
$\frac{2}{3}$ cup cornstarch
$\frac{1}{2}$ cup sugar
$3\frac{1}{2}$ cups milk
1 teaspoon vanilla extract
$3\frac{1}{2}$ cups heavy cream
5 tablespoons Grand Marnier
1 lb fresh strawberries, hulled and sliced if large
confectioners' sugar
2 large fully blown roses (pink ones for a girl, white ones for a boy) or blue borage flowers for a boy, depending on the time of year

To make the choux pastry, put the water and butter into a large saucepan and heat gently until the butter melts. Bring to a boil. Stir in the flour, all at once, and beat thoroughly. Cook over a moderate heat until the mixture forms a ball. Remove the paste from the heat and allow to cool a little, then put into the bowl of an electric mixer. Gradually beat in the eggs, a little at a time, beating well between each addition, to make a very shiny paste.

Line several large baking sheets with foil. Put some of the choux pastry into a large pastry bag fitted with a $\frac{1}{4}$-inch plain tube and pipe 20 long "S" shapes, about 4 inches long, on one of the baking sheets, spacing them apart to allow for rising. Any unpiped mixture in the pastry bag can be returned to the bowl of choux paste. These "S" shapes will form the heads and necks.

To form the "bodies," take well rounded tablespoonfuls of the choux paste and place them on baking sheets, easing the paste off the tablespoon with another tablespoon so as to keep the oval shape, spacing them well apart. Open freeze the choux shapes.

To prepare the filling, blend the cornstarch and sugar with a little of the milk to form a smooth paste. Bring the remaining milk to a boil, then pour it on the cornstarch mixture, stirring all the time. Return the mixture to a clean saucepan and bring back to a boil, stirring all the time. Take care that the custard does not burn. Reduce the heat and simmer for 2–3 minutes, stirring continuously. Beat in the vanilla extract. Pour the custard into a large mixing bowl and cover the surface closely with plastic wrap to prevent a skin from forming. Cool, then refrigerate overnight.

Bake the frozen choux shapes in a preheated 425° oven until well risen, golden brown and firm. The "bodies" will take about 35 minutes, and the "S" shapes 20 minutes. Remove the "bodies" from the oven and make a slit along the top of each one to allow the steam to escape, then return to the oven for 5–10 minutes to dry out completely. Remove the "S" shapes from the oven and make a small hole in the end of each one, then return to the oven for 5 minutes to dry. Cool on wire racks.

To complete the swans, beat the chilled cornstarch custard until it is very smooth. Whip $2\frac{1}{2}$ cups of the heavy cream with 4 tablespoons of the Grand Marnier until it is thick, but not buttery. Mix the custard and cream together.

Cut each "body" almost in half from the top to the bottom, just enough so that they can be pulled apart for filling. Three-quarters fill each one with the custard mixture, then insert an "S" shape in the end of each one to resemble the head and neck of a swan. Fill the swans with the strawberries.

Whip the remaining cream with the remaining Grand Marnier until it is thick, but not buttery. Put the cream into a pastry bag fitted with a star tube and use to decorate each swan. Sift confectioners' sugar all over the swans.

Arrange the swans on large flat serving platters, and scatter with rose petals or borage flowers. Refrigerate until ready to serve.

ST. VALENTINE'S DAY DINNER FOR 2

St. Valentine's Day is the perfect occasion for a romantic dinner for two. It doesn't matter if you've been married for years and years, you can still celebrate St. Valentine's Day.

Our menu for this special dinner begins with Gravlax, a Scandinavian dish of marinated fresh salmon served with a dill and mustard sauce. This is followed by filets mignons flambéed in brandy, with a particularly delicious sauce, accompanied by new potatoes and spinach. The dessert is entirely appropriate for the occasion—a Tropical Fruit Salad with Passion Fruit Cream.

St. Valentine's Day dinner calls for a beautifully set table, with glowing candlelight and soft music. Traditionally, red roses are a symbol of love, but a small posy of mixed pink and red roses would look very pretty on the table.

ST. VALENTINE'S DAY DINNER FOR 2

GRAVLAX WITH DILL SAUCE

FLAMBÉED FILETS MIGNONS

PARSLEYED NEW POTATOES

CREAMED SPINACH

TROPICAL FRUIT SALAD WITH PASSION FRUIT CREAM

SUGGESTED WINES: CHAMPAGNE BEFORE AND WITH THE GRAVLAX; A STURDY RED—ST. EMILION FOR EXAMPLE—WITH THE STEAKS

Gravlax with Dill Sauce

This recipe makes more than 2 servings, but the salmon will keep well in the refrigerator for at least a week, and it is so delicious that you will want to eat more on another day! Start the preparations for the salmon 3 days before St. Valentine's Day. The sauce can be made the day before.

1½-lb tail end piece of fresh salmon
2 teaspoons black peppercorns
1 teaspoon whole allspice
1 tablespoon sea or kosher salt
1½ tablespoons sugar
¼ cup chopped fresh dill
DILL SAUCE
2 tablespoons heavy cream
1 teaspoon Dijon mustard
1 tablespoon mayonnaise
1 teaspoon lemon juice
1 tablespoon chopped fresh dill
salt and pepper
GARNISH
fresh dill sprigs or watercress leaves
4 lemon wedges
6 heart-shaped pieces of buttered wholewheat bread, the edges dipped in finely chopped fresh parsley

To prepare the salmon, carefully scrape off all the scales using the back of a knife. Carefully bone the salmon by cutting along the center of the back until you reach the bones, then, keeping the knife very close to the bones, cut the flesh away from both sides.

Coarsely grind the peppercorns and allspice in an electric spice grinder, or in a mortar with a pestle. Mix the ground peppercorns and allspice with the salt and the sugar.

Sprinkle a quarter of the salt mixture over the bottom of a shallow glass dish, one that is just large enough to take the salmon. Lay one side of the salmon, skin-side down, on top of the salt mixture in the dish. Sprinkle the salmon with another quarter of the salt mixture, then cover with the chopped dill. Sprinkle another quarter of the salt mixture on top of the dill, then place the second side of the salmon, flesh-side down, on top of the dill. Sprinkle the remaining salt mixture over the top of the salmon.

Cover the salmon with plastic wrap, then place a small flat board, or oval plate, on top. Place some heavy weights, or cans of food, on top of the board or plate. Refrigerate the salmon for 3 days. Every 12 hours, remove the salmon from the refrigerator, turn it over and baste it well, inside and outside, with the juices that have formed in the bottom of the dish.

To make the dill sauce, mix all of the ingredients together, then spoon the sauce into a serving dish. Cover and refrigerate until ready to serve.

Gravlax with Dill Sauce

To serve the salmon, remove it from the dish and scrape away all the salt and dill mixture. Pat the salmon dry with paper towels. Cutting on the slant, cut thin slices from the salmon, cutting off sufficient for two servings. Cover the remaining salmon with plastic wrap and refrigerate for later use.

Arrange the salmon slices neatly on two individual serving plates. Garnish with dill or watercress leaves, lemon wedges and heart-shaped pieces of buttered wholewheat bread. Serve with the dill sauce.

133

Flambéed Filets Mignons

These succulent steaks are sauced with a mixture of artichoke hearts, brandy and cream, and are garnished with strips of red pepper. Altogether a very special dish! The steaks can be marinated, and the vegetables for the sauce and garnish cooked, several hours in advance. The accompaniments—boiled new potatoes tossed in butter and parsley, and creamed spinach subtly spiced with nutmeg—can also be prepared for cooking ahead of time.

two 6-oz filets mignons
2 tablespoons olive oil
1 garlic clove, crushed
1 teaspoon mixed dried herbs
salt and pepper
8 thin asparagus spears
2 small artichokes, trimmed down to the hearts and chokes removed
2 tablespoons unsalted butter
2 tablespoons brandy
$\frac{2}{3}$ cup beef stock
6 tablespoons heavy cream
strips of cooked red pepper, for garnish

Trim any excess fat from the steaks. Put the olive oil into a dish with the garlic, herbs and seasoning. Mix well. Add the steaks to the dish and turn them until they are well coated with the oil mixture. Cover and leave to marinate for 1–2 hours.

Thinly scrape the asparagus spears up to the tips. Remove the tips, then cut the stalks into thin slices on a slant. Thinly slice the artichoke hearts. Blanch the asparagus tips and stalks and artichokes in boiling salted water for 3–5 minutes, until tender. Drain in a colander, and refresh under a cold tap. Drain very well.

Melt the butter in a frying pan, add the steaks and cook on each side for 2–3 minutes, then drain off excess fat from the pan. Pour the brandy into the pan and set alight. When the flames go out, remove the steaks to a hot serving dish. Cover and keep warm.

Pour the beef stock into the frying pan and bring it to a boil, stirring to mix in the meat sediment, then boil gently until the stock reduces by half. Add the asparagus and artichokes to the pan and heat through for about 3 minutes, then stir in the cream. Season well. When the sauce is hot but not boiling, pour it over the steaks. Garnish with strips of red pepper and serve immediately.

Tropical Fruit Salad with Passion Fruit Cream

The syrup of this delicious fruit salad is flavored with the distinctive taste of fresh lime. It is a perfect background for the exotic mixture of mango, papaya, fresh pineapple and kiwi fruit. The passion fruit cream and the fruit salad can both be prepared in the morning for dinner that night.

$\frac{2}{3}$ cup sugar
$\frac{2}{3}$ cup water
thinly pared rind and strained juice of 2 limes
1 ripe mango
1 ripe papaya
$\frac{1}{2}$-inch thick slice of fresh pineapple
2 ripe kiwi fruit
PASSION FRUIT CREAM
4 ripe passion fruit
$\frac{2}{3}$ cup heavy cream
2 tablespoons sugar

To prepare the tropical fruit salad, put the sugar, water and lime rind and juice into a small saucepan. Heat gently until the sugar dissolves, then bring to a boil. Boil gently for 5 minutes, then strain into a mixing bowl.

Peel the mango, then cut the flesh away from the pit. Cut the mango flesh into small cubes. Cut the papaya in half and scoop out the seeds. Peel the papaya, then cut each half into two lengthwise and cut into slices crosswise. Remove all the outer skin from the pineapple, and remove the hard center core. Cut the pineapple into small pieces. Peel and slice the kiwi fruit.

Add all of the prepared fruits to the lime syrup. Cover and refrigerate until serving.

To make the passion fruit cream, cut each passion fruit in half, then scoop out the seeds into a nylon sieve placed over a small bowl. Work the seeds in the sieve with the back of a spoon until all of the juice has been extracted into the bowl.

Whip the cream with the sugar until it will hold soft peaks, then gradually fold in the passion fruit juice. Spoon the cream into a serving bowl, cover and refrigerate until ready to serve.

Transfer the tropical fruit salad to a serving bowl. Serve with the passion fruit cream.

HARVEST SUPPER FOR 20

A Harvest Supper is a lovely party to give in the fall, around harvest time. A Harvest Supper is an informal occasion with simple food. My menu is composed of tasty wholesome dishes—baked squash stuffed with a beef and vegetable mixture accompanied by a dish of thinly sliced potatoes baked with onions and spicy red cabbage cooked with green grapes. The dessert is the very essence of autumn, latticed apple pies, served with whipped cream and blackberry sauce.

A Harvest Supper can be served in the kitchen of your house, or in a barn with hay bales to sit on. To decorate the table with seasonal colors, use arrangements of copper beech leaves, small bronze-colored daisy chrysanthemums and bright red and yellow dahlias.

HARVEST SUPPER FOR 20

BAKED STUFFED SQUASH

CRISPY LAYERED POTATOES

SPICY RED CABBAGE WITH GREEN GRAPES

LATTICED APPLE PIES WITH
BLACKBERRY SAUCE AND WHIPPED CREAM

SUGGESTED WINE: A DRY ITALIAN RED, SUCH AS
BAROLO

Baked Stuffed Squash

The stuffing for the squash, and the preparation of the squash for stuffing can be done the day before the Harvest Supper. In fact, if you happen to be very busy around the time of the party, the beef stuffing for the squash can be made and frozen two or three weeks in advance. Take it out of the freezer the day before the party to thaw, ready to stuff the squash before cooking them the evening of the party.

5 lb lean chuck
4 tablespoons olive oil
3 very large onions, finely sliced
1 lb carrots, finely diced
4 beef bouillon cubes
$\frac{2}{3}$ cup flour
1 lb 3 oz canned tomatoes, sieved to make a purée
2 tablespoons mixed dried herbs
1 lb mushrooms, chopped
12 oz (3 cups) frozen peas
salt and pepper
three 4-lb large summer squash

Remove all of the fat and tissue from the chuck, then finely grind the meat. Heat the oil in a very large saucepan or two saucepans. Add the onions and carrots and fry gently for about 10 minutes until softened but not browned. Remove the onions and carrots from the pan(s) with a slotted spoon, to a large plate.

Add the ground meat to the pan(s) and fry gently for 5–10 minutes until the meat changes color.

Return the onions and carrots to the pan(s). Crumble in the bouillon cubes and stir well until dissolved. Stir in the flour, then the tomato purée, herbs, mushrooms and peas. Bring the mixture to a boil, stirring all the time. Remove from the heat and season.

If the squash do not lie flat, take a very thin slice from the bottom of each one to ensure that they do. Cut a slice from the top of each squash, about a quarter of the way down. Scoop out the seeds and the stringy center from each, using a metal spoon.

Season the inside of each squash then fill each one with the beef mixture. Replace their tops. Wrap the squash individually, in foil, then place them in roasting pans. Bake in a preheated 350° oven for about 3 hours until the squash are well cooked through, changing the position of the squash in the oven halfway through the cooking.

To serve, lift the squash, still in their foil wrappings, from the roasting pan to serving dishes, then open out and roll down the foil to about halfway down the side of each squash, or remove the foil completely. (Leaving the foil on helps to retain the shape of the squash.) Serve hot.

Crispy Layered Potatoes

———— ◆■◆ ————

This is a very convenient potato dish to serve at a party, because it involves no last minute cooking. Prepare the dish for cooking several hours in advance (or cook it ahead of time)—it will keep warm for 1–1½ hours.

10 lb potatoes, thinly sliced
2 lb onions, thinly sliced
½ lb (2 sticks) unsalted butter
salt and pepper
3 tablespoons mixed dried herbs
5 cups milk

Lightly grease 2 large ovenproof dishes each about 13 × 10 inches. Arrange a layer of potatoes in the bottom of each dish, then sprinkle with a layer of sliced onions. Dot with butter and sprinkle with herbs and seasoning. Continue to layer the potatoes and onions, ending with a layer of potatoes dotted with butter. Pour 2½ cups of milk into each dish.

Bake the potatoes, uncovered, in a preheated 425° oven for about 20 minutes, then reduce the oven temperature to 350° and continue cooking for a further 1½ hours, or until the potatoes are very soft, golden brown on the top, and have absorbed all the milk.

Spicy Red Cabbage with Green Grapes

———— ◆■◆ ————

The cabbage can be cooked on the morning of the party. Before serving, add the grapes and reheat in the butter.

6 lb red cabbage, cored and finely shredded
2 cups water
1 cup red wine vinegar
6 tablespoons sugar
salt and pepper
1 lb seedless green grapes, or larger grapes halved and seeded
8 tablespoons (1 stick) unsalted butter

Put the cabbage into a very large saucepan, or two saucepans. Add the water, vinegar, sugar, and seasoning. Cover the saucepan(s) tightly and cook gently for at least 1 hour until the cabbage is tender.

Add the grapes and continue cooking for a further 5 minutes.

Drain the cabbage well in a large colander. Melt the butter in the saucepan(s), then return the drained cabbage to the pan(s) and toss well in the hot butter. Spoon into a hot serving dish and serve hot.

Latticed Apple Pies with Blackberry Sauce and Whipped Cream

———— ◆■◆ ————

The apples for the pies can be cooked and the pastry made the day before the party. Bake the pies the morning of the party and warm through before serving.

8 lb tart apples, peeled, cored and sliced
2 lb (5 cups) sugar
thinly pared rind and the juice of 2 large lemons
PASTRY
5¼ cups all-purpose flour
¼ teaspoon salt
¼ cup sugar
12 oz (3 sticks) unsalted butter
4 large eggs, lightly beaten
little milk for glazing
little sugar for sprinkling
FOR SERVING
blackberry sauce (see right)
2½ cups whipped cream

Divide the apples equally between two large saucepans. Add half of the sugar, lemon rind and juice to each pan. Cover tightly and cook the apples gently for about 20–25 minutes, stirring occasionally, until they are soft.

Pour the cooked apples into large nylon sieves, or colanders, placed over mixing bowls and allow to drain (the juice can be kept to make drinks, topped up with soda water or 7-Up). Allow the apples to cool.

To make the pastry, sift the flour, salt and sugar into a large mixing bowl. Rub in the butter until the mixture resembles fine breadcrumbs. Mix with the beaten eggs to form a stiff dough. Cut the dough into four equal pieces.

Roll out one quarter of the dough on a lightly floured surface to a round 1 inch larger than a 10 inch diameter, 1-inch deep tart or cake pan with an edge. Line the pan with the dough, pressing it firmly onto the bottom. Do not trim the excess dough.

Fill with half the cooked apples.

Roll out another one quarter of the dough to an oblong 11 × 7 inches. Trim the edges, then cut into 14 long strips, each one ½ inch wide.

Moisten the edge of the dough in the pan with a little cold water, then arrange seven of the dough strips evenly spaced across the apple filling. Arrange the remaining strips in the opposite direction, on top of the first strips, to form a neat lattice pattern. Press the strips firmly around the edge to seal. Trim the excess dough from around the edge of the pie. Brush the lattice top with a little milk, then sprinkle with sugar. Make another pie in exactly the same way.

Bake the pies in a preheated 425° oven for 40–45 minutes, until the pastry is crisp. Serve the pies warm or cold, with blackberry sauce and whipped cream.

Latticed Apple Pie

Blackberry Sauce

Make 2 or 3 days in advance and store in refrigerator.

1½ lb blackberries, thawed if frozen
1 cup sugar

Put the blackberries into a saucepan with the sugar. Cover and cook gently until the blackberries are very soft, about 20 minutes.

Sieve the blackberries and their juice, through a nylon sieve to make a purée. Add a little more sugar to sweeten, if necessary. Pour the sauce into a jug and serve hot or cold.

137

TWENTY-FIRST BIRTHDAY PARTY FOR 30

A twenty-first birthday—and an eighteenth birthday as is sometimes celebrated—is a milestone to be celebrated in a special way.

The menu for this party is wonderful—full of delicious, savory finger foods. There are tiny tartlets of asparagus, smoked salmon and shrimp and mussels, set in a creamy cheese custard. Savory choux puffs are filled with a shrimp butter and a mixture of cream cheese and chives. There are also stuffed vegetable delicacies.

Numerous delicious and unusual "bits" are presented on sticks. Fish balls and meat balls can be served hot or cold, dipped into a spicy tomato sauce, and there is a blue cheese dip for crudités. Canapés, which look so attractive, complete the superb selection.

TWENTY-FIRST BIRTHDAY PARTY FOR 30

VEGETABLE DELICACIES

INDIVIDUAL QUICHES

SAVORY CHOUX PUFFS

LITTLE SAVORIES ON STICKS

MEAT AND FISH BALLS WITH DIPPING SAUCE

CANAPÉS

BLUE CHEESE DIP WITH CRUDITÉS

PARTY PUNCH

BIRTHDAY CAKE (SEE PAGE 186)

SUGGESTED WINES: CHAMPAGNE COULD BE SERVED AS AN ALTERNATIVE TO THE PUNCH, OR IN ADDITION TO IT, AND WITH THE BIRTHDAY CAKE

Vegetable Delicacies

You can mix each of the stuffings for the vegetables up to 2 days before the party. Keep them in covered containers in the refrigerator. Prepare the cherry tomatoes the day before the party—this is a fiddly job and good to have out of the way well beforehand! They will keep perfectly well, upside-down on paper towels, to drain away any excess moisture.

MUSHROOMS
2 lb button mushrooms
8 tablespoons (1 stick) unsalted butter
juice of 2 lemons
salt and pepper
1 lb smooth, mild-flavored liver pâté
chopped fresh parsley, and sliced, stuffed olives, for garnish

CELERY
½ lb gorgonzola cheese
2 tablespoons mayonnaise
2 tablespoons heavy cream
8 celery stalks, about 10 inches long
2 tablespoons snipped fresh chives
2 tablespoons finely chopped peanuts

CHERRY TOMATOES
60 cherry tomatoes
½ lb (1 cup) cream cheese
6 tablespoons heavy cream
4 garlic cloves, crushed
2 teaspoons mixed dried herbs
tiny fresh parsley sprigs, for garnish

CUCUMBER
2 large cucumbers
12 oz cooked fresh salmon, flaked and boned, or flaked white crabmeat or diced lobster
2 tablespoons mayonnaise
2 teaspoons lemon juice
salt and pepper
¼ cup finely chopped watercress
watercress leaves, for garnish

To prepare the mushrooms, carefully remove the stems. Put the mushroom caps aside and finely chop the stems. Melt the butter in one large, or two, frying pans. Add the mushroom caps and toss them gently in the butter until well coated, then add the lemon juice and seasoning. Cover the pan(s) tightly and cook very gently until the mushroom caps are only just tender; do not overcook, because they must retain their shape. Lift the caps from the pan(s) with a slotted spoon, and drain well on paper towels. Allow to cool.

Add the chopped mushroom stems to the butter remaining in the pan(s) and cook gently until softened. Increase the heat and boil gently until all the liquid remaining in the pan(s) has evaporated. Allow the mushroom stems to cool.

Beat the liver pâté until very soft, then beat in the mushroom stems and seasoning. Fill each mushroom

Front to back: Crudités; Individual Quiches; Vegetable Delicacies; Party Punch; Dipping Sauce; Little Savories on Sticks; Savory Choux Puffs; Blue Cheese Dip

cap with the liver mixture. Sprinkle with chopped parsley, and garnish each with a slice of stuffed olive.

To prepare the celery, mash the gorgonzola cheese with the mayonnaise and cream. Season. Fill the channel in each celery stalk with the cheese mixture, then sprinkle with chives and peanuts. Refrigerate until well chilled. Just before serving, cut crosswise into 1-inch pieces.

To prepare the cherry tomatoes, slice the top off each tomato (the opposite side to the stalk); reserve the tops or "lids." Carefully scoop out all the seeds from the inside then drain upside-down on paper towels.

Beat the cheese with the cream until it is soft, then beat in the garlic, seasoning and herbs. Pipe, or spoon, the cheese mixture into each tomato. Replace the tomato "lids," and garnish with sprigs of parsley. Refrigerate until well chilled.

To prepare the cucumber, peel them, cut in half lengthwise and scoop out the seeds. Drain well.

Mix the flaked salmon (or crab or lobster) with the mayonnaise. Add the lemon juice and seasoning. Mix in the chopped watercress. Fill the cucumber halves with the fish mixture, then refrigerate until well chilled. Just before serving, cut the cucumber halves crosswise into 1-inch slices. Garnish the serving plates with the watercress leaves and serve.

Individual Quiches

Make the quiches in batches of 12 (or less), depending on how many tartlet pans you have. The custard quantity is for 36 tartlets, so make it all and use it as you need it. Keep it in a cool place. The quiches may be made the day before the party.

PASTRY (for 12 pans)
2 cups all-purpose flour
pinch of salt
8 tablespoons (1 stick) unsalted butter
1 large egg, beaten with 1–2 tablespoons cold water
CUSTARD
12 large eggs
$2\frac{1}{2}$ cups milk
$2\frac{1}{2}$ cups heavy cream
salt and pepper
$\frac{1}{2}$ lb (2 cups) Cheddar cheese, finely grated
$\frac{1}{2}$ lb (2 cups) Gruyère or Swiss cheese, finely grated
FILLINGS
12 oz asparagus
6 oz peeled cooked shrimp
6 oz cooked shelled mussels
2 tablespoons chopped fresh parsley
12 black olives
6 oz smoked salmon, cut into thin strips
2 tablespoons chopped fresh chives
1 red pepper

To make the pastry, sift the flour and salt into a mixing bowl, then rub in the butter until the mixture resembles fine breadcrumbs. Mix to a stiff dough with the beaten egg mixture. Knead the dough very lightly on a floured surface until smooth.

Roll out the pastry to about $\frac{1}{8}$ inch thick, then cut into rounds about 5 inches in diameter, re-rolling the trimmings to obtain 12 rounds. Neatly line twelve 4-inch tartlet pans with the pastry rounds, then trim the edges. Place the lined pans on baking sheets and chill.

To make the custard, lightly beat the eggs together in a large mixing bowl with the milk and the cream. Season, then stir in the cheeses.

To make asparagus quiches, scrape the asparagus stalks to the tips using a potato peeler. Remove the tips, then slice the stalks thinly, on a slant. Blanch the asparagus in boiling salted water for 3–4 minutes, until just tender. Put into a colander and refresh under cold water. Drain the asparagus well on paper towels.

Divide the blanched asparagus equally among the pastry lined pans, then fill each one with the custard mixture. Bake in a preheated 425° oven for 20–25 minutes, until the custard has set.

Allow the quiches to cool in the pans for a short while before unmolding.

To make shrimp and mussel quiches, make another batch of pastry and line 12 tartlet pans. Divide the shrimp and mussels equally among the pans, then fill with the custard mixture. Sprinkle with parsley and garnish with olives. Bake as for asparagus quiches.

To make smoked salmon quiches, broil the red pepper until the skin is charred, turning the pepper to cook it evenly. Allow to cool, then pull off the skin. Remove the core and seeds, and cut the pepper into thin strips. Use to garnish the smoked salmon quiches. Make another batch of pastry and line 12 tartlet pans. Divide the salmon equally between the pans, and sprinkle with chopped chives. Fill with the custard mixture. Bake as for asparagus quiches. Serve the quiches warm or cold.

Savory Choux Puffs

The choux pastry may be made and piped onto the baking sheets and then frozen, ready to be baked on the morning of the party. Both fillings can be made and kept in covered containers in the refrigerator.

1 cup water
6 tablespoons unsalted butter
$\frac{3}{4}$ cup all-purpose flour
3 large eggs, lightly beaten
paprika for sprinkling
CHEESE FILLING
12 oz ($1\frac{1}{2}$ cups) cream cheese
3 tablespoons mayonnaise
salt and pepper
3 tablespoons snipped fresh chives
SHRIMP FILLING
$\frac{1}{2}$ lb (2 sticks) unsalted butter
12 oz peeled cooked shrimp, finely chopped
2 teaspoons lemon juice
salt and pepper

Line several baking sheets with baking parchment paper.

To make the choux pastry, put the water and butter into a saucepan and heat gently until the butter melts, then bring to a boil. Add the flour all at once and beat well. Cook over a moderate heat until the mixture forms into a ball at the center of the saucepan. Allow to cool slightly, then gradually beat in the eggs, adding just a little at a time, and beating well between each addition. (This can be done with an electric mixer.)

Put the choux pastry into pastry bags fitted with a $\frac{1}{2}$-inch plain tube. Pipe 80 small rounds, each about the size of a small grape, on the lined baking sheets —spacing them well apart to allow for rising. With the remaining mixture, pipe 60 short strips about $1\frac{1}{2}$ inches long.

Bake in a preheated 425° oven for about 20 minutes, until well risen and firm. Remove from the oven and pierce each one to allow the steam to escape; pierce the rounds underneath, and the oblong strips at the ends. Return to the oven to bake for a further 5–10 minutes, to dry out completely. Remove the puffs to wire racks and leave to cool.

To make the cheese filling, beat the cream cheese with the mayonnaise until very soft and creamy, season well, and then beat in the chives. Put the mixture into a pastry bag fitted with a small plain tube and fill each round choux puff through the hole made in the base. Refrigerate until well chilled.

To make the shrimp filling, beat the butter until it is very soft. Add the shrimp and continue beating until the shrimp break up and the mixture becomes smooth. Add the lemon juice and seasoning. Put the mixture into a pastry bag fitted with a small plain tube and fill each oblong choux puff through the hole made at the end. (If the shrimp mixture is not beaten sufficiently it will be difficult to pipe into the puffs. If this is the case, the puffs may be cut almost in half and filled with a spoon.) Refrigerate the puffs until well chilled.

To serve, pile the puffs in separate serving dishes and sprinkle lightly with paprika. Serve chilled.

Little Savories on Sticks

All the little savories can be prepared the day before the party. Keep them separate, wrapped in plastic wrap, in a cool place. Assemble shortly before serving.

a large melon, squash, or green cabbage for serving
SALMON AND CUCUMBER
1 large cucumber
salt and pepper
6 oz smoked salmon, thinly sliced
HAM AND NASTURTIUM
6 oz sweet-cured cooked ham, in one piece
2 tablespoons chopped fresh parsley
2 garlic cloves, crushed
salt and pepper
about 30 nasturtium blooms or sprigs of watercress or arugula
MELON WITH HAM
1 large ripe but firm melon
½ lb prosciutto, thinly sliced
capers
HERRINGS WITH GHERKINS
12 medium-sized gherkins
two 12-oz jars pickled herrings, well drained
about 100 small white cocktail onions
OLIVES WITH ANCHOVIES
four 2-oz cans anchovy fillets, well drained
about 60 stuffed green olives

To prepare the salmon and cucumber, peel the cucumber, cut in half lengthwise, then scoop out the seeds. Cut the cucumber halves in half again, lengthwise, then cut them into small cubes about ½ inch. Put the cucumber pieces into a bowl, sprinkle them lightly with salt and allow to stand for about 1 hour (the salt draws out the excess water, and crisps the cucumber). Rinse the cucumber and drain well on paper towels.

Season the cucumber pieces, then wrap each piece in a small strip of smoked salmon. Spear on toothpicks.

To prepare the ham and nasturtiums, cut the ham into small cubes, about ½ inch. Mix the parsley with the garlic and seasoning, in a mixing bowl. Add the cubed ham and toss well to coat it evenly with the parsley mixture. Wrap each piece of ham in nasturtium petals, and spear on toothpicks.

To prepare the melon with ham, cut the melon in half and scoop out the seeds. Cut the melon halves into quarters, then carefully cut away the skin. Cut the melon flesh into ½-inch cubes. Wrap each piece of melon in a strip of prosciutto, and spear on toothpicks. Top each with a caper.

To prepare the herrings with gherkins, cut the gherkins into quarters lengthwise, then cut into ½-inch pieces. Wrap each piece of gherkin in a strip of herring, then spear on toothpicks. Top each with a cocktail onion.

To prepare the olives with anchovies, cut the anchovy fillets in half lengthwise. Curl a strip of anchovy around each stuffed olive, then spear on toothpicks.

To serve, arrange attractively, by studding all over a large melon, squash or green cabbage, outer leaves laid back and a thin slice taken from the base.

Meat Balls

Fry the meat balls the day before, if they are to be served cold. If serving them hot, mix and roll them, ready for frying just before serving.

2 lb ground round
2 large onions, finely chopped
2 tablespoons chopped fresh parsley
2 teaspoons mixed dried herbs
2 garlic cloves, crushed
1 cup fresh white breadcrumbs
2 large eggs, lightly beaten
salt and pepper
a little olive oil for frying

Mix the ground round with the onions, herbs, garlic, breadcrumbs, eggs and seasoning. Shape the mixture into small balls, about 1 inch in diameter.

Fry the meat balls in a little hot olive oil until they are lightly browned on all sides—do not overcook. Drain the meat balls well on paper towels. Allow to cool, then spear each one on a toothpick. Arrange with the other savories on sticks.

Alternatively, the meat balls may be served hot—fry them just before serving.

Fish Balls

These may be made and cooked the day before if you are going to serve them cold. If to be served hot, they can be shaped and breaded, ready for frying at the last minute.

2 lb haddock fillets
$1\frac{1}{4}$ cups milk
salt and pepper
4 tablespoons unsalted butter
5 tablespoons all-purpose flour
2 tablespoons chopped fresh parsley
2 tablespoons capers, chopped
2 tablespoons mayonnaise
4 eggs, lightly beaten
4 cups fresh white breadcrumbs
oil for deep frying

Put the haddock fillets into a large saucepan with the milk and seasoning. Cover and cook gently for about 20 minutes, until the haddock flakes easily.

Strain the stock from the haddock into a measuring cup and add more milk, if necessary, to yield $1\frac{1}{2}$ cups. Remove the skin and bones from the haddock, then flake the flesh.

Melt the butter in a saucepan, and stir in the flour, then gradually stir in the fish stock. Bring to a boil, stirring all the time until the sauce thickens. Reduce the heat and simmer very gently for about 10 minutes, stirring frequently. Add the flaked haddock, parsley, capers and mayonnaise to the fish sauce and beat well together until smooth. Season. Spoon the haddock mixture onto a plate. Cover with plastic wrap and allow to cool, then refrigerate for at least 2 hours, until well chilled.

Shape the chilled haddock mixture into small balls, about 1 inch diameter, with wet hands. Return the fish balls to the refrigerator to firm up again.

Coat the fish balls with beaten egg and breadcrumbs, then deep fry in hot oil, in batches, for 3–4 minutes, until golden brown. Drain well on paper towels. Serve hot or well chilled.

Chilled fish balls may be speared onto toothpicks, and be arranged with the other savories on sticks.

Party Punch

Dipping Sauce

This sauce is to accompany the fish and meat balls.

2 tablespoons olive oil
2 large onions, finely chopped
2 garlic cloves, crushed
2 tablespoons curry powder
$2\frac{1}{2}$ lb canned tomatoes
2 tablespoons mango chutney
2 tablespoons garam masala

Heat the oil in a saucepan, add the onions and fry gently for about 10 minutes, until softened but not browned. Stir in the garlic and curry powder and continue cooking for one minute. Add the tomatoes, including their juice, and the chutney and stir well. Bring to a boil, stirring all the time, then reduce the heat, partially cover and simmer gently for about 40–45 minutes, until thickened.

Purée the sauce in a blender or food processor, or pass through a nylon sieve. Season the sauce with garam masala, adding a little more or less, to suit your own taste. Reheat the sauce if serving it hot.

Party Punch

The melon and pineapple base mixture can be prepared a day in advance.

1 large ripe pineapple
1 large ripe melon
$2\frac{1}{2}$ cups Grand Marnier
$3\frac{1}{2}$ cups brandy
2 large oranges, thinly sliced
2 large lemons, thinly sliced
1 lb fresh strawberries, hulled and sliced
1 or 2 large blocks of ice
6 bottles of champagne, well chilled
fresh mint sprigs and a few fresh flowers, such as nasturtium blooms, geranium petals or borage flowers, to decorate

Cut away all the skin from the pineapple, then cut the flesh into quarters lengthwise, and cut away the hard center core. Cut the pineapple slices into small pieces.

Cut the melon in half and scoop out the seeds. Scoop the flesh from the melon with a melon baller directly into a very large punch bowl. Add the pineapple pieces, then stir in the Grand Marnier and brandy. Cover the bowl and refrigerate for at least 6 hours.

One hour before serving the punch, add the orange and lemon slices to the fruit mixture.

Just before serving, add the strawberries and ice, then pour in the champagne. Stir well, decorate with mint and flower blooms, and serve immediately.

Canapés

Canapés take a little time and patience to make, but are very rewarding as they look so attractive when completed, and arranged for serving. Rye bread is used here for the bases, because it has a delicious flavor, especially suited to canapés, and its close texture prevents it from becoming soggy.

3 large loaves, light or dark rye bread, preferably sliced lengthwise $\frac{1}{8}$ inch thick

BUTTERS

12 oz (3 sticks) unsalted butter
3 tablespoons prepared white horseradish
2 garlic cloves, crushed
1 tablespoon Dijon mustard
salt and pepper

TOPPINGS

$\frac{1}{2}$ lb pastrami, thinly sliced
$\frac{1}{2}$ lb garlic sausage, thinly sliced
$\frac{1}{2}$ lb smoked salmon, thinly sliced
12 oz cooked chicken breast meat, thinly sliced
1 lb cooked ham, sliced about $\frac{1}{8}$ inch thick
1 lb pickled herrings, well drained

GARNISHES

about 10 medium-size gherkins, thinly sliced
about 10 stuffed olives, sliced
watercress leaves
5–6 hard-boiled eggs, sliced
small strips black olives
thinly sliced red onion rings
2 green apples, quartered, cored and thinly sliced
thinly sliced cucumber
about 25 small cooked asparagus tips
thin strips of cooked red pepper
1 quart aspic (page 182)
finely chopped fresh parsley

You can cut the canapés into any shape you wish, but remember that they must be bite-size, and easy to pick up. Rounds and ovals look very pretty, but they do mean that some of the bread and topping ingredients will be wasted when cutting out. Squares, oblongs, triangles and diamonds do not waste any of the ingredients.

To make the butters, beat the butter until it is very soft, then divide it equally into three portions. Beat the horseradish into one third, the garlic into another third, and the mustard into the remaining third. Season each butter.

Butter some of the slices of bread with horseradish butter, and trim off the crusts. Arrange the pastrami on some of the buttered bread, and when it is used up, arrange the sausage on the other slices, buttering more slices as necessary. Cut into the desired shapes. Place on wire racks and cover with plastic wrap to prevent the meats from drying out.

Next, butter slices of bread and trim off the crusts. On some arrange the smoked salmon, and on others the sliced chicken. Cut into shapes, put onto wire racks and cover with plastic wrap.

Butter the remaining slices of bread with mustard butter and trim off the crusts. On these arrange the sliced ham and the herrings. Cut into shapes, put onto wire racks and cover with plastic wrap.

Garnish the pastrami canapés with thinly sliced gherkins; garnish the sausage canapés with sliced stuffed olives and watercress leaves; garnish the ham canapés with sliced hard-boiled eggs and strips of black olive; garnish the herring canapés with rings of red onion looped over slices of apple; garnish the smoked salmon canapés with cucumber slices; garnish the chicken canapés with asparagus tips and strips of red pepper.

Chill the aspic until it is almost on the point of setting, then carefully spoon it over each canapé to glaze evenly. Sprinkle the pastrami canapés with a little chopped parsley before the aspic sets. Season the smoked salmon with pepper. Refrigerate the canapés until the aspic sets firmly.

Blue Cheese Dip with Crudités

The dip and vegetables can be completely prepared the day before the party. Keep the vegetables in tightly closed plastic bags in the refrigerator.

12 oz gorgonzola or other blue cheese
1 lb ricotta cheese
3 garlic cloves, crushed
2 cups heavy cream
salt and pepper

CRUDITÉS

1 large bunch of celery
2 red peppers, cored and seeded
2 green peppers, cored and seeded
2 yellow peppers, cored and seeded
1 large cucumber, halved lengthwise and seeded
1 lb carrots, peeled

To make the dip, beat the blue cheese with the ricotta cheese until very soft. Beat in the garlic, cream and seasoning. Spoon the dip into a large serving dish, cover with plastic wrap and refrigerate until ready to serve.

To prepare the crudités, cut all of the vegetables into sticks about 2–3 inches long.

To serve, place the bowl of cheese dip in the center of a large platter, then arrange the vegetables around it.

EASTER LUNCH FOR 8

E aster is a very special religious festival. Easter Day itself is a day of happiness: after the gloom of Good Friday there is the joy of the resurrection. In celebration, it is a wonderful day to give a lunch party. At this time of the year, all the early flowers—primroses and violets in particular—come as such a treat after the virtually flower-less winter months, and the table for an Easter lunch party can be decorated with simple posies in small pots or vases. The simpler the presentation the better: such flowers don't need to be arranged.

If there are children present an Easter lunch can be followed by an Easter egg hunt—outside, weather permitting, or inside if it's rainy.

The menu for my Easter lunch starts with broiled avocados—the avocado skins are filled with a mixture of the avocado flesh, celery, apples and shrimp bound with mayonnaise, sprinkled with grated Gruyère cheese and broiled. To follow, there is baked sea bass, with a pungent pepper, tomato and mussel stuffing. The fish has a delicious herb and anchovy butter to accompany it.

The dessert for this Easter lunch is Paskha, a traditional Russian Easter specialty. It is a sort of rich cheesecake, full of candied peel and fruit.

EASTER LUNCH FOR 8

BROILED AVOCADOS

STUFFED SEA BASS
WITH MONTPELLIER BUTTER

NEW POTATOES

TOSSED GREEN SALAD

PASKHA

SUGGESTED WINES: A GOOD CHABLIS, DOMESTIC
OR IMPORTED

Broiled Avocados

Grate the Gruyère cheese the day before. If using fresh shrimp, cook and shell them the day before; keep them in a covered container in the refrigerator. The filling for the avocado doesn't take a minute to assemble on Easter morning before lunch.

4 large ripe avocados
2 celery stalks, very thinly sliced
2 red-skinned apples, quartered, cored and sliced
6 oz peeled cooked shrimp
$\frac{1}{4}$ cup mayonnaise
salt and pepper
1$\frac{1}{2}$ cups finely grated Gruyère or Swiss cheese
lemon twists and parsley sprigs, for garnish

Cut each avocado in half and remove the pit. Carefully scoop out the flesh, in neat teaspoonfuls or using a melon ball cutter, and place it in a mixing bowl. Set the avocado skins aside.

Add the celery, apples, shrimp and mayonnaise to the avocado flesh and season very well with salt and pepper. Mix thoroughly together.

Re-fill the avocado skins with the avocado mixture. Place in heatproof avocado dishes, or directly on the rack of a broiler pan. Sprinkle the avocados with the Gruyère, then cook under a very hot broiler until the cheese melts and turns golden brown. Garnish each avocado with a twist of lemon and sprigs of parsley and serve immediately.

Stuffed Sea Bass with Montpellier Butter

Make the Montpellier butter the day before and keep it in the refrigerator. Make the stuffing for the sea bass also on the Saturday. On Easter Sunday prepare the sea bass for cooking and stuff it. The potatoes to accompany the fish can be scrubbed well in advance and the salad vegetables prepared to be assembled. Salad dressing can also be made ahead of time.

5-lb sea bass
watercress, for garnish
MONTPELLIER BUTTER
1 small onion, skinned
about 8 spinach leaves
1 large fresh parsley sprig
½ cup chopped watercress
1 tablespoon capers
4 anchovy fillets
3 hard-boiled egg yolks
6 tablespoons unsalted butter, softened
STUFFING
4 tablespoons unsalted butter
1 large onion, finely chopped
1 small red pepper, cored, seeded and finely chopped
1 small green pepper, cored, seeded and finely chopped
1 small yellow pepper, cored, seeded and finely chopped
1¼ lb can peeled plum tomatoes, drained, seeded and roughly chopped
2 large garlic cloves, crushed
salt and pepper
1 lb cooked shelled mussels

To make the Montpellier butter, bring a small saucepan of water to a boil, then add the onion and cook gently for 5 minutes, to soften. Add the spinach, parsley and watercress to the water, and cook for 1 minute. Pour into a colander, then refresh under a cold tap. Squeeze the spinach, parsley and watercress dry. Very finely chop the spinach, parsley, watercress, onion, capers and anchovies.

Press the egg yolks through a nylon sieve. Beat the sieved yolks and all of the chopped ingredients into the butter, beating well until very smooth and creamy.

Alternatively, put all of the ingredients, unchopped, into a blender or food processor and blend for about 2 minutes. Spoon the Montpellier butter into a serving bowl, cover and refrigerate until ready to serve.

To prepare the stuffing, melt the butter in a large frying pan, add the chopped onion and the peppers and fry gently for 10 minutes, until very soft, without browning. Add the chopped tomatoes and garlic and stir. Continue cooking gently until the mixture becomes thick, about 20 minutes. Season very well with salt and pepper. Allow to cool, then mix in the mussels. Set aside while preparing the bass.

To prepare the bass, remove the scales using the back of a small strong knife. (The scales on a bass are quite large and strong, and can fly to unwanted places in the kitchen when they are being removed. To prevent this happening, the bass may be scaled inside a very large plastic bag.) Remove the fins using strong kitchen scissors. Slit the bass along the belly, then remove the entrails. Wash the bass under cold water, then dry thoroughly with paper towels. Using a very small, sharp knife, carefully remove the bones from the bass—loosen each of the long bones, that are at each side of the backbone, individually. Then, keeping the knife close to the bones, cut the flesh away from the backbone. Cut the backbone free, at the head and the tail end of the fish. Remove and discard the bones.

Season the bass, then fill it with the mussel stuffing. Sew the bass up with fine string or very strong thread. Wrap the bass tightly in foil, then place it on a very large baking sheet. (If you do not have one very large baking sheet, place two flat baking sheets side-by-side on the oven shelf, then place the bass on top.) Bake in a preheated 400° oven for 35–45 minutes, until the flesh will flake easily when tested with a fork.

To serve, very carefully remove the cooked bass from the foil onto a long, hot serving dish. Remove the string or thread. Garnish with watercress, and serve with the Montpellier butter.

Paskha

This traditional Russian Easter specialty is normally made in a special tall paskha mold, but you can use a clay flower pot instead. The flower pot should have a hole in the bottom, and be scrupulously clean—it is a good idea to buy one specially for making paskha, and keep it with your other kitchen equipment. For the following recipe you will need a 6½-inch wide flower pot that is about 5 inches deep. You will also need some clean cheesecloth. Make the paskha the day before it is to be served.

12 tablespoons (1½ sticks) unsalted butter
finely grated rind of 1 lemon
finely grated rind of 1 orange
1 cup sugar
2 large eggs
1 teaspoon vanilla extract
2 lb small curd cottage cheese or ricotta cheese
⅔ cup heavy cream
3 tablespoons chopped citron peel
3 tablespoons chopped candied lemon peel
3 tablespoons chopped candied orange peel
⅔ cup (4 oz) chopped raisins
½ cup (2 oz) chopped blanched almonds
⅓ cup chopped glacé cherries
⅓ cup chopped glacé pineapple

146

Paskha

DECORATION
citron peel
glacé cherries
glacé pineapple
blanched almonds, halved and lightly toasted
fresh violets or primroses (optional)

Beat the butter with the lemon and orange rind and the sugar until very light and fluffy. Beat in the eggs one at a time, beating well between each addition. Add the vanilla extract and the cheese and beat well together until very smooth. Beat in the cream, then mix in the remaining ingredients and set aside.

Place the flower pot in the center of a large square of cheesecloth, then make a diagonal cut to the center of the cheesecloth. Line the flower pot smoothly with the cheesecloth; the cut will enable the cloth to be over-lapped for a smoother lining. If there are too many bumps in the cloth, these will mark the paskha and spoil its finished appearance.

Fill the flower pot with the paskha mixture, then bring the overhanging cheesecloth up and over the mixture to enclose it completely. Place a small flat plate on top of the paskha, then place some heavy weight, or cans of food, on top of the plate, to compress the mixture. Stand the flower pot on a plate, then refrigerate overnight. (It is important to stand the pot on a plate as a certain amount of liquid will drain away from the paskha as it is com-pressed.)

To unmold the paskha, open out the cheesecloth on the top, then place a flat serving plate on top of the paskha. Invert the plate and the flower pot together. Remove the flower pot, then very carefully peel away the cheesecloth.

Decorate the paskha attractively with strips of citron peel, cherries, pineapple, almonds—and violets and primroses if liked. Keep the paskha refrigerated until ready to serve.

ST. ANDREW'S NIGHT DINNER FOR 8

The feast of St. Andrew, the patron saint of Scotland, falls on November 30th, two days after my husband Godfrey's birthday, so sometimes we combine celebrations! Traditionally on St. Andrew's Night the food served has a truly Scottish flavor. And whatever else you decide to put on your menu for St. Andrew's Night, there must be haggis—a traditional dish which is always store-bought. The haggis is served after the first course and before the main course, and is usually "addressed," after being brought into the dining room with some ceremony, hopefully with a piper in attendance. The address is the immortal Ode to the Haggis by Robert Burns. (Any non-Scot present will need a translator.) When the address is finished, a toast is drunk to the haggis, then a very small amount of haggis is given to each guest— really just a token mouthful or two.

ST. ANDREW'S NIGHT DINNER FOR 8

KINLOCH CREAMY SMOKED HADDOCK SOUP

HAGGIS

ROAST VENISON WITH
ROWAN AND APPLE JELLY
BOILED POTATOES WITH FRIED OATMEAL
ROAST PARSNIPS
SPICY RED CABBAGE WITH APPLES, ONIONS AND
RAISINS

ICED WHISKEY AND HONEY CREAMS

SUGGESTED WINES: A FINE SHERRY WITH THE
SOUP; SCOTCH WITH THE HAGGIS; A GOOD FRENCH
BURGUNDY WITH THE VENISON

Kinloch Creamy Smoked Haddock Soup

This soup tastes delicious and looks most attractive. It needs no garnishing—its garnishes are in the soup itself. By adding the parsley at the last minute it keeps its bright, fresh color.

The soup may be prepared in the morning for dinner that night.

2 lb smoked haddock, on the bone if possible
1 quart each milk and water mixed
4 tablespoons unsalted butter
1 tablespoon oil
2 onions, fairly finely chopped
4 potatoes, diced
freshly grated nutmeg
pepper
4 tomatoes, skinned, seeded and diced
1 tablespoon finely chopped fresh parsley

Put the smoked haddock into a saucepan with the mixture of milk and water. Bring the liquid to simmering point, then simmer very gently for 5 minutes. Remove from the heat and leave to cool for 15–20 minutes.

Meanwhile, in another saucepan, melt the butter with the oil. Add the onions and cook for about 5 minutes, stirring occasionally. Add the diced potatoes and cook gently for a further 10–15 minutes, stirring from time to time to prevent sticking. Strain the liquid from the haddock and add to the vegetables. Simmer until the pieces of potato are soft. Purée the vegetables and liquid in a blender or food processor. Pour into a clean saucepan. Season with freshly grated nutmeg and pepper— the smoked haddock will have enough saltiness without you needing to add extra salt.

Flake the fish, removing all bones and skin. Stir the flaked fish and the diced tomatoes into the soup. Heat through gently. Just before serving, stir in the parsley.

Kinloch Creamy Smoked Haddock Soup; Haggis

Roast Venison

— ◆ —

Venison should be hung for 10–14 days after it is shot (the length of time depends on the weather). In the morning on St. Andrew's Day, prepare the vegetables and put them in the roasting pan with the venison on top, all ready to put into the oven for roasting.

3 tablespoons good beef drippings
2 onions, chopped
3 carrots, chopped
3 parsnips, chopped
$\frac{1}{4}$ turnip, chopped
1 celery stalk, sliced
$\frac{1}{2}$ lb mushrooms, roughly sliced
1 haunch of venison, weighing about 6 lb
$1\frac{1}{4}$ cups red wine
$1\frac{1}{4}$ cups milk
2 teaspoons red currant jelly
2 wineglasses port wine
salt and pepper

Melt the drippings in a saucepan and add the vegetables. Cook for 7–10 minutes, stirring occasionally to prevent them from sticking.

Put the venison in a roasting pan. Pour the partially cooked vegetables, drippings and all, over the venison. Roast in a preheated 425° oven for 30 minutes. At the end of this time, baste with the drippings and lower the temperature to 350°. Pour the red wine and milk over the venison. Cover with foil and continue roasting for $1\frac{1}{2}$–2 hours.

Transfer the venison to a warmed platter and keep warm in the oven. Skim the fat off the surface of the cooking juices and vegetables in the roasting pan, then pour the juices and vegetables into a blender or food processor. Add the red currant jelly and port and blend until smooth. Pour this sauce into a saucepan. Taste and adjust the seasoning, then reheat. Serve in a sauce boat or a jug, with the venison.

Rowan and Apple Jelly

— ◆ —

Rowan jelly—made from the berries of the mountain ash—is traditionally served with venison in Scotland; it is also very good served with roast lamb. It is made several months in advance of the feast day.

2 lb apples, quartered
2 lb rowan berries or red currants
5 cups water
1 cinnamon stick
sugar

Put the quartered apples, rowan berries, water and cinnamon into a large saucepan. Simmer until the apples and rowan berries are soft and pulpy, then pour into a jelly bag or large piece of cheesecloth. Leave to strain into a bowl for several hours—overnight, if convenient.

Measure the juice which has dripped from the bag into the bowl: to each $2\frac{1}{2}$ cups of juice add $2\frac{1}{2}$ cups of sugar. Put this into a saucepan, and heat until the sugar has dissolved in the juice. Bring to a boil and boil fast for 5 minutes, then remove the pan from the heat and test for a set: drip a little of the juice onto a saucer and leave to cool for several minutes, then push the jelly with your fingertip. If the jelly wrinkles, you have a set. If it doesn't wrinkle, boil for a further few minutes, then test again. Pack into jars.

Boiled Potatoes with Fried Oatmeal

— ◆ —

Fry the oatmeal and leave it to drain on paper towels on the day before or in the morning. Prepare the potatoes ready for cooking well in advance. If you peel them, be sure to keep them covered with cold water to prevent discoloration.

16 medium potatoes
4 tablespoons unsalted butter
1 teaspoon salt
$\frac{1}{2}$ cup oatmeal

Cut each potato to a uniform size, so that they cook evenly. Cook in boiling salted water until tender.

Meanwhile, melt the butter in a saucepan, add the salt and oatmeal and fry, stirring continuously, until the oatmeal is golden brown. Drain on paper towels.

Drain the potatoes well, and steam over heat for a few moments, to dry off any excess moisture. Turn into a warmed serving dish and sprinkle with the oatmeal.

Roast Parsnips

Peel the parsnips and halve them ready for cooking, when convenient. Keep them covered with cold water to prevent discoloration, but drain and pat dry thoroughly before cooking.

8 tablespoons good beef drippings, or a mixture of sunflower oil and butter
16 parsnips, halved lengthwise

Heat a coating layer of drippings (or oil and butter) in a roasting pan. Add the parsnips and turn to coat with the fat. Roast in a preheated 375° oven for 45–50 minutes or until tender. Turn them occasionally during roasting so they brown evenly. They will keep warm very well in a cool oven, on a serving dish.

Spicy Red Cabbage with Apples, Onions and Raisins

This is such a convenient vegetable dish to prepare, because it can all be made in the morning and reheated for dinner that night. The flavors of red cabbage, apples and onions all go very well with venison, and with all game.

3 tablespoons oil
2 tablespoons unsalted butter
2 onions, finely sliced
1 medium head red cabbage, trimmed of its outer leaves and finely shredded
3 apples, cored and chopped
$\frac{1}{3}$ cup (2 oz) raisins
2 tablespoons wine vinegar
1 teaspoon ground allspice
salt and pepper

Heat the oil in a large saucepan or flameproof casserole and melt the butter in it. Add the onions and cook for 2–3 minutes, then add the cabbage, apples, raisins, vinegar, allspice and seasoning. Cook over a gentle heat for about 30 minutes, stirring from time to time so that it cooks evenly.

Iced Whiskey and Honey Creams

These iced creams need no decoration, in my opinion, but if you like, a sprinkling of grated chocolate looks pretty. They will keep well in the freezer, and so may be made well in advance.

$\frac{1}{4}$ cup thick honey
4 large egg yolks
$1\frac{1}{4}$ cups heavy cream
$\frac{1}{4}$ cup whiskey
grated chocolate, to decorate (optional)

Put the honey into a saucepan and heat until the honey is very hot and runny. Beat the egg yolks, then gradually add the hot honey, beating until the mixture is pale in color, thick and mousse-like.

Whip the cream, whipping in the whiskey one spoonful at a time. Fold together the egg yolk mixture and the cream mixture. Divide evenly between 8 ramekins. Put the ramekins on a tray and into the freezer. Cover and freeze until firm.

151

CHILDREN'S BIRTHDAY PARTY FOR 12

This party is designed to suit children from the ages of 6 to 12 years. After the age of 6 or 7, children's birthday parties cease being a trial and become fun for the parents and other adults present, as well as for the younger guests.

The menu for this party is refreshingly straightforward, without endless different plates full of a variety of food. The Squirrel Platters contain miniature cakes decorated with tiny stars of lemon buttercream and candy diamonds, and midget vanilla cookies. Anything scaled down in size—like these cakes and cookies—is instantly appealing to children. The main course of the party menu is a choice of three different types of burger—beef, sausage or tuna. Each burger is served in a warmed bun, itself wrapped in a paper napkin, and accompanied by a selection of relishes. If the weather permits, you could barbecue the burgers. For dessert there is a delectable "mountain" gelatin mold made from fresh strawberry purée, and decorated with rosettes of whipped cream and strawberries. To drink there are fresh banana milk shakes, with a decoration of grated chocolate on each glassful. The finale is a Sparkling Butterfly Cake, decorated with chocolate butterflies and dramatically lit by sparklers.

CHILDREN'S BIRTHDAY PARTY FOR 12

SQUIRREL PLATTERS

BURGER SELECTION

STRAWBERRY MOUNTAIN

BANANA MILK SHAKES

SPARKLING BUTTERFLY CAKE

Squirrel Platters

These are for nibbling while the burgers cook. They will appeal to all ages, and they don't just look pretty, they taste delicious too. Both the cakes and the cookies can be made the day before the party. Arrange the mini cakes with the little vanilla cookies on doily-lined trays to make a sweet platter. Make up a platter with potato chips and cooked cocktail sausages as well.

8 tablespoons (1 stick) unsalted butter, softened
$\frac{2}{3}$ cup sugar
2 large eggs
$\frac{3}{4}$ cup self-rising flour
DECORATION
5 tablespoons unsalted butter
2 cups confectioners' sugar, sifted
finely grated rind of 1 lemon
2 teaspoons hot water
diamond-shaped candies

Place about 50 petits fours cases on one large baking sheet, or on two smaller baking sheets.

Put the butter, sugar, eggs and self-rising flour into a mixing bowl and beat well together for about 2 minutes, until well blended and smooth. Put the cake batter into a pastry bag fitted with a $\frac{1}{2}$-inch plain tube. Pipe the batter into the paper cases, filling each one half full. (The cake batter may also be spooned into the cases, but it is very much quicker to pipe it in.)

Bake the cakes in a preheated 375° oven for 15–20 minutes, until they are well risen, lightly browned and firm to the touch. Cool on wire racks.

To make the decoration, beat the butter until soft, then beat in the confectioners' sugar, lemon rind and hot water. Continue beating until the buttercream is very light and creamy. Put the buttercream into a pastry bag fitted with a medium-size star tube. Pipe a star of buttercream on the top of each little cake, then decorate with the candy diamonds.

Little Vanilla Cookies

Makes 60.

8 tablespoons (1 stick) unsalted butter
$\frac{3}{4}$ cup confectioners' sugar, sifted
$\frac{1}{2}$ teaspoon vanilla extract
1 cup flour
pinch of salt
confectioners' sugar, to decorate

Grease several baking sheets. Beat the butter until soft, then beat in the confectioners' sugar and vanilla. Sift in the flour and salt and mix well, working the mixture together by hand, until smooth.

Cut the dough into two equal pieces. Shape each piece into a long roll about 8 inches long and $1\frac{1}{2}$ inches in diameter. Wrap each roll in plastic wrap and refrigerate for at least 3 hours or overnight.

Taking one roll of dough at a time, cut it into slices about $\frac{1}{8}$ inch thick—cutting straight across or on a slant. You could cut one roll straight across to make round cookies and the other on a slant to make oval cookies. There should be about 60 slices.

Place the cookies on the baking sheets, spacing well apart. Bake in a preheated 350° oven for 10–15 minutes, until the cookies are colored very slightly around the edges. Allow the cookies to cool on the baking sheets for about 2 minutes, then remove them with a spatula to wire racks to cool completely. The cookies will crisp up as they cool.

To serve, very lightly sift confectioners' sugar over the cookies, then arrange neatly on doily-lined trays with the mini-cakes.

Burger Selection

Each of the following recipes make 12 burgers, so you can decide whether to make one or more types of burger, depending on the age and appetites of your guests. You can make and freeze the beef and sausage burgers in advance; allow 3–4 hours thawing at room temperature before cooking.

HAMBURGERS
$2\frac{1}{2}$ lb chuck
1 large onion, skinned
1 cup fresh white breadcrumbs
1 egg, lightly beaten
salt and pepper
SAUSAGE BURGERS
$1\frac{1}{2}$ lb pork sausage
1 onion, finely chopped
2 tablespoons ketchup
2 teaspoons mixed dried herbs
salt and pepper
TUNA BURGERS
four 7-oz cans tuna fish in oil, well drained
3 cups fresh white breadcrumbs
3 tablespoons mayonnaise
2 large eggs, lightly beaten
salt and pepper
oil for frying
FOR SERVING
fresh buns, warmed
selection of relishes

To make the hamburgers, remove all of the fat and the connective tissue from the chuck. Finely grind the meat with onion in a meat grinder or food processor. Mix the meat and onion with the breadcrumbs, egg and sea-soning. Divide the mixture equally into 12 pieces. On a lightly floured surface, shape each piece into a flat round about $3\frac{1}{2}$ inches in diameter. Alternatively, shape the burgers in a burger press if you have one. Place the burgers on trays lined with wax paper and refrigerate until required for cooking.

To make the sausage burgers, put the sausage, onion, ketchup, herbs and seasoning into a mixing bowl, and beat well together. Divide the mixture into 12 equal-sized pieces. On a lightly floured surface, shape each piece into a flat round about $3\frac{1}{2}$ inches in diameter. Place the burgers on trays lined with wax paper and re-frigerate until required for cooking.

To make the tuna burgers, put the tuna fish in a large mixing bowl with the breadcrumbs, mayonnaise and eggs. Season and mix thoroughly together. Divide the mixture into 12 equal-sized pieces. Shape each piece into a flat round about $3\frac{1}{2}$ inches in diameter. Place on trays lined with wax paper, and refrigerate until required for cooking.

To cook the burgers, heat 2–3 tablespoons of oil in 2 large frying pans, add the burgers and cook gently for 4–5 minutes on each side, until golden brown and cooked through. The tuna burgers will take only 3–4 minutes each side.

To serve, place each burger inside a warmed, or toasted, bun then wrap in a paper napkin and serve immediately, accompanied by a selection of relishes.

The burgers may also be cooked on a barbecue at an outdoor party.

Banana Milk Shakes

This recipe makes 2–4 drinks, depending on the age and appetite of the children. Banana milk shakes are quite delicious but rather filling, so smaller amounts per guest will leave more room for other goodies.

2 very ripe bananas, sliced
$2\frac{1}{2}$ cups ice cold milk
1 cup (2 large scoops) vanilla ice cream
grated chocolate, to decorate

Put the bananas into the goblet of an electric blender. Add the milk and ice cream. Cover, and blend at full speed for about 1 minute.

Pour the milk shakes into tall glasses, insert straws, and sprinkle with grated chocolate. Serve immediately. Make more milk shakes in the same way.

Sparkling Butterfly Cake

Make the cake the day before the party—or bake the cake a week or two ahead and freeze it if this is more convenient for you; fill and assemble it the day before. The chocolate butterflies can be made the day before the party, but don't store them in the refrigerator as the chocolate may develop a "bloom." Keep them in a cool place. The orange syrup can be made a day or two ahead, and kept in the refrigerator.

½ lb (2 sticks) unsalted butter
1 cup sugar
3 tablespoons corn syrup
6 oz semi-sweet chocolate, melted
4 large eggs
1¾ cups self-rising flour
BUTTERFLIES
3 oz semi-sweet chocolate, melted
ORANGE SYRUP
⅔ cup water
⅔ cup sugar
thinly pared rind of 2 large oranges
FILLING AND DECORATION
1 lb semi-sweet chocolate
½ cup water
6 egg yolks
2 cups heavy cream
4 oz chocolate flakes or vermicelli
4 small sparklers

To make the butterflies, put about 2 teaspoons of the melted chocolate into a small paper pastry bag, then cut a small hole in the bottom of the bag. Place a small square of wax paper over the diagram for the butterfly wings. Carefully pipe the chocolate around the outside edge of the wings (just as though you were tracing it with a pencil). Having outlined the wings, fill in the center with joining squiggley lines, to give a lace-like effect. Fill in the "body" with a solid spiral of chocolate. For the antennae, simply pipe two straight lines, with a dot at the top of each one. Carefully move the wax paper to a flat tray.

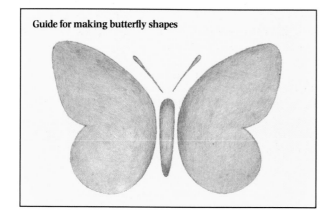

Guide for making butterfly shapes

Make more butterflies in the same way: you will need about 8 butterflies for decoration, but make a few more to allow for breakage.

Put the butterflies in a cool place to set hard. Once the chocolate has hardened, the butterflies may be stored in a tin, in a cool place.

Other animals, such as dogs, cats and squirrels may be made instead of butterflies. These will look better if they are completely filled in with chocolate—the lace effect looks best on more delicate shapes, such as the butterflies.

To make the cake, grease and flour a 10-inch round deep cake pan. Beat the butter, sugar and corn syrup together until very light and fluffy. Beat in the melted chocolate, then beat in the eggs one at a time, beating well between each addition. Gently fold in the flour.

Spoon the cake batter into the prepared pan and spread evenly. Bake in a preheated 350° oven for about 1 hour until the cake shrinks very slightly from the side of the pan and a skewer inserted in the center comes out clean. Carefully turn the cake out onto a rack to cool.

To make the orange syrup, put the water, sugar, and orange rind into a small saucepan. Heat very gently until the sugar dissolves, then bring to a boil, and boil gently for 5 minutes until syrupy. Allow to cool, then remove the orange rind.

To make the filling, break the chocolate into small pieces and put them into a mixing bowl with the water. Place the bowl over a pan of hot water and heat until the chocolate melts. Stir frequently to ensure that the chocolate melts smoothly. Beat the egg yolks into the melted chocolate, then remove the bowl from the saucepan. Cool the mixture until it is cold, but not set.

Whip the cream until it will hold soft peaks. Fold the cream and the chocolate mixture together.

To assemble the cake, slice the cake into two equal layers. Place the bottom layer of cake on a board or plate. Brush evenly with half of the orange syrup, then spread with a generous layer of the chocolate cream. Brush the cut side of the second layer of cake with orange syrup, then place it, cut side down, on top of the chocolate cream.

Spread an even layer of chocolate cream around the side of the cake, then coat it evenly with chocolate flakes or vermicelli.

Spread an even layer of chocolate cream over the top of the cake, and mark it roughly with a long narrow spatula. Put the remaining chocolate cream into a pastry bag fitted with a star tube. Pipe rosettes or shells around the top and bottom edges of the cake.

Pipe 8 short lines—about 1 inch long—of chocolate cream on top of the cake, evenly spaced apart around the outside edge, and pointing toward the center. Carefully remove a pair of butterfly wings from the wax paper. Insert a wing on either side of one of the short lines of cream, then place a "body" piece in the center and insert a pair of antennae. Repeat with the remaining butterflies.

Refrigerate the cake overnight, then remove it from

Sparkling Butterfly Cake; Squirrel Platters; Strawberry Mountain; Burger Selection

the refrigerator about $1\frac{1}{2}$ hours before serving.

To serve the cake, place 4 sparklers on top of the cake, spaced apart. Light the sparklers, then take the cake, sparkling, to the table. If wished, traditional candles may also be put on top of the cake, to be lit after the sparklers have gone out.

Warning:
While the sparklers are alight, do not place the cake on a table covered with a paper table cloth. Keep the cake held high until the sparklers have finished burning.

Strawberry Mountain

This gelatin can be made a day or two before the day of the party, and turned out and decorated shortly before serving.

4 lb fresh strawberries, hulled, or frozen strawberries, thawed
$1\frac{1}{3}$ cups sugar
four 6-oz packages of strawberry-flavored gelatin
DECORATION
$\frac{2}{3}$ cup heavy cream
$\frac{1}{2}$ lb fresh strawberries, hulled
little paper flags (optional)

Cut the strawberries up roughly, and put them into a large mixing bowl. Sprinkle the sugar over the strawberries, cover and leave to stand for about 1 hour.

Purée the strawberries in a blender or food processor. Pass the strawberry purée through a very fine sieve. (If you do not have a very fine sieve, squeeze the purée, a little at a time, through cheesecloth.) Add water, if necessary, to yield 2 quarts.

Dissolve the gelatin in 1 cup boiling water, then stir into the strawberry purée.

Pour into a $2\frac{1}{2}$-quart mold, a tall one if possible. Refrigerate overnight.

To unmold the gelatin, dip the mold up to the rim in very hot water for 5 seconds. Place a flat plate on top of the mold, then invert the mold and plate together. Holding the plate and the mold firmly together, give the gelatin a sharp shake to free it from the mold. Carefully lift off the mold.

To decorate the gelatin, whip the cream until it is thick, but not buttery. Spoon the cream into a pastry bag fitted with a large star tube. Pipe rosettes of cream around the base of the gelatin. Decorate with strawberries, and with small flags, each one bearing the name of a party guest. Keep refrigerated until serving.

CHRISTMAS DINNER FOR 8-10

My first favorite for dinner at Christmas is turkey—a fresh bird, never a frozen turkey—but to make a change, I am choosing goose as the main course for this Christmas Dinner. Each year more and more people seek an alternative to turkey, and goose is a very good one.

Goose is a rich meat, so I suggest a light first course: fish marinated overnight in a mixture of lemon juice and white wine vinegar. To accompany the goose I suggest roast potatoes and a creamy purée of Brussels sprouts, flavored with nutmeg and leeks braised with tomatoes.

This recipe for plum pudding, which was given to my mother by the wife of our vicar in our village in the north west of England years and years ago, contains neither flour nor breadcrumbs, so is particularly light. As an alternative to Christmas pudding, I like Iced Apricot and Orange Mousse.

CHRISTMAS DINNER FOR 8–10

MARINATED TURBOT WITH TOMATO MAYONNAISE

ROAST GOOSE WITH APPLE AND PRUNE STUFFING

ROAST POTATOES

BRUSSELS SPROUT PURÉE WITH TOASTED CASHEW NUTS

LEEKS BRAISED WITH TOMATOES

PLUM PUDDING

BRANDY BUTTER WITH ORANGE AND CINNAMON

OR

ICED APRICOT AND ORANGE MOUSSE

SUGGESTED WINES: CHAMPAGNE BEFORE DINNER; A FRUITY DRY WHITE WINE, WITH THE GOOSE, SUCH AS A GOOD CROZES HERMITAGE OR CHATEAUNEUF DU PAPE BLANC. FOLLOW WITH A RICH SAUTERNES OR GERMAN BEERENAUSLESE

Marinated Turbot with Tomato Mayonnaise

You can use any firm-fleshed white fish for this dish— monkfish or halibut for example. The fish is cut into small pieces and marinated in lemon and white wine vinegar overnight. For serving, it is drained, arranged on a bed of shredded lettuce and accompanied by a tomato mayonnaise. The pink of the mayonnaise, with its green flecks of parsley, looks very pretty against the white fish. The mayonnaise can be prepared well in advance, and the lettuce shredded on Christmas Eve and kept in a plastic bag in the refrigerator.

2 lb turbot fillet
$1\frac{1}{4}$ cups white wine vinegar
$1\frac{1}{4}$ cups fresh lemon juice
1 head iceberg lettuce, shredded
MAYONNAISE
1 egg
1 egg yolk
1 tablespoon tomato paste
salt and pepper
$1\frac{1}{2}$ teaspoons sugar
$\frac{1}{2}$ garlic clove, skinned
$\frac{2}{3}$ cup mixed sunflower and olive oil
3 tablespoons wine vinegar
1 handful of fresh parsley, stems removed

To prepare the fish, trim it of any bones and skin. Cut the fish into pieces about $\frac{1}{2}$ inch in size and put them into a shallow non-metallic dish. Pour the vinegar and lemon juice over and leave to marinate overnight in a cool place. In the morning, give the pieces of fish a stir, so that they get mixed up in the marinade and are coated evenly.

To make the mayonnaise, put the whole egg, egg yolk, tomato paste, seasoning, sugar and garlic into a blender or food processor and blend briefly. Add the oil, drop by drop, still blending. When about half the oil has been added, the remainder may be added more quickly. Blend in the vinegar and parsley. Taste the mayonnaise and adjust the seasoning if necessary. Store the mayonnaise in a screw-top jar, or a bowl with a lid, in the refrigerator.

To serve, drain the fish. Divide the lettuce between the serving plates and arrange the fish on top. Either put a spoonful of the mayonnaise on the side of each plate, or serve it separately.

Roast Goose with Apple and Prune Stuffing

Goose produces a lot of fat during cooking, and halfway through the cooking time it can be drained off and used to cook the roast potatoes. All over Britain, goose fat has many other interesting applications—in the north west of England, farmers and keen gardeners put goose fat around their roses. It is also thought to be good for bad chests—and for cows' udders! So don't just throw it away. The stuffing for the goose can be prepared the day before, and the goose stuffed on Christmas morning. Cook your goose to have it ready about 40 minutes before you want to serve it. It will keep hot very well in a cool oven and will enable you to have a peaceful drink before dinner.

11-lb oven-ready goose
1 tablespoon all-purpose flour
2½ cups chicken stock (see page 181)
gravy browning (optional)
¼ cup dry vermouth
salt and pepper
STUFFING
2 tablespoons oil
2 onions, finely chopped
1 celery stalk, finely sliced
3 large tart apples
lemon juice
⅔ cup (4 oz) chopped prunes
½ cup raw brown rice, cooked
1 teaspoon chopped fresh lemon thyme, or
½ teaspoon dried thyme
salt and pepper

To make the stuffing, heat the oil in a saucepan, add the onions and celery and cook for about 5 minutes, until softened, stirring from time to time.

Meanwhile, peel, core and dice the apples, dropping them into a bowl of water with lemon juice.

Drain the apples, and mix together with the onion and celery mixture, the prunes, rice, lemon thyme and seasoning. Stuff the goose with this, then truss.

Put the goose in a large roasting pan. Roast in a preheated 425° oven for about 2½ hours. Halfway through the cooking time, drain off the fat.

When the goose is cooked—test it with a skewer: the juices that run out should be clear—remove it to a serving platter. Cover with foil and keep warm.

To make the gravy, pour most of the fat out of the roasting pan. Sprinkle in enough flour to absorb the fat, and cook on top of the stove for a minute or two, scraping the pan and stirring well to prevent the flour from burning. Gradually stir in the chicken stock and bring to a boil, still stirring. Color with a few drops of gravy browning, if you wish, and stir in the dry vermouth and seasoning.

Roast Potatoes

The potatoes can be peeled up to 3 days before Christmas Day, but remember to change the cold water covering the potatoes every day.

3 lb potatoes, peeled
goose fat

Cut the potatoes into equal-sized pieces. If prepared in advance, keep them in a bowl of cold water to prevent discoloration. When ready to cook, drain the potatoes and pat them dry. Heat the goose fat in a roasting pan in the oven with the goose. Add the potatoes and turn them to coat evenly with the fat. Roast for 1–1¼ hours or until tender and golden brown, turning the potatoes over from time to time.

Brussels Sprout Purée with Toasted Cashew Nuts

Make the sauce a day or two in advance. When cool, press buttered wax paper onto the surface (this prevents a skin from forming) and store in the refrigerator. The actual cooking and puréeing of the sprouts doesn't take a minute, especially if you have a food processor. The sprouts can be prepared for cooking up to 2 days in advance, and the cashew nuts toasted, sprinkled with salt and kept in a screw-top jar for several days ahead.

2 lb Brussels sprouts
1¼ cups basic white sauce (see page 184)
freshly grated nutmeg
salt and pepper
½ cup chopped toasted cashew nuts

Put the sprouts into a saucepan and pour boiling water over them to a depth of about 1 inch. Cover with a lid, and cook over high heat for about 10–15 minutes until tender.

Meanwhile, reheat the sauce, stirring occasionally. Drain the sprouts and put them in a blender or food processor with the hot sauce, and nutmeg and seasoning to taste. Blend until smooth. Put into a warmed serving dish, and sprinkle over the toasted cashew nuts. Keep warm until you are ready to serve.

157

Leeks Braised with Tomatoes

The leeks and tomatoes can be prepared for cooking on Christmas Eve. Then all you need to do on Christmas Day is gently cook them together.

3 lb leeks, washed and trimmed
2 tablespoons oil
1 lb fresh ripe tomatoes, skinned, seeded and diced or canned chopped tomatoes
salt and pepper

Cut the leeks into pieces about 2 inches long. Heat the oil in a flameproof casserole which has a lid. Add the prepared leeks and cook over a moderate heat for 5 minutes, turning the leeks from time to time. Add the tomatoes and seasoning. Cover with the lid and cook gently for 10–15 minutes. Serve warm.

Plum Pudding

Plum puddings can be made at any time—whenever it is convenient for you. But as they really do improve with keeping, try to make them in the fall if you can. This recipe is wonderful—light and not at all stodgy because it contains no flour or breadcrumbs, just fruit and suet and brandy, bound together with beaten eggs. You can even leave out the sugar if you wish.

2 cups ($\frac{3}{4}$ lb) golden raisins
3 cups shredded suet
2 cups ($\frac{3}{4}$ lb) raisins, halved if large
1 cup (6 oz) currants
1 cup (6 oz) chopped candied peel
$\frac{3}{4}$ cup (3 oz) slivered almonds, toasted
grated rind of 1 lemon
1 cup dark brown sugar
$\frac{3}{4}$ teaspoon freshly grated nutmeg
6 eggs, beaten
1 wineglass brandy
1 cup milk

Combine all the ingredients, mixing thoroughly. Put the mixture into a buttered 2-quart steaming mold. Cover with a circle of wax paper. If you are using a steaming mold with a clip-on lid, just clip it on. Otherwise, tie on a cloth cover and knot the corners on top to prevent them from trailing in the water. Put the pudding into a saucepan and half fill the pan with boiling water. Cover the pan with a lid, and put onto the heat. Steam the pudding for 5–6 hours, replenishing the boiling water in the saucepan from time to time, to prevent it boiling dry. Allow to cool, then recover with a fresh cloth or paper. To reheat the pudding on Christmas Day, steam again for $1\frac{1}{2}$–2 hours.

Brandy Butter with Orange and Cinnamon

This can be made 10–14 days before Christmas, and stored in a covered container in the refrigerator. Remember to take the brandy butter out of the refrigerator at least 2 hours before serving.

$\frac{1}{2}$ lb (2 sticks) unsalted butter
$1\frac{1}{3}$ cups light brown sugar
$\frac{1}{2}$ cup brandy
grated rind of 1 orange
$1\frac{1}{2}$ teaspoons ground cinnamon

Beat the butter until softened, then gradually add the soft brown sugar. Beat until fluffy. Beat in the brandy, a spoonful at a time. Beat in the grated orange rind and cinnamon. Chill in a covered container.

Iced Apricot and Orange Mousse

This makes a refreshing alternative to plum pudding. It is delicious and easy to make, and will keep well in the freezer for several weeks.

1 lb dried apricots, soaked overnight and drained
4 eggs, separated
$\frac{2}{3}$ cup sugar
$1\frac{1}{4}$ cups heavy cream
grated rind of 1 orange
$\frac{1}{4}$ cup orange liqueur such as Cointreau

Purée the apricots in a blender or food processor.

Put the egg yolks into a bowl and beat, adding the sugar gradually. Continue beating until the mixture is thick, pale and mousse-like. Fold in the apricot purée.

Whip the cream, adding the grated orange rind and liqueur. Beat the egg whites until stiff. Fold the whipped cream into the apricot mixture. Lastly, using a large metal spoon, fold in the egg whites gently but thoroughly.

Spoon the mousse into a freezerproof container or serving dish and freeze until firm.

Transfer the mousse to the refrigerator just before serving the first course, to allow the dessert to soften.

Plum Pudding

THEME PARTIES

Theme parties were greatly in vogue in the Thirties, and they are coming back into fashion with a vengeance! There are so many ideas for theme parties, and here I give you suggestions, with appropriate menus.

The food you serve at your theme party is only part of the occasion. The rest of the atmosphere is created by props, such as china, pictures, flowers, lighting, music and, more than anything else, the clothes you and your guests wear. The latter helps to create the atmosphere for the evening in two ways—by their very appearance, and also because there is a great anticipation of the event through planning and wearing a costume. There is an added bonus: coming in costume is a natural ice-breaker, getting the evening started with the best ingredient for a successful party—laughter!

Procuring the right props for a theme party does not mean spending a fortune acquiring a collection of cloths, costumes, backdrops, china, etc., because such things are to be found in abundance at garage sales and in second-hand markets. You can find wonderful props for your party, such as brocade curtains or bedcovers which can be used as a table covering or hung on the wall as a backdrop for an Arabian evening.

Pink Party for 25 (see page 178)

A TASTE OF THE CARIBBEAN

One of the most evocative sounds of the Caribbean is that of a steel band, so if you can, get some records of steel band music and play them and reggae music throughout the evening. Palm trees, whether plastic or made out of papier maché, will create a Caribbean atmosphere, and for a humorous touch, scatter coconuts about under the palm trees. Ask your guests to wear Caribbean-style clothes, with brightly colored floral designs—straw hats too, if they wish.

The food completes the Caribbean atmosphere. The first course is a salad of salt cod spiced with chili and partnered by slices of avocado. This is served with cornbread. The main course is delicious Creole Beef—broiled marinated steaks flamed in rum and garnished with exotic fruits. Baked sweet potatoes and green beans are excellent accompaniments. Finally, there is a creamy mousse of guava scented with lime.

Salt Cod Salad with Avocado; Sweet Cornbread

Salt Cod Salad with Avocado

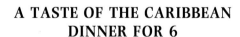

You can soak and cook the fish the day before the party, and make the fish salad in the morning on the day.

1½ lb salt cod
1 cucumber, peeled and sliced
2 medium tomatoes, skinned and sliced
1 green chili pepper, seeded and finely chopped
2 tablespoons lime juice
3 tablespoons sunflower oil
pepper
3 avocados
2 tablespoons chopped fresh coriander or parsley

Place the fish in a large bowl, cover with cold water and leave to soak for 2 hours, changing the water twice. Drain. Place the fish in a pan with fresh cold water to cover and bring to a boil. Simmer for 20 minutes, then drain. Remove the skin and bones and flake the fish. Leave to cool. Mix together the fish, cucumber, tomatoes and chili. Pour over the lime juice, oil and pepper.

Peel, halve and pit the avocados. Slice them lengthwise. Arrange a fan of avocado slices on each serving plate with a serving of fish salad beside it. Sprinkle the salad with a little parsley and serve at once.

**A TASTE OF THE CARIBBEAN
DINNER FOR 6**

SALT COD SALAD WITH AVOCADO

SWEET CORNBREAD

BEEF CREOLE

BAKED SWEET POTATOES

GREEN BEANS

GUAVA MOUSSE

SUGGESTED WINES: DRY SHERRY WITH THE FIRST
COURSE, AND A ROBUST RED WINE, SUCH AS
AUSTRALIAN HERMITAGE OR RHONE VALLEY, WITH
THE STEAKS

Sweet Cornbread

Make this bread on the day of the party.

$1\frac{1}{3}$ cups all-purpose flour
1 tablespoon baking powder
1 teaspoon salt
$1\frac{1}{4}$ cups cornmeal
2 tablespoons sugar
2 eggs, beaten
4 tablespoons butter, melted
$1-1\frac{1}{4}$ cups milk

Sift the flour, baking powder and salt into a bowl. Stir in the cornmeal and sugar. Make a well in the center and add the eggs, butter and a little milk. Beat with a wooden spoon, adding the remaining milk a little at a time until you have a smooth batter.

Turn the mixture into a greased 7-inch square pan and smooth the top. Bake in a preheated 375° oven for 30–35 minutes, until golden brown and firm to the touch. Cool in the pan for 10 minutes, then turn out onto a wire rack to cool completely. Cut into squares to serve.

Beef Creole

You can marinate the steaks overnight, if it is more convenient for you. This will give the marinade longer to impart its flavor to the meat, too.

six 6–8 oz boneless sirloin steaks
2 garlic cloves, crushed
6 tablespoons olive oil
1 tablespoon wine vinegar
salt and pepper
1 lb mixed fruits, e.g., pineapple, papaya, mango,
watermelon, prepared and sliced
1 teaspoon Dijon mustard
2 tablespoons lemon juice
6 tablespoons dark rum

Arrange the steaks, in one layer, in a shallow dish. Mix the garlic, 2 tablespoons oil, the vinegar and seasoning together and pour over the steaks. Leave to marinate for at least 1 hour, turning once.

Meanwhile, arrange the fruit around the edge of a serving platter. Cover tightly and set aside. Place the mustard, lemon juice, remaining oil and seasoning in a screw-top jar and shake well to mix.

Broil the steaks for 6–8 minutes, turning once, until done to your liking. Meanwhile, warm the rum.

Pour the dressing over the fruit. Arrange the steaks in the center of the platter. Pour over the rum and ignite. Serve when the flames have subsided.

Guava Mousse

This is a wonderful mousse—the lime brings out the flavor of the guava beautifully. Make the night before the party, but add the decoration only an hour or so before serving.

4 guavas
3 eggs, separated
$\frac{1}{2}$ cup sugar
$\frac{1}{2}$ teaspoon grated lime rind
2 teaspoons unflavored gelatin
2 tablespoons lime juice
$1\frac{1}{4}$ cups heavy cream
DECORATION
$\frac{1}{2}$ cup heavy cream
crystallized or glacé fruits

Peel and halve the guavas. Remove the black pits with a teaspoon. Purée the flesh in a blender or food processor. Place the egg yolks and sugar in a bowl and beat until thick and fluffy. Beat in the puréed guavas and lime rind. Sprinkle the gelatin over the lime juice in a small bowl. Place the bowl in a pan of simmering water and leave to dissolve. Cool slightly, then stir into the fruit mixture. Whip the cream and fold into the mixture. Beat the egg whites and fold in. Transfer to a serving bowl and leave to set in the refrigerator.

Whip the cream for the decoration until it just holds its shape. Spread over the mousse. Decorate with small pieces of crystallized or glacé fruits.

ARABIAN NIGHTS

Try to create the interior of a Bedouin tent for this Arabian Nights feast. This is not as difficult as you may think—with colored sheets or thin material billowing from the ceiling, Persian rugs on the floor, and cushions for your guests to recline on as they eat, you will soon have the impression of a tent's interior. If you can find a volunteer to do a belly dance, that will only add to the Arabian atmosphere!

This menu begins with 3 unusual appetizers—a sesame, almond and yogurt dip served with spiced pita bread; artichoke hearts in garlic-flavored olive oil; and tiny deep-fried chicken meatballs flavored with lemon and cumin. The main course is a stew of lamb with quinces and chick peas, warmly spiced. It is accompanied by zucchini and raisin couscous. You might want to offer a simple tomato and onion salad, too. Then, for dessert, there is a compôte of oranges and figs in a honey syrup. Turkish coffee will provide the finishing touch.

ARABIAN NIGHTS DINNER FOR 8

TAHINI WITH YOGURT AND ALMONDS, WITH
SPICED PITA BREAD
ARTICHOKE HEARTS IN OLIVE OIL
CHICKEN KOFTAS

LAMB AND QUINCE STEW
RAISIN AND ZUCCHINI COUSCOUS
TOMATO AND ONION SALAD

HONEY AND ORANGE FIGS

SUGGESTED WINE: A MEDIUM DRY WHITE SUCH AS
CALIFORNIAN SAUVIGNON OR CHENIN BLANC WITH
THE MAIN COURSE, OR ANY CABERNET SAUVIGNON

Tahini with Yogurt and Almonds

1 garlic clove, crushed
$\frac{2}{3}$ cup tahini (sesame paste)
$\frac{2}{3}$ cup plain yogurt
6 tablespoons lemon juice
$\frac{1}{2}$ teaspoon ground cumin
salt and pepper
3 tablespoons (1 oz) ground almonds
almond halves, for garnish

Mix the garlic and tahini paste together. Stir in the yogurt, then gradually add the lemon juice until the mixture is creamy, beating well. Add the cumin and seasoning. Stir in the ground almonds.

Place in a serving bowl. Serve with spiced pita bread.

Spiced Pita Bread

The pita bread can be made well in advance and frozen. To reheat, put the bread under the broiler and cook for 4–5 minutes before serving.
Makes 10.

2 teaspoons cumin seeds
2 tablespoons sesame seeds
$\frac{1}{2}$ teaspoon sugar
3 teaspoons active dry yeast
$1\frac{1}{2}$ cups lukewarm water
$3\frac{1}{2}$ cups all-purpose flour
$\frac{1}{2}$ teaspoon salt
2 teaspoons ground coriander
1 tablespoon oil

Scatter the cumin and sesame seeds over a sheet of foil and place under the broiler. Toast for 2–3 minutes, stirring to prevent burning. Remove and cool.

Dissolve the sugar and yeast in the water. Place the flour, salt, coriander and toasted spices in a large bowl and mix well. Make a well in the center and add the yeast liquid and oil. Mix with a large fork to a soft dough.

Knead the dough on a lightly floured surface for about 10 minutes, until it feels smooth and no longer sticky. Return it to the mixing bowl, cover with plastic wrap and leave to rise in a warm place about 1 hour, until double in size.

Knead the dough again to remove any large air bubbles. Divide into 10 equal pieces. Roll out each piece of dough to an oval 9 inches long. Place them on greased and floured baking sheets. Brush with water and sprinkle with flour. Leave to rise again for about 30 minutes. Bake in a preheated 450° oven for 8–10 minutes, until puffed but not browned. Serve warm or cool.

Lamb and Quince Stew

This tastes even better if it is made the day before the party. Skim any fat from the surface before reheating.

3 lb lean boneless lamb, such as leg
2 onions, finely chopped
$\frac{1}{2}$ teaspoon cayenne
2 teaspoons ground coriander
1 teaspoon ground cinnamon
$\frac{1}{4}$ teaspoon powdered saffron
1 red pepper, cored, seeded and diced
$1\frac{1}{2}$ cups cooked chick peas or drained canned chick peas
12 oz quinces, peeled, quartered and cored
2 tablespoons chopped fresh parsley
salt and pepper

Trim off excess fat from the lamb and cut the meat into cubes. Place in a pan with the onions, spices, saffron and $2\frac{1}{2}$ cups water. Bring gently to a boil and skim off any scum that rises to the surface. Reduce the heat, cover, and simmer for 30 minutes.

Add the red pepper and chick peas. Add the quinces with the parsley and seasoning. Simmer for a further 30–40 minutes, until the lamb is very tender. Serve hot.

From the Back: Lamb and Quince Stew; Raisin and Zucchini Couscous; Tomato and Onion Salad

Artichoke Hearts in Olive Oil

Make these on the morning of the party, and keep them in a cool place.

6 tablespoons lemon juice
8 globe artichokes
6 tablespoons olive oil
2 garlic cloves, peeled
salt and pepper

Add 2 tablespoons of the lemon juice to a large bowl of cold water. Remove the stems and outer leaves from the artichokes. Using a sharp stainless steel knife, slice off the remaining leaves to within $\frac{1}{2}$ inch of the heart. Remove the chokes with a teaspoon. As the artichoke hearts are prepared, plunge them quickly into the acidulated water to cover them completely. This will prevent them discoloring. Place 2 cups of water in a saucepan with the remaining lemon juice, the olive oil, whole garlic cloves and seasoning. Bring to a boil, then add the artichoke hearts and simmer for 20–25 minutes, until tender.

Remove the artichoke hearts with a slotted spoon. Boil the cooking liquid until reduced by half, then strain a little over the artichoke hearts. Leave to cool, then cut the hearts into quarters.

Chicken Koftas

These delicious little chicken meatballs can be prepared in the morning ready to fry in the evening. Or, if serving cold, fry them ahead of time.

$\frac{1}{2}$ lb cooked chicken meat, skinned
1 cup fresh white breadcrumbs
1 egg, lightly beaten
2 teaspoons lemon juice
little grated nutmeg
salt and pepper
flour
oil for deep frying
lemon wedges, to serve

Grind or process the chicken finely and set aside. Soak the breadcrumbs in a little water for 5 minutes, then squeeze dry with the hands. Mix the breadcrumbs with the chicken, egg, lemon juice, nutmeg and seasoning. Continue mixing for a few minutes until all the ingredients are well blended. Shape the mixture into tiny balls and toss lightly in flour.

Heat the oil to 360°. Fry the Koftas, in 2 batches, for 3–4 minutes, until golden brown. Drain well on paper towels. Serve warm or cold, with wedges of lemon.

Raisin and Zucchini Couscous

This delicious accompaniment to the lamb and quince stew is very easy to prepare in the afternoon of the party, ready to cook in the early evening.

2 cups (1 lb) couscous
12 oz small zucchini, thinly sliced
$\frac{2}{3}$ cup (4 oz) raisins
salt
1 teaspoon paprika
2 tablespoons unsalted butter, melted

Put the couscous in a large bowl and cover generously with cold water. Leave to soak for 20 minutes, then drain well, pressing out as much water as possible.

Mix together the couscous, zucchini, raisins, salt and paprika. Place in a colander placed over a pan of boiling water or a couscousier and steam over simmering water for 30 minutes, until tender.

Transfer to a warmed serving dish and drizzle over the butter. Mix it in lightly with a fork and serve.

Honey and Orange Figs

This is very easy and quick to prepare. It can be made the day before the party, and kept in a cool place.

$\frac{1}{2}$ cup fresh orange juice
2 tablespoons lemon juice
$\frac{1}{4}$ cup clear honey
8 ripe figs, peeled and sliced
4 oranges, peeled and segmented

Mix together the orange and lemon juices. Add the honey and stir until it has dissolved. Add the figs and oranges.

Chill for at least 1 hour. Serve in tiny dishes.

CHINESE FIRE POT

For this Chinese evening, set your table with Oriental dishes—small plates, bowls, teapot and cups all made in China—and chopsticks. You'll find all these for sale, very cheaply, in the Chinatown district of any big city. As a centerpiece for the table, a simple arrangement of orchids would be appropriately Oriental. (This will have to be removed when the main course is served.) Ask your guests to wear silk pajamas—the men could even paint on black mandarin-style moustaches.

The menu begins with a platter of seasoned pork and Chinese-style vegetables, served cold. To follow, there is a choice of two Oriental-style fondues. One is a Peking lamb hotpot, a simple presentation of lamb, Chinese cabbage, rice noodles and beansprouts, which the diners cook themselves in a seasoned stock. The alternative is the more elaborate ten variety hotpot, which offers chicken, duck, pork, scallops and shrimp as well as a variety of vegetables. Boiled rice is the only accompaniment needed. To complete this most convivial of meals, there are deep-fried sweet dumplings, filled with dates, crystallized fruits and sesame seeds.

CHINESE FIRE POT DINNER FOR 8

CHINESE COLD PLATTER

PEKING LAMB HOTPOT
OR
TEN VARIETY HOTPOT

BOILED RICE

CRYSTALLIZED FRUIT DUMPLINGS

SUGGESTED WINE: A DRY TO MEDIUM DRY WHITE
WINE, SUCH AS A CENTRAL EUROPEAN RIESLING OR
THE VERY PLEASANT CHINESE WINE DYNASTY.
SERVE JASMINE TEA WITH OR AFTER THE MEAL,
TOO, IF YOU LIKE

Chinese Cold Platter

Make the Chinese chicken stock 1 or 2 days before your party, keeping it in the refrigerator. Cook the pork the day before the party. Blanch the vegetables the morning of the party, but only dress them shortly before serving.

2 lb boned loin of pork, excess fat removed
5 cups Chinese chicken stock (see page 168)
3 slices ginger root
3 scallions
2 star anise
2 teaspoons five spice powder
$\frac{1}{3}$ cup sugar
2 tablespoons soy sauce
salt
4 oz Chinese cabbage, shredded
4 oz (1 cup) broccoli stems and flowerets, sliced
2 teaspoons sesame seeds
1 tablespoon oil
2 teaspoons sesame oil
$\frac{1}{2}$ lb (5 cups) beansprouts
1 small red chili pepper, seeded and finely chopped
3 tablespoons vinegar
2 tablespoons soy sauce
scallions, for garnish

Place the pork in a pan with the stock, ginger, scallions, star anise, five spice powder, sugar, soy sauce and a little salt. Bring to a boil, then cover and simmer for $1\frac{1}{2}$ hours, until the pork is tender. Remove the pork from the stock, and strain the stock into a bowl. Leave the pork and stock until cold, then wrap the pork in foil and chill. Set the stock aside.

Blanch the Chinese cabbage for 1 minute and the broccoli for 5 minutes. Refresh the vegetables under cold running water to stop further cooking.

Place the Chinese cabbage and broccoli in separate bowls. Mix together the sesame seeds, oil and sesame oil. Divide between the vegetables, turning until they are evenly coated.

Mix the beansprouts with the chili, vinegar and soy sauce.

Slice the pork thinly. Divide between 8 plates. Spoon a little of the cooking liquid over each piece of meat. Place a little of the broccoli, Chinese cabbage and beansprouts on each plate. Garnish with scallions.

Chinese Chicken Stock

Makes about 2 quarts.

2 lb chicken wings
2 slices fresh ginger root
3 scallions
2 garlic cloves, bruised
½ teaspoon salt

Using a heavy cleaver, chop the chicken pieces through the bones into small pieces. Place in a large pan with the ginger, scallions, garlic, salt and 3 quarts water. Bring slowly to a boil, skimming off any scum that rises to the surface, then simmer for 2 hours, skimming occasionally, until the stock is clear.

Strain the stock into a large bowl and leave to cool if not using immediately.

Peking Lamb Hotpot

The stock can be made 1 or 2 days in advance. You can prepare all the dips in their little dishes on the morning of the party, and also cut the lamb into wafer-thin slices.

4 lb boneless lean lamb, such as leg
½ lb rice noodles
1 quantity Chinese chicken stock (see above)
1 lb bok choy or Chinese cabbage, shredded
½ lb beansprouts
DIPS
soy sauce, hoisin sauce, chili sauce, vinegar, rice wine or sherry, finely chopped scallion, finely grated fresh ginger root

For this Oriental-style fondue you will need a Mongolian hotpot or meat (metal) fondue pot, 8 small wire baskets on long handles, chopsticks and bowls.

Cut the lamb into wafer-thin slices, about 1 × 3 inches. Soak the noodles in warm water for 15 minutes, until softened, then drain. Bring the stock to boiling point in the Mongolian hot pot or fondue pot. You will need a heat source on the table, either the traditional charcoal burner or a small electric plate.

Put the lamb, noodles, bok choy or Chinese cabbage and beansprouts in separate dishes on the table. Place all the dips in small separate dishes on the table.

Bring the bubbling stock to the table; the pot must remain simmering for the length of the meal. The diners fill their wire baskets with raw ingredients and plunge them into the simmering stock to cook to their taste. The food imparts additional flavor to the stock which is ladled into the bowls and drunk at the end of the meal.

Ten Variety Hotpot

Make the Chinese chicken stock 1 or 2 days in advance. Prepare the dips in their little dishes on the morning of the party. Cut up the chicken, duck and pork into small cubes on the morning of the party, and prepare the rice noodles and all the vegetables.

2 lb boneless chicken breast, skinned
1 lb boneless duck breast, skinned
2 lb lean boneless pork
4 tablespoons oil
soy sauce
1 quantity Chinese chicken stock (see left)
½ lb rice noodles
2 oz dried Chinese mushrooms
½ lb bay scallops
½ lb peeled cooked shrimp
½ lb (2 cups) beansprouts
½ lb (2 cups) Savoy cabbage or Swiss chard, shredded and blanched
½ lb (2 cups) broccoli, sliced and blanched
DIPS
soy sauce, hoisin sauce, chili sauce, vinegar, rice wine or sherry, chopped scallion, grated fresh ginger root

For this Oriental-style fondue, you will need a Mongolian hot pot or meat (metal) fondue pot, 8 small wire baskets on long handles, chopsticks and bowls.

Cut the chicken, duck and pork into small cubes. Stir-fry the chicken in a little oil, then add a sprinkling of soy sauce and a little hot water or stock and simmer for 5 minutes. Remove from the wok or pan. Stir-fry the duck in the same way, then simmer for 10 minutes. Place the pork in the pan with a little soy sauce and 2½ cups of the Chinese chicken stock and bring to a boil. Simmer for 20 minutes, then drain.

Meanwhile, soak the noodles in warm water for 15 minutes, until softened, then drain. Soak the dried mushrooms in warm water for 20 minutes, then drain, squeeze out excess water and remove the stems.

Pack some of each ingredient—chicken, duck, pork, scallops, shrimp, beansprouts, noodles, mushrooms, cabbage and broccoli—in sections around the hot pot. Place all the remaining ingredients in bowls on the table. Place the dips in small dishes on the table. You will need a heat source at the table, either the traditional charcoal burner or a small electric plate.

Bring the remaining stock to a boil and pour over the ingredients in the hot pot. Return to a boil and simmer, covered, for 5 minutes. Bring to the table.

Diners start off by helping themselves to morsels from the hot pot using their wire baskets. More ingredients are then added to the bubbling stock as the meal continues. Guests select from the dips, which can be mixed together to create variations. At the end of the meal the stock is ladled into the bowls and drunk.

Ten Variety Hotpot

Crystallized Fruit Dumplings

You can use whatever crystallized fruits you like, but my favorite is crystallized pineapple; it has a tangy taste which stops the dumplings from being too sweet. The dumplings can be prepared several hours ahead, ready to be fried at the last minute.

2 cups glutinous (sweet) rice flour
$\frac{1}{4}$ cup finely chopped dates
3 tablespoons finely chopped crystallized or glacé fruits
1 tablespoon toasted sesame seeds
3 tablespoons brown sugar
oil for deep frying
confectioners' sugar for sprinkling

Put the flour in a bowl and gradually stir in $\frac{3}{4}$–1 cup warm water to form a soft smooth dough. Shape into a roll about $1\frac{1}{2}$ inches thick. Slice rounds off the roll about $\frac{1}{4}$ inch thick.

Mix together the dates, fruits, sesame seeds and sugar. Place a little of the mixture in the center of each round of dough. Wrap the dough around the filling to enclose it completely.

Heat the oil to 350° or until a cube of bread dropped into the oil instantly rises to the surface. Fry the dumplings, a few at a time, until they are golden brown. Drain on paper towels and serve hot, dredged with confectioners' sugar.

HALLOWEEN PARTY

This is a wonderful menu for a children's party. Our children love Halloween, dressing up as ghosts and witches—and one wizard—and going trick-or-treating! Coming home, in from the cold night air, to a delicious party like this, makes a never-to-be-forgotten evening for the children—and any lucky grown-ups who happen to be present too! If possible, serve the food in your kitchen, lit entirely by candlelight, but make sure that you have enough candles so that your guests can see what they are eating.

With a pumpkin carved into a jack-o'-lantern as the centerpiece for your table, the atmosphere is really set for this Halloween party.

Spooky Soup

This tomato-based soup is full of tiny pasta shapes—stars, moons and suns. It is a good and tasty soup. The soup can be made entirely the day before Halloween with the pasta shapes added to cook as the soup reheats before the party.

$2\frac{1}{2}$ cups chicken (see page 181) or beef stock
four 2-lb cans tomatoes
1 lb onions, chopped
4 celery stalks, chopped
4 carrots, chopped
juice of 3 oranges
3 bay leaves
salt and pepper
PASTA SHAPES
$\frac{3}{4}$ cup all-purpose flour
1 egg
1 teaspoon oil
pinch of salt
1–2 teaspoons water

Place all the soup ingredients in a large pan, bring to a boil and simmer for 40 minutes.

Meanwhile, sift the flour into a mixing bowl. Make a well in the center and add the egg, oil and salt. Work into the flour with your fingers, adding the water a few drops at a time until the dough is smooth and pliable. Knead thoroughly for 10 minutes, then cover and leave to rest at room temperature for 30 minutes.

Roll out the dough on a lightly floured surface until it is as thin as possible. Using tiny cutters, cut into moons, stars and suns.

Discard the bay leaves, then purée the soup, in batches, in a blender or food processor. Return to the pan. Taste and adjust the seasoning.

Add the pasta shapes to the soup and simmer for 10–15 minutes, until cooked.

HALLOWEEN PARTY FOR 25

SPOOKY SOUP

DEVILED BONES
BAKED POTATO SKINS
RAW VEGETABLE STICKS

PUMPKIN PIES

SUGGESTED DRINK: HOT CINNAMON CHOCOLATE

Spooky Soup

Deviled Bones

These lamb chops with a sinister name are eaten in the fingers, so have plenty of paper napkins handy to wipe sticky fingers! The deviled mixture can be made the day before the party. Keep, covered, in the refrigerator.

25 lamb chops
1 lb unsalted butter, softened
2 tablespoons Worcestershire sauce
2 tablespoons ketchup
$\frac{1}{4}$ cup mustard powder
salt and pepper

Trim excess fat from the chops. Place in 2 roasting pans and bake in a preheated 400° oven for 20–25 minutes, until almost cooked.

Meanwhile, mix together the remaining ingredients. Spread a little deviled mixture over each chop and return to the oven to bake for a further 5 minutes. Serve the chops piping hot.

Baked Potato Skins

You could substitute grated Cheddar cheese for the sour cream in the potato skins if you think your young guests would prefer it. The potatoes can be baked several hours in advance. Brush them with oil, reheat and fill with the hot bacon mixture just before serving.

13 large baking potatoes, scrubbed and pricked
oil
1 lb bacon, chopped
1 lb mushrooms, sliced
pepper
$3\frac{1}{2}$ cups sour cream
paprika

Bake the potatoes in a preheated 400° oven for about 1 hour, until soft.

Cut each potato in half and scoop out the insides to within $\frac{1}{2}$ inch of skin. Use the scooped-out potato for another dish. Brush the insides of the potato shells with oil and return to the oven to bake for 15 minutes, until crispy.

Meanwhile, fry the bacon, without additional fat, until crispy and golden. Add the mushrooms and pepper and cook until softened, about 5 minutes. Drain well on paper towels.

Fill the center of each potato skin with the bacon filling and top with sour cream. Sprinkle with paprika and serve hot.

Pumpkin Pies

Delicious little individual pies, these have a sweet, spicy pumpkin filling. Make them the day before the party. If serving warm, reheat in a preheated 350° oven for 10–15 minutes, or in a microwave.

$1\frac{1}{2}$ quantities Kinloch pastry (see page 183)
2 lb pumpkin, seeded, peeled and diced
milk, for cooking
3 eggs, lightly beaten
$\frac{1}{2}$ cup brown sugar
$\frac{1}{4}$ cup corn syrup
1 cup heavy cream
1 teaspoon ground cinnamon
1 teaspoon ground ginger
grated nutmeg, to sprinkle
whipped cream, to decorate (optional)

Roll out the pastry and cut into 25–30 rounds to line cupcake or muffin tins. Chill.

Cook the pumpkin in a little milk until tender, about 20 minutes. Drain well, then mash or purée in a blender or food processor. Mix thoroughly with all the remaining ingredients, except the nutmeg and whipped cream.

Spoon a little pumpkin mixture into each pastry case. Sprinkle a little grated nutmeg over each. Bake in a preheated 375° oven for 25–30 minutes, until the filling has set and the pastry is light golden. Serve warm or cold, with a swirl of cream on each if liked.

Hot Cinnamon Chocolate

This is a perfect drink for your small chilly guests to sip when they come in out of the cold. The cinnamon enhances the chocolate flavor perfectly. The recipe makes 12 drinks, so make 2 batches in 2 saucepans.

12 oz semi-sweet chocolate, grated
$7\frac{1}{2}$ cups milk
1 cup light brown sugar
$\frac{1}{2}$ teaspoon vanilla extract
ground cinnamon

Place the chocolate, milk, sugar and vanilla extract in a saucepan and heat gently, stirring all the time, until the chocolate has melted. Do not allow to boil. Beat the mixture until bubbles form, then pour into mugs. Sprinkle with cinnamon and serve hot.

PROVENÇAL EVENING

For a Provençal evening, set your table with a cloth of Provençal printed cotton. Light the table with candles stuck into old wine bottles—if you can, dribble lots of candle wax down the sides of the bottles. Have a board with melons and grapes arranged on it for the centerpiece, and somewhere in the room have a bowl full of herbs from Provence—their fragrance will help to set the scene.

The food on this menu will complete the Provençal impression. The first course consists of a piquant paste of black olives, anchovies, capers and garlic, which is spread on toasted French bread and eaten with a salad. To follow this there is porgy, a succulent fish, stuffed with lettuce and sorrel. The delicate flavor of the stuffing for the fish complements it so well, and it is easy to prepare if you ask your fishmonger to fillet the fish for you. The main course is Provençal roast lamb seasoned with herbs, garlic and olive oil. There is a pumpkin gratin to serve with the lamb. An almond peach tart completes the feast—sweet ripe peaches on an almond shortbread base, served with a vanilla-flavored cream.

Composed Salad with Tapénade

The tapénade can be made 2 or 3 weeks in advance and kept in a small jar, covered with a thin layer of olive oil, in the refrigerator. Prepare as many of the salad ingredients as possible the morning of the party and store, tightly covered, in the refrigerator.

selection of salad leaves, e.g., mâche, red leaf lettuce, radicchio, escarole
6 canned artichoke hearts, halved
1 whole fennel, thinly sliced
1 head Belgian endive, separated into leaves
3 hard-boiled eggs, halved
4 oz button mushrooms
$\frac{1}{2}$ lb cherry tomatoes
2 cups grated carrots
6 tablespoons French dressing (see page 185)
1 small French bread, thinly sliced and toasted
TAPÉNADE
1 lb large black olives, pitted
2 garlic cloves, peeled
2-oz can anchovies, drained
$\frac{1}{3}$ cup drained capers
3 tablespoons olive oil
pepper

Place all the tapénade ingredients in a blender or food processor and blend until smooth. Divide the mixture between 6 small dishes.

Arrange the salad ingredients on 6 large plates and drizzle over a little dressing. Serve with the tapénade and toasted French bread. The anchovy-flavored tapénade is spread over the bread.

PROVENÇAL EVENING FOR 6

COMPOSED SALAD WITH TAPÉNADE

PORGY STUFFED WITH LETTUCE AND SORREL

PROVENÇALE ROAST LAMB
PUMPKIN GRATIN
SNOW PEAS OR PETITS POIS

ALMOND PEACH TART

SUGGESTED WINE: A DRY CÔTES DE PROVENCE
ROSÉ

Porgy or Scup Stuffed with Lettuce and Sorrel

Mix the sorrel and lettuce stuffing for the fish the day before your party, then on the day of your party all you need do is to stuff the fish, wrap it in the lettuce leaves, and cook it.

3-lb porgy or scup
4 tablespoons butter
2 shallots, finely chopped
1 head iceberg or romaine lettuce
4 oz sorrel leaves
2 teaspoons chopped fresh tarragon
2 tablespoons chopped fresh chervil or parsley
1 tablespoon lemon juice
salt and pepper
$\frac{1}{2}$ cup dry white wine
$\frac{1}{2}$ cup heavy cream
carrots, for garnish

Ask the fishmonger to skin and bone the fish to leave you with two large fillets.

Melt half the butter in a small pan and fry one shallot until softened, about 5 minutes. Set aside.

Separate the lettuce and sorrel leaves. Quickly plunge into boiling salted water, then drain under cold running water, taking care not to damage the leaves. Select about 15 large outer lettuce leaves and reserve them. Squeeze all the excess water from the remaining lettuce and sorrel leaves. Very finely chop the leaves, then mix with the fried shallot, herbs, lemon juice and seasoning.

Arrange about 6 of the reserved large lettuce leaves, overlapping, along a board. Put one fish fillet on top. Season, then spread with the chopped lettuce mixture. Cover with the other fish fillet and season this. Wrap the leaves around the fish, placing the remaining whole leaves over the top to enclose it completely.

Sprinkle the remaining shallot over the bottom of a shallow buttered baking dish large enough to take the fish. Place the fish carefully in the dish. Dot with the remaining butter and sprinkle over the wine. Cover with buttered parchment paper and bake in a preheated 350° oven for 30 minutes.

Remove the fish to a warmed serving plate and keep warm. Strain the cooking liquid into a small pan and boil hard until reduced by half. Reduce the heat and stir in the cream. Taste and adjust the seasoning if necessary. Peel the carrots and cut into 1-inch lengths. Pare at each end to form barrel shapes.

Serve the fish in slices, with a little sauce poured over the top. Garnish each plate with a few steamed barrel-cut carrots.

Provençal Roast Lamb

Make the herb and garlic paste the day before the party. If you like, rub it over the lamb the day before, too.

3 tablespoons chopped mixed fresh herbs, e.g., rosemary, savory, marjoram and thyme
3 garlic cloves, crushed
salt and pepper
$\frac{1}{4}$ cup olive oil
4-lb leg of lamb, boned weight
$\frac{1}{2}$ cup red wine
2 tablespoons unsalted butter cut into 6 pieces

Pound the herbs in a mortar with the garlic to form a paste. Season and gradually work in the olive oil.

Rub this mixture over all the surfaces of the meat, particularly in the cavity. Tie into a neat shape and place in a roasting pan. Leave at room temperature for 2 hours.

Roast in a preheated 425° oven for 15 minutes, then reduce the heat to 350° and continue roasting for 1 hour 25 minutes. The meat will be pink inside, so if you prefer it well done, roast for 20–25 minutes longer. Baste occasionally with the wine during cooking.

Remove the lamb to a warmed serving platter and keep warm while you make the sauce. Pour off most of the fat from the roasting pan. Heat the remaining fat and sediment until it is very hot, then pour in the wine, scraping down the sediment and stirring all the time. Reduce the heat and simmer for 5 minutes, stirring. Swirl the butter into the pan, a piece at a time to thicken.

Slice the meat and pour a little sauce over each slice.

Pumpkin Gratin

Prepare up to baking in the morning.

3 tablespoons olive oil
1 large onion, thinly sliced
2 lb pumpkin, peeled, seeded and cut into small chunks
2 teaspoons chopped fresh thyme
salt and pepper
$\frac{1}{4}$ cup grated Parmesan cheese

Heat 2 tablespoons oil in a pan, add the onion and fry for about 10 minutes, until softened and lightly browned.

Meanwhile, parboil the pumpkin in salted water for 10 minutes. Drain, reserving 3 tablespoons of the cooking liquid. Mix the pumpkin with the reserved liquid, the thyme, remaining oil and seasoning.

Spread the onion over the bottom of a gratin dish. Put the pumpkin on top. Bake in a preheated 375° oven for 30 minutes. Sprinkle with the Parmesan and bake for 15 minutes longer.

Provençal Roast Lamb and Pumpkin Gratin

Almond Peach Tart

◆◆

Make the pastry the day before the party and store it, wrapped, in the refrigerator. Bake the pastry base and complete the tart on the afternoon of the party.

PASTRY
$\frac{3}{4}$ cup all-purpose flour
3 tablespoons sugar
3 tablespoons ground almonds
1 teaspoon grated lemon rind
6 tablespoons unsalted butter, diced
1 egg yolk
FILLING
4 ripe peaches, peeled, pitted and thinly sliced
2 tablespoons sugar
2 tablespoons apricot jam
$\frac{1}{4}$ cup toasted slivered almonds
CRÈME CHANTILLY
1 egg white
2 tablespoons sugar
$1\frac{1}{4}$ cups heavy cream
few drops of vanilla extract

Mix together the flour, sugar, almonds and lemon rind. Add the butter and rub in lightly with the fingertips. Add the egg yolk and mix to a firm dough. Wrap in plastic wrap and chill for 20 minutes.

Roll out the dough to a 10-inch round and place on a baking sheet. Pinch around the edge and prick the base several times. Bake in a preheated 375° oven for 15 minutes.

Arrange the peach slices on the pastry base in two rings. Sprinkle evenly with the sugar and return to the oven. Bake for 10 minutes longer.

Warm the jam and brush evenly over the peaches. Sprinkle with toasted almonds and allow to cool.

To make the Crème Chantilly, whip the cream until softly stiff. In a separate bowl beat the egg white until stiff. Add the sugar and beat again to make a soft meringue. Fold into the cream with the vanilla. Serve with the tart.

SASHIMI AND SAKE

The charm of Japanese entertaining is its simplicity. If your party happens to be in the late spring time, a few branches of cherry blossom in as plain a vase as possible will look very Japanese. Ask your guests to wear kimonos, and greet them in a very polite way—as is typical of the Japanese.

The first course is unmistakably Japanese—the thinnest slices of beautifully fresh raw fish. This sashimi is served with a dipping sauce—soy sauce made as hot as you like with Japanese horseradish. Following is a clear soup with watercress and cubes of tofu—soybean curd—floating in it. The main course is a dish of beef steak strips stir-fried with mushrooms and beansprouts. Plain boiled rice is the only accompaniment required, in addition to the unusual eggplant relish. To complete the meal, serve a selection of fresh fruits.

Sake, the famous Japanese rice wine, is suggested to accompany the dinner. This wine should be warmed to body temperature and served in small china flasks to be poured into very small cups—only a mouthful or so in each. To warm the sake, stand the closed bottle in a bucket of hot water—heating it in a pan would drive off the alcohol.

SASHIMI AND SAKE FOR 6

SASHIMI

CLEAR SOUP WITH TOFU AND WATERCRESS

BEEF WITH MUSHROOMS AND BEANSPROUTS
BOILED RICE
EGGPLANT RELISH

FRESH FRUITS IN SEASON

SUGGESTED DRINK: SAKE (JAPANESE RICE WINE)

Sashimi

Use only perfectly fresh, best quality fish for this dish. Clean the fish carefully, removing all the skin and bones. Do not prepare the fish much more than 1 hour before serving.

$1\frac{1}{2}$ lb raw seafish, e.g., porgy or scup, bass, tuna, turbot, salmon, trout
$\frac{1}{2}$ lb white radish (daikon), peeled and finely grated
2 carrots, finely grated
2 baby turnips, grated
2 tablespoons Japanese horseradish (wasabi)
$\frac{2}{3}$ cup light soy sauce

Using a razor-sharp knife, cut the fish into the thinnest possible slices. Arrange the slices of fish attractively on 6 platters, traditionally oblong. Garnish with the radish, carrot and turnip in small piles. Cover with plastic wrap and chill for 1 hour.

Mix the horseradish with sufficient water to make a paste. Place a little on each platter beside the fish. Give each diner a small dish of soy sauce.

Each guest dips the fish into the wasabi, then soy sauce, or mixes a little wasabi into the soy sauce.

Clear Soup with Tofu and Watercress

If you are unable to obtain the ingredients for the dashi (stock), substitute the Chinese chicken stock (page 168). Make the dashi on the morning of the party.

$\frac{1}{2}$ oz kelp seaweed (kombu)
$\frac{1}{2}$ oz dried bonito shavings (katsuobushi)
2 teaspoons light soy sauce
1 teaspoon salt
$\frac{1}{2}$ lb tofu (soybean curd), cut into small cubes
2 scallions, finely chopped
1 bunch watercress, coarsely chopped

Bring 2 quarts of water to a boil in a saucepan and add the seaweed. Simmer for 5 minutes, stirring well. Add the bonito shavings, and remove from heat. When the pieces have settled to the bottom of the pan, strain the stock. Return it to the pan.

Add the soy sauce and salt to the dashi and bring back to a boil. Add the tofu, scallions and watercress and simmer for 2 minutes, until heated through. Serve in bowls.

Beef with Mushrooms and Beansprouts

Prepare the beef, mushrooms and carrot in the afternoon, ready to cook that night.

$1\frac{1}{2}$ lb boneless sirloin steak
salt and pepper
1 tablespoon cornstarch
2 tablespoons oil
6 large mushrooms, very thinly sliced
1 carrot, very thinly sliced
4 oz ($2\frac{1}{2}$ cups) beansprouts
2 tablespoons light soy sauce

Cut the beef into thin strips across the grain. Sprinkle with salt and toss in cornstarch.

Heat the oil in a wok or large frying pan. Add the beef and stir-fry quickly until evenly browned. Remove with a slotted spoon and keep warm. Add the mushrooms, carrot and beansprouts and stir-fry quickly until just beginning to brown. Return the beef to the pan with the soy sauce and a sprinkling of pepper. Stir-fry for 1 minute, then turn out onto a warmed serving plate.

Eggplant Relish

You can make this the day before the party.

$\frac{1}{2}$ lb eggplant, sliced
salt
1 tablespoon mustard powder
1 tablespoon mirin (sweetened rice wine)
3 tablespoons light soy sauce

Put the eggplant in a colander and sprinkle with salt. Place a plate on top and leave to drain for 30 minutes. Rinse and pat dry with paper towels.

Mix the mustard to a smooth paste with a little water. Add the mirin and soy sauce. Place the eggplant in a bowl and mix in the mustard mixture. Place a plate on top and weight down. Leave for 2 hours.

Before serving, cut the eggplant slices into dice and place in individual bowls.

Sashimi; Clear Soup with Tofu and Watercress

177

PINK PARTY

Having a color theme party is great fun, and pink is probably the easiest color of all, because there are so very many shades of pink—from the palest pink to brilliant fuchsia—and pink is a very flattering color both for food and drink, and also for clothes!

This menu consists of a rich cream cheese and ham terrine, with a surprising layer of pink peppercorns; individual smoked trout quiches, with a tomato cream sauce and a Cheddar and Parmesan pastry; and an impressive yet simple centerpiece of shrimp arranged in tiers, served with a green mayonnaise. There is also a salad of beet and orange, dressed with sour cream and horseradish. A tossed salad featuring red cabbage and radicchio is also a good complement. The puddings are an exotic pomegranate sherbet, with frosted pink fruits and pink sugared cookies, and a tart filled with raspberries and pears first poached in red wine. The tart is even served with a pink cream!

PINK PARTY FOR 25

HAM AND PINK PEPPERCORN TERRINE

SMOKED TROUT CUPS

SHRIMP CENTERPIECE

BEET AND ORANGE SALAD

TOSSED SALAD

POMEGRANATE SHERBET

WITH

PINK SUGAR COOKIES

GLAZED PEAR AND RASPBERRY TART

SUGGESTED WINES: PINK CHAMPAGNE, KIR ROYALE (CHAMPAGNE AND CRÈME DE CASSIS), SPARKLING ROSÉ WINE, PREFERABLY CHILEAN WHICH IS FAIRLY DRY, OR SLOE GIN WITH TONIC WATER

Ham and Pink Peppercorn Terrine

This can be made the day before the party, and kept, wrapped, in the refrigerator.
Makes two 2-lb terrines.

$\frac{1}{2}$ lb grape leaves
2 lb cooked ham, roughly chopped
2 lb cream cheese
6 tablespoons lemon juice
2 tablespoons tomato paste
4 egg yolks
8 egg whites
$\frac{1}{4}$ teaspoon cayenne
$\frac{1}{4}$ cup pink peppercorns, lightly crushed
radicchio, to serve

Place the grape leaves in a bowl and pour over boiling water to cover generously. Leave to soak for 20 minutes, then drain and soak in cold water for 5 minutes.

Meanwhile, put the ham in a food processor and chop it very finely. Add the cheese, lemon juice, tomato paste and egg yolks and blend until smooth. Beat the whites lightly and fold into the mixture with the cayenne. Taste and add salt if necessary.

Drain the grape leaves. Line two 9 × 5 × 3-inch loaf pans with overlapping grape leaves. Half fill each pan with the ham mixture and smooth the top. Sprinkle the peppercorns evenly over the top. Spoon the remaining ham mixture over and smooth it evenly. Top with the remaining grape leaves.

Cover the pans with oiled foil. Place them in a large roasting pan and add boiling water to a depth of 1 inch. Bake in a preheated 300° oven for 1 hour, until firm to the touch. Leave to cool, then chill. Serve cut into thin slices on a bed of shredded radicchio leaves.

Smoked Trout Cups

You can make the cheesey pastry cups and the tomato sauce for the filling the day before the party, but don't fill the tartlets until a couple of hours before the party.
Makes 50.

PASTRY
$1\frac{3}{4}$ cups wholewheat flour
$1\frac{3}{4}$ cups all-purpose flour
$\frac{1}{2}$ lb (2 sticks) unsalted butter, diced
1 cup grated sharp Cheddar cheese
$\frac{1}{4}$ cup grated Parmesan cheese
1 tablespoon Dijon mustard
1 egg, lightly beaten
1–2 tablespoons water

FILLING
½ lb ripe tomatoes, chopped
fresh thyme sprig
1 bay leaf
1 teaspoon paprika
2 shallots, chopped
salt
⅔ cup heavy cream
2 lb smoked trout fillets, chopped
fresh dill, for garnish

Mix together the flours and add the butter. Rub in with the fingertips until the mixture resembles fine breadcrumbs. Stir in the cheeses, then add the mustard, egg and water and mix to a firm dough.

Roll out the dough and cut into 3-inch rounds. Use to line 50 cupcake or muffin tins. Prick the bottoms and bake blind in a preheated 400° oven for 15 minutes, until crisp and lightly browned. Cool on a wire rack.

Place the tomatoes, thyme, bay leaf, paprika, shallots and salt in a small pan. Bring to a boil, then simmer for about 10 minutes, until thickened. Press through a sieve and leave to cool. Just before serving, whip the cream lightly and fold into the tomato sauce. Adjust seasoning.

Place a small piece of trout in each pastry cup and spoon a little sauce over each. Garnish and serve.

Shrimp Centerpiece

Make the green mayonnaise the day before and store it in a covered container in the refrigerator. Have an empty bowl handy for the shrimp shells.

4 lb jumbo shrimp in shells
3 lemons or limes, sliced
GREEN MAYONNAISE
4 oz spinach, washed
2 tablespoons finely chopped watercress
1 tablespoon finely chopped fresh parsley
1¼ cups mayonnaise
½ teaspoon grated lemon rind
salt and pepper

Select four of five shallow glass or white china dishes of varying sizes and stack into a pyramid with an upturned glass bowl between each.

Hang the shrimp over the edge of the dishes until they are completely covered. Any leftover shrimp can be piled into the top dish.

Make a cut in each lemon or lime slice from the center to the outside edge. Hang between the shrimp.

Cook the spinach with just the water clinging to the leaves until it wilts, about 3 minutes. Drain thoroughly. Very finely chop the spinach and mix with the watercress, parsley, mayonnaise and lemon rind. Taste and season. Serve as a dipping sauce for the shrimp.

Beet and Orange Salad

If the thought of grated raw beets doesn't appeal to you (although it is, in fact, delicious) boil the beets first. Then, when they are cooked, peel their skins off and cut them into matchsticks.

2 red onions, thinly sliced
2 lb raw young beets, peeled and coarsely grated
4 oranges, peeled and segmented
1¼ cups sour cream
2 teaspoons prepared horseradish
salt and pepper
3 tablespoons snipped fresh chives

Mix together the onions, beets and oranges. Mix the sour cream, horseradish and seasoning and stir into the salad just before serving. Sprinkle the top with snipped fresh chives.

Pomegranate Sherbet; Pink Sugar Cookies

Pomegranate Sherbet

This is a marvelously fragrant sherbet. It can be made days or even weeks in advance of the party. If you have a food processor, put the half-frozen sherbet into it and whizz, then refreeze. If you repeat this process a couple of times, your sherbet will be beautifully smooth.

2 quarts water
3 lb ($7\frac{1}{2}$ cups) sugar
16–18 pomegranates

Put the water and sugar in a saucepan and heat gently, stirring, until the sugar has dissolved. Bring to a boil, then boil rapidly for 15 minutes, until you have a light syrup. Leave to cool.

To extract the pomegranate juice, squeeze and press the skin firmly to crush the seeds. Hold the fruit in a sieve over a bowl and slit the skin. The juices will flow out. You need 5 cups of pomegranate juice.

Mix together the sugar syrup and pomegranate juice. Pour into 2 or 3 shallow freezerproof containers and freeze for 2–3 hours, until the sherbet is set 1 inch in from the edges.

Turn the sherbet out into a bowl and break down the ice crystals with a fork. Return to the containers and freeze until firm, a further 2–3 hours.

Serve in chilled glasses, with pink sugar cookies.

Pink Sugar Cookies

Make 1–2 days before the party and store in an airtight tin.
Makes 30–35.

8 tablespoons (1 stick) butter
$\frac{2}{3}$ cup sugar
1 teaspoon vanilla extract
1 egg, lightly beaten
$1\frac{3}{4}$ cups all-purpose flour
$\frac{1}{4}$ teaspoon baking powder
2 tablespoons raspberry jelly
red food coloring
$\frac{1}{3}$ cup sugar cubes, lightly crushed

Beat together the butter and sugar until light and fluffy, about 5 minutes. Beat in the vanilla extract and egg. Sift the flour and baking powder into the bowl and mix in lightly and evenly. Gently stir in the raspberry jelly, then a few drops of food coloring to give a pink tint.

Fill a pastry bag fitted with a large star tube with the mixture. Pipe small rosettes of the mixture, spaced a little apart, onto greased baking sheets. Sprinkle a little crushed sugar over the top of each. Bake in a preheated 375° oven for 8–10 minutes. Cool on a wire rack.

Glazed Pear and Raspberry Tart

This is a stunning tart, extremely decorative. Make the pastry the day before the party and keep it in the refrigerator. Fill the pastry cases only a few hours before serving.
Makes three 10-inch tarts.

PASTRY
$4\frac{1}{4}$ cups all-purpose flour
$\frac{3}{4}$ cup sugar
10 oz ($2\frac{1}{2}$ sticks) unsalted butter
2 eggs
1 tablespoon water
1 teaspoon vanilla extract
FILLING
$2\frac{1}{2}$ cups red wine
2 tablespoons orange juice
$1\frac{1}{3}$ cups sugar
15 firm ripe pears, peeled, halved and cored
$\frac{2}{3}$ cup red currant jelly
1 lb raspberries
$\frac{1}{4}$ cup finely chopped almonds
red food coloring
PINK CREAM
$2\frac{1}{2}$ cups heavy cream
4 oz raspberries, sieved
3 tablespoons sugar

Mix together the flour and sugar. Rub in the butter until the mixture resembles fine breadcrumbs. Beat together the eggs, water and vanilla extract. Add to the dry ingredients and mix to a firm dough. Knead lightly, then wrap in plastic wrap and chill for 30 minutes.

Divide the dough into 3 portions. Roll out the dough and use to line three 10-inch tart pans. Prick the bottoms and bake blind in a preheated 400° oven for 15–20 minutes, until golden brown. When cooked, allow to cool.

Meanwhile, place the red wine, orange juice and sugar in a saucepan and bring slowly to a boil, stirring to dissolve the sugar. Simmer for 5 minutes. Add the pears, in batches, and cook for 8–10 minutes, until slightly softened. Remove with a slotted spoon and cool.

Boil the wine mixture vigorously until reduced to $1\frac{1}{4}$ cups. Add the red currant jelly and simmer, stirring, until melted and smooth.

Cut each pear half into thin slices and arrange attractively in the pastry cases. Fill in the spaces with raspberries. Brush the red wine glaze liberally over the top and over the edge of the pastry.

Mix the almonds with a little coloring to tint pink. Sprinkle carefully around the pastry edge.

Whip the cream until stiff. Fold in the raspberry purée and sugar. Serve with the tarts.

BASIC RECIPES
STOCKS

There are no two ways about it: there is no substitute for stock, the real thing, as opposed to the ubiquitous bouillon cube or stock from a can. It doesn't matter what you are making; if the recipe includes stock as one of its ingredients, the end result will be far better if you use homemade. Don't be put off, as I used to be, by the thought of making stock—it isn't an endless chore. It can be thrown together in two ticks, be it chicken, vegetable, fish or game, and can be left simmering away quietly for a couple of hours. If you don't happen to have a chicken carcass lying in your refrigerator, and you want to make soup needing chicken stock, just make a vegetable stock. It is far, far better than a bouillon cube, and has some goodness in it too.

Chicken Stock

Make more than you need and freeze half the quantity. If you are short of space in your freezer and don't want to make as much as in this recipe just halve the water quantity. If you are going to use the stock for a light summery soup, skin the onions. Otherwise, leave the skins on as they color the stock a warm, rich brown.
Makes about 3 pints.

2 chicken carcasses
small handful of black peppercorns
2 bay leaves
4 onions, quartered
3–4 carrots, halved
handful of fresh parsley
some celery leaves, or 2 celery stalks
1 tablespoon salt

Put all the ingredients into a large saucepan and add $3\frac{1}{2}$ quarts of water. Bring to a boil, then half cover and leave to simmer for 2–3 hours. Cool.

Strain the stock into a bowl, jug or plastic container and store in the refrigerator. If kept for more than a few days, boil for a good 15 minutes every other day.

Vegetable Stock

Vegetable stock is wonderfully tasty and can be substituted for any other stock. All vegetables are perfectly delicious in vegetable stock except potatoes and turnips. Somehow turnips make the stock taste bitter, and potatoes make it taste sour and go cloudy. The following recipe is only a guide; you can put in whatever you have on hand in the vegetable line.
Makes about 3 pints.

4 onions, quartered
4 large carrots, halved
2 large parsnips, halved
2 celery stalks
4 leeks, quartered
2 garlic cloves, halved
small handful of black peppercorns
2 teaspoons salt
handful of fresh parsley
2 bay leaves

Put all ingredients into a large saucepan and add $3\frac{1}{2}$ quarts of water. Bring to a boil. Half cover the saucepan and simmer gently for 2 hours. Strain the stock, and keep in the refrigerator or freezer.

Fish Stock

Fish stock is the quickest of all to make: you can have delicious fish stock an hour after you put it on to cook. If you buy your fish from a fishmonger's, your fish will be sold to you already filleted, so do remember to ask for the skin and bones as well. The bones and skin of turbot and skate have very gelatinous properties so the resulting stock from them, when cold, sets to quite a firm jelly—delicious!
Makes about $2\frac{1}{2}$ pints.

fish bones, skin and trimmings
$2\frac{1}{4}$ cups white wine
2 onions, sliced
small handful of black peppercorns
large handful of fresh parsley
few celery leaves (optional)

Put all the ingredients into a saucepan and add 2 quarts water. Bring the liquid to a boil. Cover the pan tightly and simmer for 45–60 minutes. Remove from the heat and leave to cool, then strain the stock. Use the same day.

Game Stock

Game stock is the basis for one of the best of all soups—game soup. Up until a few years ago, game anything had rather elite connotations, as game was associated with the privileged few rather than the average household. This is not true now, with pheasants and other game birds being widely available, comparatively cheaply, and venison being farmed more and more. You can put any game you have on hand into game stock.
Makes about 3 pints.

2 pheasants (either whole, if you have an abundance, or their carcasses)
1 rabbit
2 old grouse or partridge
2 squabs
4 onions, quartered
2 celery stalks
4 carrots
bacon rinds (optional)
about 12 juniper berries, crushed
small handful of black peppercorns
2 teaspoons salt
2 bay leaves
pared rind of 1 lemon
pared rind of 1 orange
handful of fresh parsley

Put all the ingredients into a large saucepan and add $3\frac{1}{2}$ quarts of water. Bring to a boil. Half cover the pan and simmer gently for 3–4 hours. Cool. Strain the stock, and keep, covered, in the refrigerator. If you don't use the stock immediately, boil it up for 15 minutes every other day.

Aspic Jelly

Makes $3\frac{1}{2}$ cups.

two 14-oz cans consommé
3 tablespoons gelatin

Pour the consommé into a small bowl. Sprinkle in the gelatin and leave to soak for 5 minutes. Stand the bowl in a saucepan of boiling water and heat gently until dissolved, stirring all the time.

PASTRIES

Some people are excellent pastry makers, some are not quite so good. My basic pie pastry—for want of a better word to describe what we make and use here at Kinloch as pie pastry—can be made by anyone, with good results. It has no water or egg yolks in it and has to be patted around the sides of the tart or pie pan, instead of being rolled out. It is a very rich, very delicious pastry. Please don't be put off by the confectioners' sugar in the savory pastry. I really do mean to put it in, and increase the amount of confectioners' sugar for sweet tarts.

Kinloch Pastry

Makes enough to line an 8–9-inch tart pan, which I
reckon serves 6–8 people.

$1\frac{3}{4}$ cups all-purpose flour
12 tablespoons ($1\frac{1}{2}$ sticks) cold unsalted butter, cut into pieces
4 teaspoons confectioners' sugar
1 teaspoon salt (optional)

Put all the ingredients into a food processor and blend
until it resembles fine crumbs. Pat around the sides and
base of the tart pan, then chill for at least 1 hour.

To bake blind, prick well and bake in a preheated 350°
oven for 25 minutes, until a pale biscuit color.

If the pastry is to be used for a tart with a sweet filling,
reduce the amount of flour to $1\frac{1}{2}$ cups and use $\frac{3}{4}$ cup
confectioners' sugar.

Suet Pastry

Steak and kidney pudding is what comes mouth-
wateringly to my mind at the very mention of the
words suet pastry. Steamed puddings are so easy to
make, and so appreciated by those who eat them, I
can't think why I don't make them more often than I
do.
Makes enough to line a $1\frac{1}{2}$-quart steaming mold.
Makes about 1 lb.

$2\frac{1}{3}$ cups self-rising flour
$2\frac{1}{2}$ teaspoons baking powder
$1\frac{1}{4}$ cups (6 oz) shredded suet
salt and pepper

Sift the flour and baking powder into a bowl and stir in
the suet and seasoning. Add sufficient cold water to
make a firm dough. Knead in the bowl for 3–5 minutes,
then divide the pastry into two portions, one twice the
size of the other. The smaller portion is to be rolled out for
the top of the pudding, and the larger portion used to line
the mold.

If you like, you can use half self-rising flour and half
wholewheat flour, but increase the quantity of baking
powder to 1 tablespoon if you do.

SAUCES

A flavorful home-made sauce does so much to
enhance a meal. Many people are wary of
making sauces, but you shouldn't be. A rich, warm
hollandaise sauce, for example, turns even simple
vegetables, such as asparagus, into a special dish.

Hollandaise Sauce

Makes 1 cup.

$\frac{1}{4}$ cup white wine vinegar
1 bay leaf
blade of mace (optional)
6–8 black peppercorns
few fresh parsley sprigs
4 egg yolks
12 tablespoons ($1\frac{1}{2}$ sticks) unsalted butter,
cut into 6 equal pieces

Put the vinegar, bay leaf, mace, peppercorns and parsley
stalks into a small saucepan and bring to a boil. Simmer
until the liquid has reduced by about half.

Put the egg yolks into a bowl, and beat with a wire
whisk. Beat in the strained seasoned vinegar. Put the
bowl over a saucepan half full of hot water and place
over a medium heat. Add the pieces of butter one at a
time, beating each in well before adding the next. When
all the butter has been incorporated, the sauce will be
thick and golden.

Leave in the roasting pan of hot water, off the heat,
beating from time to time, until you are ready to serve. If
the sauce separates, beat frantically, adding a small
ladleful of hot water from the roasting pan and the sauce
will come together again—disaster averted! Try not to
keep the sauce warm for much more than 20–25
minutes.

Tomato Sauce

This sauce is one of the most valuable of all sauces to have in your repertoire. It is so versatile—delicious with vegetables, fish, or in pizzas—and it has the added bonus of being low in calories, too. If making the sauce in summer, when fresh basil is available, add the basil when you purée the sauce. I think that fresh basil loses its pungency in cooking.
Makes about 3½ cups.

5 tablespoons olive oil
2 onions, chopped
1 celery stalk, cut into 1-inch chunks (optional)
1 red pepper, cored, seeded and chopped
2-lb can tomatoes, or 1½ lb fresh tomatoes, skinned, halved and seeded
½ teaspoon sugar
1 large garlic clove, chopped
salt and pepper
small handful of fresh basil leaves, or 1 teaspoon dried basil

Heat the oil in a saucepan, add the onions and cook for 5 minutes, stirring occasionally. Add the celery and red pepper. Cook for a further 2–3 minutes, then add the tomatoes, sugar, garlic, seasoning and basil, if you are using dried basil. Let the sauce simmer, uncovered, for 25–30 minutes. Allow to cool slightly, then pour into a blender or food processor. Add the fresh basil, if using, and blend until smooth.

This sauce freezes beautifully, and keeps very well in the refrigerator for 2–3 days.

Basic White Sauce

A well made white sauce, with a glossy sheen to it, is the basis of so many other sauces and dishes. With cheese and mustard added to it, it becomes a sauce delicious with cauliflower, leeks and broiled fish. It is the basis of many hot soufflés, and simply flavored with a few spoonfuls of finely chopped fresh parsley or mixed herbs it becomes the perfect companion for all vegetables (particularly with lima beans), fish and ham. More and more when I make this sauce for our family, I use wholewheat flour instead of white flour. The taste is better, but I must admit that the color is not attractive so I add a liberal amount of chopped parsley!
Makes 2½ cups.

4 tablespoons butter
5 tablespoons all-purpose or wholewheat flour
2½ cups milk
freshly grated nutmeg
salt and pepper

Melt the butter in a saucepan. Add the flour and stir it in well, then cook for a couple of minutes. Gradually add the milk, stirring continuously until the sauce boils. Simmer for a couple of minutes, stirring all the time, until thickened and smooth. Remove the pan from the heat and add nutmeg and seasoning to taste.

Brandy Butter

Traditionally, brandy butter, or hard sauce, is eaten at Christmas time with the rich steamed fruit pudding and mince pies. But it is also delicious on a hot dried fruit salad, made with prunes, figs, dried apples and stem ginger, or used to bake bananas for a quick and easy winter dessert. So make a lot. It keeps so well in the refrigerator and it is maddening to run short before the Christmas holidays—and the mince pies—have finished. You can substitute white sugar for the brown sugar if you prefer, and also leave out the grated orange rind if you would rather have just the flavor of brandy.
Makes about 4 cups.

1 lb unsalted butter
2⅔ cups (1 lb) dark brown sugar
¾ cup brandy
finely grated rind of 2 oranges

Put the butter into a large bowl and beat hard until soft, creamy and pale in color. Still beating, slowly add the sugar and beat until the mixture is fluffy. Still beating, add the brandy at a steady trickle but no faster. Beat in the grated orange rind. Scoop the brandy butter into a container, cover and chill.

Chocolate Sauce

—•—

I am such a chocolate addict and how I wish I wasn't, but it is just one of those things you have to learn to live with! This sauce fills my best expectations of all that a chocolate sauce should be.
Makes about 1¼ cups.

1⅓ cups dark brown sugar
3½ tablespoons cocoa powder, sifted
6 tablespoons unsalted butter
2 teaspoons instant coffee powder
1 teaspoon vanilla extract
3 tablespoons corn syrup

Put all the ingredients into a saucepan and add 1¼ cups boiling water. Heat until smooth, then bring to a boil. Simmer gently, stirring occasionally, for 5 minutes.

This sauce keeps well, in a jar in the refrigerator, but it becomes thick and fudgy when cold. To reheat, stand the jar in a warm place and then pour the sauce into a saucepan.

Vanilla Fudge Sauce

—•—

This is a most delicious sauce, good with everything that could possibly be enhanced by fudge sauce—from vanilla and coffee ice cream, to pears and peaches, and meringues. It is also extremely quick and easy to make. It keeps well in the refrigerator, stored in a sealed container.
Makes about 1¼ cups.

12 tablespoons (1½ sticks) unsalted butter
1⅓ cups dark or light brown sugar
1 teaspoon vanilla extract
1¼ cups heavy cream

Put all the ingredients into a saucepan and heat gently until smooth. Bring to a boil and let the sauce boil fairly fast for at least 5 minutes—no need to stir as it boils. Serve hot.

French Dressing

—•—

The seasoning for French dressing is a very individual thing: some people love a small amount of sugar in their dressing—I do—and others loathe it; some people love mustard in their dressing, while others don't. This is how I like French dressing, but juggle around with the ingredients to suit your own tastes.
Makes about ⅔ cup.

2 teaspoons sugar
1 teaspoon salt
1 teaspoon mustard powder
pepper
1 garlic clove, finely chopped (optional)
finely chopped fresh herbs (optional)
2 tablespoons wine vinegar
3 tablespoons olive oil
3 tablespoons sunflower oil

Mix together the dry ingredients, then add the vinegar and oils, stirring well. Alternatively, put all the ingredients into a screw-top jar and shake well. Store in a screw-top jar in the refrigerator, but not too long or the garlic and herbs will make the dressing taste stale.

Mayonnaise

—•—

Like French dressing, seasoning mayonnaise is a matter of individual taste. I personally like sugar in mine, and I don't like making mayonnaise with all olive oil as I find the flavor of olive oil alone too obtrusive. This is how I make mayonnaise, but change the amounts of the ingredients to suit your own tastes.
Makes about 1 cup.

2 egg yolks
1 teaspoon salt
1¼ teaspoons mustard powder
pepper
1¼ teaspoons sugar
¼ cup olive oil
⅔ cup sunflower oil
2–3 tablespoons wine vinegar

Put the egg yolks, salt, mustard, pepper and sugar into a blender or food processor. Blend together. With the motor running, slowly add the oils, in a very thin trickle. As the mayonnaise thickens, add the oil in a slightly faster trickle, until it is all used up. Add 2 tablespoons of the vinegar, then taste and add more if you like. Keep in a covered bowl in the refrigerator.

To this basic recipe you can add tomato paste, finely chopped garlic, finely chopped mixed fresh herbs, grated lemon or lime rind, or puréed avocado.

CAKES

No special occasion—be it a Christening or silver wedding anniversary—is complete without a lovingly made rich fruitcake. The joy of a fruit-cake rather than sponge is that it can be made so far in advance.

Celebration Cakes

To give the cake time to mature, make it at least 1 month ahead, longer if possible.

CAKES

Christening Cake
$3\frac{1}{2}$ cups ($1\frac{1}{4}$ lb) golden raisins
$2\frac{2}{3}$ cups (1 lb) currants
$2\frac{2}{3}$ cups (1 lb) raisins
2 cups ($\frac{3}{4}$ lb) glacé cherries, halved
$\frac{2}{3}$ cup (4 oz) chopped mixed candied peel
finely grated rind of 1 orange
finely grated rind of 1 lemon
3 tablespoons Grand Marnier
$\frac{1}{2}$ lb (2 sticks) + 1 tablespoon unsalted butter
$\frac{2}{3}$ cup light brown sugar
$\frac{3}{4}$ cup dark brown sugar
7 large eggs
$\frac{3}{4}$ cup (4 oz) ground almonds
2 cups all-purpose flour

Silver Wedding Cake and 21st Birthday Cake
$5\frac{1}{3}$ cups (2 lb) golden raisins
4 cups ($1\frac{1}{2}$ lb) currants
4 cups ($1\frac{1}{2}$ lb) raisins
$3\frac{1}{3}$ cups ($1\frac{1}{4}$ lb) glacé cherries, halved
1 cup (6 oz) chopped mixed candied peel
finely grated rind of 2 oranges
finely grated rind of 2 lemons
6 tablespoons Grand Marnier
1 lb less 2 tablespoons unsalted butter
$1\frac{1}{4}$ cups light brown sugar
$1\frac{1}{3}$ cups dark brown sugar
12 large eggs
$1\frac{1}{4}$ cups (6 oz) ground almonds
$3\frac{1}{2}$ cups all-purpose flour

Extra Spirit for Soaking Baked Cake
$\frac{1}{4}$ cup brandy, whiskey, or rum

ALMOND PASTE

Christening Cake
3 cups (1 lb) ground almonds
$1\frac{1}{3}$ cups granulated sugar
3 cups confectioners' sugar, sifted
$\frac{1}{2}$ teaspoon almond extract
8 large egg yolks
1 egg white

Silver Wedding Cake
$4\frac{1}{2}$ cups ($1\frac{1}{2}$ lb) ground almonds
2 cups sugar
2 cups confectioners' sugar, sifted
1 teaspoon almond extract
12 large egg yolks
1 egg white

21st Birthday Cake
$3\frac{3}{4}$ cups ($1\frac{1}{4}$ lb) ground almonds
2 cups sugar
2 cups confectioners' sugar, sifted
$\frac{1}{2}$ teaspoon almond extract
10 large egg yolks
1 egg white

ROYAL ICING

Christening Cake
8 large egg whites
9 cups (3 lb) confectioners' sugar, sifted
$1\frac{1}{2}$ tablespoons glycerin

Silver Wedding Cake and 21st Birthday Cake
8 large egg whites
12 cups (4 lb) confectioners' sugar, sifted
$1\frac{1}{2}$ tablespoons glycerin
few drops lemon juice

DECORATIONS

Christening Cake
$5\frac{1}{3}$ cups (1 lb) confectioners' sugar
2 egg whites
few drops acetic acid
3 yards of 2-inch wide ribbon

Silver Wedding Cake
13-inch round cake board
9-inch round cake board
$1\frac{3}{4}$ yards of 2-inch wide lace
about 20 sugar silver leaves
sugar silver balls
4 cake pillars & 2 orchids

21st Birthday Cake
14-inch square cake board
21 white birthday cake candles, and white holders
2 yards of 2-inch wide satin ribbon for side

To Make and Bake Cakes

To make the cake, put the golden raisins, currants, raisins, cherries, peel and orange and lemon rinds into a large mixing bowl. Add the Grand Marnier and mix well. Cover and let stand for 2–3 hours.

For the Christening cake, line a 4-inch deep 10-inch cake pan with a double thickness of wax paper. Cut a strip of thick brown paper, double thickness, long enough to fit around the pan, and as deep as the pan. Use a 4-inch deep 12-inch square pan for the 21st Birthday cake; for the Silver Wedding cake, use a 4-inch deep 10-inch round pan and a 4-inch deep 7-inch round pan.

Beat the butter with the sugars until very light, soft and fluffy. Beat in the eggs, one at a time, beating well after each addition. Fold in the ground almonds and flour. Add the soaked fruit, and mix thoroughly.

Spoon the cake mixture into the prepared pan(s) and spread evenly. When filling the pans for the silver wedding cake, to ensure that each tier is exactly the same depth, insert a clean ruler in the center of each cake—they should measure about $2\frac{1}{2}$ inches deep. Wrap the brown paper strips(s) around the pan(s) and secure with string.

Bake in a preheated 300° oven. For the 10-inch round cakes allow 4–$4\frac{1}{2}$ hours; for the 7-inch round cake allow 3–$3\frac{1}{2}$ hours; for the 12-inch square cake allow $5\frac{1}{2}$–6 hours, until a skewer inserted in the center of the cake comes out clean. Allow the cake(s) to cool in the pan(s) for at least 1 hour, then turn out very carefully onto a wire rack to cool completely.

To store, wrap the cold cake(s) in plastic wrap and then in foil. Store in a cool, dry, airy cupboard. Start to marzipan and ice the cake(s) 2 weeks before the celebration date.

To Make the Almond Paste

Mix the almonds and sugars together in a large mixing bowl. Add the almond extract and egg yolks and mix together to make a stiff paste. Knead only just enough to smooth the paste. Do not overwork it as this will cause the oil in the almonds to seep out, which will, in turn, spoil the royal icing.

To Make the Royal Icing

Lightly whisk the egg whites, then gradually beat in the confectioners' sugar, beating until the icing is very white. Beat in the glycerin (see special notes for each cake before adding the glycerin).

To Cover Cakes with Almond Paste

Remove cake(s) from wrapping and place upside-down on a cake board. Prick the cake(s) all over with a fine skewer, then carefully pour the chosen spirit over the top, a little at a time, and allow it to soak in.

Cut off one-third of the almond paste and set it aside. For a round cake, roll out the remaining almond paste to a long strip, long enough and wide enough to fit around the side of the cake. Brush the strip with a little beaten egg white, then fit it around the cake (egg white side to cake) and press firmly into position. Roll a clean jam jar gently around the side of the cake until the almond paste is smooth, and the ends are joined well together. Trim the almond paste level with the top of the cake, if necessary.

For a square cake, divide the remaining almond paste into 4 equal pieces. Take one piece and roll it out until it is the same length and depth as one side of the cake. Brush with a little beaten egg white, and place firmly in position against the side of the cake. Repeat with the remaining pieces. Make sure that the corners retain a good square shape.

Roll the reserved almond paste out to a round or square, large enough to fit the top of the cake. Brush the top of the cake with egg white, then place the almond paste on top, and roll gently into position with a rolling pin. Smooth the seams with a small metal spatula. Leave in a cool place for 24 hours before icing.

To Ice Cakes with Royal Icing

Spread a good layer of the icing over the top of the cake with a metal spatula, working the knife backwards and forward to expel air bubbles. Pull a ruler, preferably a metal one, across the top of the cake to smooth the icing. Spread the sides of the cake with icing (one side at a time for a square cake), spreading it as smoothly as possible. Pull a cake scraper around the side, or along the side, to smooth the icing—put a round cake on a turntable, if possible. Leave overnight, in a cool place, to dry. Put the remaining icing into a clean mixing bowl and cover the surface closely with plastic wrap. Cover the bowl with additional plastic wrap and refrigerate until the next day. Beat the icing well before using again. Store the icing in this way after each application.

Next day, scrape away the rough icing from the top edge of the cake, and from the board with a small sharp knife. Brush off loose icing from the cake with a clean dry pastry brush. Give the cake 3 more coats of icing, allowing each coat to dry overnight before applying the next. Reserve the remaining icing for decoration.

To Decorate Cakes

Christening Cake The cake is decorated with swans, made from royal icing, and ribbon. If you feel unable to make the swans, you can decorate the top of the cake with flowers, or a bought decoration of your own choice.

You only need 3 swans, but it is advisable to make a few extra to allow for breakage. Make up royal icing as above but add a few drops of lemon juice to harden the icing. Cut several squares of baking parchment paper, just large enough to cover each part of the swan (see diagram). Make a small pastry bag by folding a 10-inch square of waxed paper diagonally in half, then roll into a cone. Fold the points inwards to secure them and snip off the tip of the bag to make a small hole. Put a little confectioners' sugar in the bag.

Place a piece of the paper over a right-hand swan body. Trace the outline of the body, just as if you were drawing with a pencil. Fill the outline in completely with icing. Then, to smooth the icing out—gently rub a small spatula from side-to-side under the paper, holding the

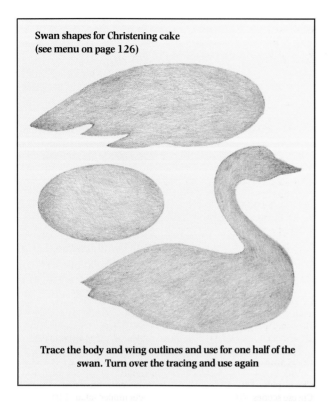

Swan shapes for Christening cake
(see menu on page 126)

Trace the body and wing outlines and use for one half of the
swan. Turn over the tracing and use again

paper firmly on the work surface. Make 4–5 more right-hand body pieces. Make an equal number of left-hand body pieces. Lay the pieces on a large baking sheet to dry.

To make the wings, put a little more icing into a new paper pastry bag and cut a small hole in the bottom. Making one wing at a time, place a piece of the paper over a wing diagram, then start to pipe from the tip of the wing in a continuous line from side to side across the wing, each line touching the other. Make a pair of wings for each swan. Place on the baking sheet with the swan bodies. Make a base for each swan in the same way as making the bodies. Dry in a cool place for at least 24 hours before assembling.

To assemble the swans, put the body pieces into pairs, then join them together with a little icing. Pipe a small blob of icing on one of the base pieces, then place a swan body on top. Pipe a good blob of icing at either side of the body, then carefully place the wings in position—angling the wings out slightly. To support the swan until the icing has set hard, stand it on a flat tray and place an egg cup at each side, just behind each wing—this will take the weight and prevent the swan falling over. Repeat with the other swans.

To decorate the cake, mark a row of evenly spaced scallops around the side of the cake so that they end just about halfway down the side of the cake. Put a little icing

into a small paper pastry bag and cut a small hole in the bottom of the bag. Pipe continuous squiggly lines to give a filligree effect. Put some more icing into a paper pastry bag fitted with a small star tube and pipe a star edge to each scallop. Tie a thin pink, or blue, ribbon around the side of the cake, just under the scallops, ending with a neat bow. Secure ribbon around the edge of the cake board.

Decorate the top edge of the cake with 3 rows of stars, then pipe a row of stars around the bottom edge. To complete the cake, make 3 pretty bows with ribbon and place one across each swan neck. Place the swans on top of the cake, with their wings pointing toward the center.

Silver Wedding Cake To decorate the cake, put the lace around the side of each cake, securing it neatly with pins (trim the lace neatly so that it overlaps to make a concealed seam).

Put some of the remaining icing into a paper pastry bag fitted with a small star tube. Decorate the top of each cake with a shell border, piping one shell on the top of the cake at a slight angle, then piping the next shell on the side of the cake, so that it very slightly overlaps the end of the shell piped on the top of the cake. Continue all around the edges. Decorate with silver balls—see page 115.

To complete the larger cake, pipe the same shell pattern around the bottom of the cake, then decorate with silver leaves. To complete the smaller cake, pipe a single row of shells around the bottom edge of the cake, then decorate with silver balls. Allow the decoration to dry for 24 hours before assembling the cake.

To assemble the cake, place the 4 pillars in the center of the cake, spacing them evenly apart. Carefully place the small cake on the top, then decorate the top of the cake with orchids.

21st Birthday Cake To decorate the cake, put the candles into their holders and put aside. Put a little of the icing into a paper pastry bag fitted with a small plain tube. Pipe a straight line of icing across the top of the cake, from one corner, diagonally, to the opposite corner. Continue to pipe straight lines $\frac{1}{4}$ inch apart, parallel to the first line, to cover one side of the cake. Pipe more lines across the top of the first lines to make a lattice pattern. Put more icing into another paper pastry bag fitted with a small star tube. Pipe a shell or star border around the top and bottom edge of the cake. Then pipe a row across the center of the cake to neaten the lattice pattern. Allow the icing to dry, then tie the satin ribbon around the side of the cake, finishing it with a neat bow. Arrange the candles neatly on top of the cake. You can pipe happy birthday or a special message in the plain space left on top of the cake. Or, for a girl, put a small arrangement of flowers on the top.

INDEX

190

ACKNOWLEDGMENTS

The publishers would like to thank R. J. Brimacombe, R. B. Jakeman, M. H. Macrae,
J. Burgis, J. R. A. Walker, Hilary Close, Suzanne Woolf and the staff at Harrods for
their invaluable assistance and co-operation in the making of this book.
The publishers would also like to thank Mrs. Kenward, Anne Charlish and Peter Banyard.